Beer Lover's
Washington

Beer Lover's Washington

First Edition

Logan Thompson

Guilford, Connecticut

To buy books in quantity for corporate use
or incentives, call **(800) 962-0973**
or e-mail **premiums@GlobePequot.com.**

All the information in this guidebook is subject to change.
We recommend that you call ahead to obtain current information
before traveling.

Copyright © 2013 Morris Book Publishing, LLC

All photos by the author.

Editor: Kevin Sirois
Project Editor: Staci Zacharski
Layout Artist: Casey Shain
Text Design: Sheryl P. Kober
Maps: Alena Joy Pearce © Morris Book Publishing, LLC

ISBN 978-0-7627-8634-3

Printed in the United States of America
10 9 8 7 6 5 4 3 2 1

Contents

About the Author

Logan Thompson has lived most of his life in the state of Washington, where he fell in love with craft beer and the amazing culture surrounding it. He owns BlogAboutBeer.com, a popular blog focused on helping people discover and appreciate quality beer. Logan is an amateur homebrewer who enjoys eating ridiculously spicy foods and pairing them with hoppy Northwest brews.

Acknowledgments

While writing a book on beer in the great state of Washington was a lot of fun, it also took up a lot of my time. For that I'd like to thank my beautiful wife, Renee, for putting up with me as I spent many evenings writing, traveling, and drinking beer, especially with the added stress of sleepless nights and extra work our newborn daughter brought to the family. I'd also like to thank my two incredible daughters, Brynna and Macy, for encouraging me to keep on writing.

I was lucky enough to have a lot of friends and family help out with getting this book together. My biggest help came from my cousin and friend Ryan Van Brunt who was always willing to travel with me, help contact breweries, and add some extra flair to the book. Also thanks to Ryan Larrabee, Joe Sousa, and Jeremy Tucker for help with the photography and my good beer drinking and homebrewing buddy Sean Suarez for helping me track down a few beers that I wanted included.

If it weren't for the great state of Washington and the craft beer industry blossoming here, this book wouldn't be nearly as exciting. Thanks to all the breweries producing delicious beers for us beer drinkers to enjoy. To all those working hard in the Washington craft beer industry, thanks!

Introduction

Beer. Synonymous with the Northwest and the state of Washington, it's more than just a crop of hops from the Yakima Valley or a truckload of malted grains from Vancouver's Great Western Malting. It defines a part of our culture, past, present, and future. So much more than just a beverage, beer brings people together, it helps build community, and it is a beautiful canvas masterfully crafted by artisans who put their hearts into its creation for our enjoyment.

Washington has had a long love affair with brewing. From breweries founded in the 1800s, such as the Rainier Brewing Company and Olympia Brewing Company, to the craft brewers of our day, the state has embraced beer with open arms. The state has also been filled with innovation. When Bert Grant opened the nation's first brewpub in Yakima in 1982, little did anyone know that someday just about every city would have at least a brewpub or two to call its own.

Today as the industry grows rapidly, we are seeing some exciting and new creations and trends. From new styles being brewed to the return of beer in cans, the Washington craft-beer industry is forging new ways for us to experience beer. Because today's marketplace offers so many unique as well as traditional styles, everyone can find a beer to connect with and love—although sometimes it takes some work trying them out to figure what that is.

I've lived in Washington most of my life, in both Vancouver and Bellingham, and have fallen in love with the beer this state produces and sells. My hope with this book is that you, too, will gain some insight and be able to connect with and support those producing beer in this wonderful state.

So sit back, crack open a cold beer, and read about what Washington has to offer. Cheers!

How to Use This Guide

Did you know that in the US, Washington is second only to California in the total amount of breweries per state (at the time of this writing)? With over 150 breweries in the state and growing, it can be tough to keep track of them all. In fact, by the time this book prints there will probably be another 10 breweries opened in the state with even more opening shortly after that. Look at this book as a guide to Washington beer, but just understand that it isn't going to cover every brewery, brewpub, and beer bar there is. If it did, it would never get printed, given the growth rate of the industry in the state.

The bulk of *Beer Lover's Washington* highlights breweries, brewpubs, and beer bars, broken down by area. Breaking Washington into sections is a bit tricky and some placements could fit into multiple categories, but don't get too caught up in that. The designations are just meant to help organize them by location.

Under the brewery listings you'll find those that bottle, can, or keg their beer mostly for distribution outside of their location. With each brewery listing you'll find a **Beer Lover's Pick,** a look at one suggested beer to try. Some are year-round and others are seasonal, but all are worth a try if you can find them.

The brewpub listings are made up of establishments that sell the majority of their beer at their location along with a restaurant.

Next you'll find a handful of beer bars in each area. This is by no means a comprehensive listing, but a stepping stone of a few suggestions. There could easily be another book written covering just the beer bars in the state.

After the brewery, brewpub, and beer bar listings, you'll find sections on:

Beer Festivals: A look at a few of the larger beer festivals in the state that occur annually.

BYOB: Brew Your Own Beer: Part of Washington's growth of breweries has stemmed from a high number of homebrewers. In this section you'll find a few suggested homebrew shops as well as clone recipes of Washington beers you can brew at home.

In the Kitchen: Did you know that beer is the perfect ingredient for a lot of foods? This section is all about recipes you can cook at home using Washington beers.

Pub Crawls: If you're visiting a city or want to experience multiple places at once, a pub crawl is the way to go. This section covers six itineraries from around the state that will have you jumping into the local beer scene.

Glossary of Terms

ABV: Alcohol by volume—the percentage of alcohol in a beer. A typical domestic beer is a little less than 5 percent ABV.

Ale: Beer brewed with top fermenting yeast. Quicker to brew than lagers, and most every craft beer is a style of ale. Popular styles of ales include pale ales, amber ales, stouts, and porters.

Altbier: A German style of ale, typically brown in color, smooth, and fruity.

Barleywine: Not a wine at all but a high-ABV ale that originated in England and is typically sweet. American versions often have large amounts of hops.

Barrel of beer: Production of beer is measured in barrels. A barrel equals 31 gallons.

Beer: An alcoholic beverage brewed with malt, water, hops, and yeast.

Beer bar: A bar that focuses on carrying craft or fine imported beers.

Bitter: An English bitter is an English-style ale, more hoppy than an English mild, but less hoppy than an IPA.

Bock: A German-style lager, typically stronger than the typical lager.

Bomber: Most beers are packaged in 12-ounce bottles. Bombers are 22-ounce bottles.

Brewpub: Typically a restaurant, but sometimes a bar, that brews its own beers on premises.

Cask: Also known as real ales, cask ales are naturally carbonated and are usually served with a hand pump rather than forced out with carbon dioxide or nitrogen.

Clone beer: A homebrew recipe based on a commercial beer.

Contract brewery: A company that does not have its own brewery and pays someone else to brew and bottle its beer.

Craft beer: High-quality, flavorful beer made by small breweries.

Double: Two meanings. Most often meant as a higher-alcohol version of a beer, most typically used in reference to a double, or imperial, IPA. Can also be used as an American translation of a Belgian Dubbel, a style of Belgian ale.

ESB: Extra-special bitter. A traditional malt-heavy English pub ale with low bitterness, usually served on cask.

Gastropub: A beer-centric bar or pub that exhibits the same amount of care selecting its foods as it does its beers.

Growler: A half-gallon jug of beer. Many brewpubs sell growlers of their beers to go.

Gypsy brewer: A company that does not own its own brewery, but rents space at an existing brewery to brew it themselves.

Hops: Hops are flowers used in beers to produce aroma, bitterness, and flavor. Nearly every beer in the world has hops.

IBU: International bittering units, which are used to measure how bitter a beer is.

Imperial: A higher-alcohol version of a regular-strength beer.

IPA: India Pale Ale. A popular style of ale created in England that has taken a decidedly American twist over the years. Often bitter, thanks to more hops used than in other styles of beer.

Kölsch: A light, refreshing German-style ale.

Lager: Beer brewed with bottom-fermenting yeast. Takes longer and is harder to brew than ales. Popular styles of lagers include black lagers, Doppelbocks, Pilsners, and Vienna lagers.

Malt: Typically barley malt, but sometimes wheat malt. Malt provides the fermentable sugar in beers. The more fermentable sugar, the higher the ABV in a beer. Without malt, a beer would be too bitter from the hops.

Microbrewery: A brewery that brews fewer than 15,000 barrels of beer a year.

Nanobrewery: A brewery that brews four barrels of beer per batch or less.

Nitro draft: Most beers that are served on draft using kegs pressurized with carbon dioxide. Occasionally, particularly with stouts, nitrogen is used, which helps create a creamier body.

Pilsner: A style of German or Czechoslovakian lager, usually light in color. Most mass-produced beers are based on this style.

Porter: A dark ale, similar to the stout but with fewer roasted characters.

Pounders: 16-ounce cans.

Quad: A strong Belgian-style ale, typically sweet and high in alcohol.

Regional brewery: A brewery that brews up to 6 million barrels of beer a year.

Russian imperial stout: A stout is a dark, heavy beer. A Russian imperial stout is a higher-alcohol, thicker-bodied version of regular stouts.

Saison: Also known as a Belgian or French farmhouse ale. It can be fruity, and it can also be peppery. Usually refreshing.

Seasonal: A beer that is brewed only at a certain time of year to coincide with the seasons.

Session beer: A low-alcohol beer, one you can have several of in one long drinking "session."

Stout: A dark beer brewed with roasted malts.

Strong ale: A style of ale that is typically both hoppy and malty and can be aged for years.

Tap takeover: An event where a bar or pub hosts a brewery and has several of its beers on tap.

Triple (Tripel): A Belgian-style ale, typically lighter in color than a Dubbel but higher in alcohol.

Wheat beer: Beers, such as Hefeweizens and Witbiers, are brewed using wheat malt along with barley malt.

Yeast: The living organism in beer that causes the sugars to ferment and become alcohol.

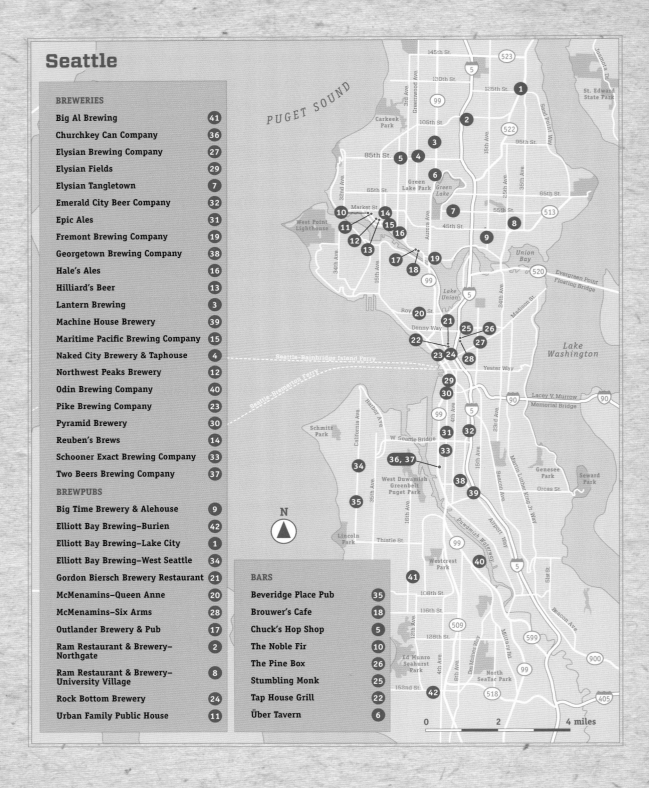

Seattle

BREWERIES

Big Al Brewing	41
Churchkey Can Company	36
Elysian Brewing Company	27
Elysian Fields	29
Elysian Tangletown	7
Emerald City Beer Company	32
Epic Ales	31
Fremont Brewing Company	19
Georgetown Brewing Company	38
Hale's Ales	16
Hilliard's Beer	13
Lantern Brewing	3
Machine House Brewery	39
Maritime Pacific Brewing Company	15
Naked City Brewery & Taphouse	4
Northwest Peaks Brewery	12
Odin Brewing Company	40
Pike Brewing Company	23
Pyramid Brewery	30
Reuben's Brews	14
Schooner Exact Brewing Company	33
Two Beers Brewing Company	37

BREWPUBS

Big Time Brewery & Alehouse	9
Elliott Bay Brewing–Burien	42
Elliott Bay Brewing–Lake City	1
Elliott Bay Brewing–West Seattle	34
Gordon Biersch Brewery Restaurant	21
McMenamins–Queen Anne	20
McMenamins–Six Arms	28
Outlander Brewery & Pub	17
Ram Restaurant & Brewery–Northgate	2
Ram Restaurant & Brewery–University Village	8
Rock Bottom Brewery	24
Urban Family Public House	11

BARS

Beveridge Place Pub	35
Brouwer's Cafe	18
Chuck's Hop Shop	5
The Noble Fir	10
The Pine Box	26
Stumbling Monk	25
Tap House Grill	22
Über Tavern	6

Seattle

Not many places in the country have as great of a love for beer as Seattle. Pretty much anywhere you go in the city you'll be able to find a pint of finely crafted beer. Even if you happen to find yourself at a Seahawks or Sounders game at Century Link Field, your options will be better there than most restaurants elsewhere in the country. Pretty much every neighborhood in Seattle has multiple alehouses serving beer produced right in the city, while breweries are located in just about all corners. Not only that but you'll also find a whole host of festivals and events happening around the city just about every week of the year dedicated to our favorite beverage.

From longtime standards such as Pike Brewing, Elysian Brewing, and Pyramid Breweries to up-and-coming newer breweries, beers to match just about every taste preference are being produced. Bottled and canned beers are easily available, while having multiple tasty brewpubs to choose from makes dining out enjoyable for beer lovers. Seattle is truly one of the best places to live or visit if you love beer culture. This chapter is all about Seattle breweries, brewpubs, and just a handful of the great beer bars the city has to offer.

Breweries

BIG AL BREWING

9832 14th Ave. SW, Seattle, WA 98106; (206) 453-4487; BigAlBrewing.com; @Big_Al_Brewing

Founded: 2008 **Founders:** Alejandro Brown and Noelle Brown **Brewer:** Alejandro Brown **Flagship Beer:** Irish Red **Year-Round Beers:** Irish Red, Smoked Porter, Rat City Blonde, Big Hoppa India Pale Ale, Tutta Bella Amber Ale, The Bridge Bitter **Seasonals/ Special Releases:** Winter Warmer, Hop Villain, Hop Soup Double IPA, Local Hero Series, and many more **Tours:** No **Taproom:** Yes

Although Seattle is packed with breweries, the south-end neighborhood of White Center has very few breweries to call its own. Pacific Rim Brewing opened in 1997 and started to make a name in the craft beer scene for a decade or so. Sadly, the owners suffered some hard times and had to close their doors. Fortunately for the neighborhood, though, the building and equipment were purchased by local homebrewer Alejandro Brown and turned into Big Al Brewing in 2008. They have since been brewing some of the best beer Washington state has to offer.

Brown keeps close to his homebrewing roots and does what he can to support other local brewers. As part of their **Local Hero series,** they celebrate homebrewers' recipes by collaborating to brew special beers that are available in the tasting room. You can find 6 year-round beers: **Irish Red, Smoked Porter, Rat City Blonde, Big Hoppa India Pale Ale, Tutta Bella Amber Ale** (crafted to pair perfectly with pizza from local restaurant Tutta Bella), and **The Bridge Bitter** (brewed for Emerald City Supporters, the largest soccer support club in Seattle). Throughout the year you can also find rotating seasonals and specialty brewed beers available in bottles as well as in small batches just for the tasting room.

This production brewery produces a range of beer on draft and in bottles, and also features a tasting room and lounge. The tasting room itself doesn't offer food, but Big Al Brewing frequently hosts "soup-offs," where customers bring homemade soups to share and enter into competitions. In the summer they offer grills outside where you can barbecue your own meats while enjoying a cold one. You'll also find plenty of entertainment ranging from live music to a friendly game of darts. Or if kicking back and relaxing is more your style, you'll find the upstairs lounge is a great place to hang out.

Smoked Porter
Style: Porter
ABV: 4.8%
Availability: Year-Round

Just like the name implies, Big Al Brewing's Smoked Porter is a tasty porter with plenty of smokiness from peated malt. The dark black color, along with a very small tan head, gives it an almost mysterious yet inviting appearance. Dark chocolate, roasted malt, and plenty of smoke fill the aroma and flavor, with some espresso and bitter chocolate playing in the background. With the smokiness playing such a big role in this porter, this is a perfect beer to pair with a plate of barbecue just about any time of the year.

Seattle

CHURCHKEY CAN COMPANY

4700 Ohio Ave. S., Ste. B, Seattle, WA 98134; ChurchkeyCanCo.com; @ChurchkeyCanCo
Founded: 2012 **Founders:** Adrian Grenier and Justin Hawkins **Brewers:** Lukas Jones and Sean Burke **Flagship Beer:** Churchkey Pilsner **Year-Round Beers:** Churchkey Pilsner **Seasonals/Special Releases:** None **Tours:** No **Taproom:** No

The craft-beer world expands and evolves each and every year, so breweries need to work hard if they want to find ways to stand out from the crowd. While most concoct new ideas to advance the craft, Churchkey Can Company has flipped the model by stepping back in time to create a throwback experience.

Churchkey Pilsner
Style: Pilsner
ABV: 4.9%
Availability: Year-Round
This might be the only beer that Churchkey Can Company produces, but it scores major points for charm and old-school appeal. Let's be honest: Outside of your college shotgunning days, where else do you get to puncture a can before drinking? If you've never used a churchkey opener before, you'd better get a six-pack. You'll need to practice before you get the hang of opening these vintage cans. Inside, you'll find this is a classic Pilsner, golden in color. Aromas of hay, bread, floral hops, and grains fill the air with a sweetness that makes way for a touch of bitterness in the finish.

The brewery, based in Seattle's SoDo neighborhood, is the creation of former Nike designer Justin Hawkins and actor Adrian Grenier (who is best known for his lead role on HBO's show *Entourage*). The two met through a mutual friend and started discussing beer can designs from across America's brewing history. After some talks, the two decided to open up a brewery that would bring back an iconic style of beer can, unseen since the invention of the pull-tab top in the early 1970s. In just a few short years, those talks came to life. The Churchkey Can Company stands apart by packaging beer in flat-top beer cans that require a steel opener—a churchkey—to puncture two holes in the top of the can.

The company hired Portland-based homebrewers Lukas Jones and Sean Burke to create a Pilsner recipe that is now the single beer that Churchkey brews. Brewing takes place through a partnership with Seattle-based Two Beer Brewing Company. Currently their beer is available in the Seattle and Portland areas, but there are plans for growth to keep up with demand.

ELYSIAN BREWING COMPANY
1221 E. Pike St., Seattle, WA 98122; (206) 860-1920; ElysianBrewing.com;
@ElysianBrewing
Founded: 1995 **Founders:** Dick Cantwell, Joe Bisacca, and David Buhler **Brewer:** Dick Cantwell **Flagship Beer:** The Immortal IPA **Year-Round Beers:** Avatar Jasmine IPA, Dragonstooth Stout, The Immortal IPA, Men's Room Original Red, Perseus Porter, The Wise

ESB, Zephyrus Pilsner **Seasonals/Special Releases:** Apocalypse Series, Bete Blanche Tripel, Bifrost Winter Ale, Dark o' the Moon, Great Pumpkin Ale, Loser Pale Ale, Manic IPA Series, Night Owl Pumpkin Ale, and many more **Tours:** By appointment **Taproom:** Yes

Since their first brewpub opened in May 1996 in Seattle's Capitol Hill neighborhood, Elysian Brewing Company has grown into one of the most beloved breweries the state has to offer. The original location is in a 1919 Packard storage building that oozes the feel of a classic American brewpub. You'll find high ceilings, exposed timber, and plenty of visible brewery tanks. Along with a full selection of food on the menu, the pub features the core lineup of Elysian beers along with several seasonal brews

Beer Lover's Pick

Dragonstooth Stout
Style: Oatmeal Stout
ABV: 7.5%
Availability: Year-Round
Elysian's Dragonstooth is a truly huge stout that needed a hefty name to match. This beast of a beer draws its name from Greek mythology: When the Phoenician prince Cadmus sowed the teeth of a slain dragon, the warrior founders of Thebes sprang up. The dark-as-night brew has a beautiful chocolate head and an aroma of smooth coffee, roasted malts, molasses, and cocoa. The sweet flavor mimics the smell and adds the slightest touch of bitterness in the finish, creating a delicious beer of mythological proportions.

that fill out their 18 taps. In 2003 a much smaller location opened in Seattle's south Greenlake area, known as Tangletown. Although it has a smaller bistro-style feel, you will still find 18 taps pouring an array of beers, many of which are experimental or one-off beers brewed on site. The third and newest location, the Elysian Fields, opened in 2006. This much larger pub is near both Century Link and Safeco Fields. With 22 taps and 2 beers on casks, there is a wide array of options to choose from.

Elysian hosts many events throughout the year, but the **Great Pumpkin Beer Festival** is one of the largest. This 3-day festival features a whopping 60-plus pumpkin beers, 13 of which are created by Elysian brewers. One of their most sought-after seasonal beers is the **Night Owl Pumpkin Ale,** which is available in 22- and 12-ounce bottles or on draft. The light-bodied and easy-drinking beer is like Grandma's pumpkin pie in beer form. In other seasons, look out for special collaboration beers. Elysian occasionally partners up with other breweries like New Belgium, The Bruery, Stone, and Green Flash to bottle up some unique brews.

EMERALD CITY BEER COMPANY

3100 Airport Way S., Seattle, WA 98134; (206) 708-7329; EmeraldCityBeer.com; @EmeraldCityBeer

Founded: 2010 **Founder:** Rick Hewitt **Brewer:** Rick Hewitt **Flagship Beer:** Dottie Seattle Lager **Year-Round Beers:** Dottie Seattle Lager, Ivana Pale Lager, Betty Black Lager **Seasonals/Special Releases:** Whiskey Dottie's Lager, Gold Lager, Sounders Amber Lager, Barrel Betty, Barrel Dottie **Tours:** Wed–Fri 4–8 p.m., Sat noon–4 p.m. **Taproom:** Yes

The Northwest is packed with hundreds of breweries that fashion hopped-up ales to please the region's hop-loving beer drinkers. But Rick Hewitt, founder and head brewer of Emerald City Beer Company, looked around the beer scene and noticed most West Coast breweries were giving little attention to lagers. Seeing this as an opportunity to enter the market, he launched Emerald City Beer Company with a lager focus and an aim to create approachable yet flavorful beers. The brewery and tasting room was opened up in the old Rainier Brewery building. From the beginning, their flagship beer, the **Dottie Seattle Lager,** has been the face of the brewery. The amber lager is a true session beer at 4.9% ABV with plenty of flavor to enjoy pretty much any time of the year. What really sets Dottie apart is the unique artwork that represents her (seen both on the 16-ounce cans and in advertisements). A local pinup artist drew a busty brunette in a short emerald-green dress to be the, uh, face that lures in thirsty beer fans. The name Dottie, however, represents a sweeter, more innocent story. It's derived from Hewitt's grandmother, who was the daughter of German hop farmers.

Dottie Seattle Lager

Style: Amber Session Ale

ABV: 4.9%

Availability: Year-Round

Few companies set out to target the Northwest beer market with a flagship lager in a can. Dottie Seattle Lager aims to take that challenge head-on by offering an easy-drinking session lager with plenty of flavor. Dottie isn't exactly the picture of class, but she sure is likeable. Crack open the 16-ounce can and you'll find a medium-bodied brew that's a tad heavy on sweet malt flavor. This beer is sure to convert a few micro drinkers into full-fledged craft-beer fans.

Seattle

Aside from Dottie Seattle Lager, you can find other beers such as **Ivana Pale Lager** and **Betty Black Lager** on draft in the tasting room and around the area. Both of these brews have their own pinup-girl icon to represent them on the tap handles. You can also visit the taproom and find experimental and small-batch beers on draft that are concocted in the Beer Lab, Emerald City Beer Company's small brewing system. While their tasting room doesn't serve food, you are welcome to bring in your own snacks to munch on while relaxing and sipping on their great selection of lagers.

EPIC ALES

3201 1st Ave. S., Ste. 104, Seattle, WA 98134; (206) 351-3637; EpicAles.com; @EpicAles
Founded: 2009 **Founder:** Cody Morris **Brewer:** Cody Morris **Flagship Beer:** Solar Trans Amplifier **Year-Round Beers:** Solar Trans Amplifier, Simple Ale **Seasonals/Special Releases:** OTTO-Optimizer, Terra-saurus, Lyli, The Fuj, Simple Summer, Project One, Beatrice, Mathilda, SAD Winter Beer, Orchard, Pumpkin Pie Gose, La Mesa Negra, Forest Ale, Beet Down, Bog, Late Night Party Time, and many more **Tours:** No **Taproom:** Yes

Epic Ales, not to be confused with Epic Brewing Company out of Utah, is the epitome of a creative nanobrewery that isn't afraid to bend the rules of what beer is supposed to be. Founded by homebrewer Cody Morris inside the K. R. Trigger building in Seattle's SoDo neighborhood, the brewhouse is one of the smallest in the state. In fact, the one-barrel brewery Cody got his start on was crammed inside just 180 square feet that also doubled as the tasting room. As the brewery has grown, they were able to expand the tasting room into what is now called the Gastropod. You can come for a visit here and try around 6 different beers at any given time.

While beer is generally brewed with the 4 main ingredients of water, malt, hops, and yeast, it seems Cody looks at anything as a possible ingredient. A few examples would be **Bog,** a wild ale brewed with shiitake mushrooms and peat-smoked malt; **Beatrice,** a beer inspired by the European beverage Kvass that's brewed with rye, brown sugar, Szechuan peppercorns, and cinnamon; and **Mathilda,** a sour rye ale brewed with spearmint and brown sugar. Each beer is crafted with a variety of spices, herbs, fruits, and sugars, much like a chef would create a tasty dish in a nice restaurant. While they're delicious on their own, each beer is made to pair well with certain foods, and pushes the limits on how beer and food work together.

Since the brewery is small, most of its beers can be found sparingly outside of the tasting room. However, you can find 22-ounce bottles around the Seattle area as well as a few kegs on draft around town. Make sure to check their Facebook page for tasting room hours.

Solar Trans Amplifier
Style: Witbier
ABV: 6%
Availability: Year-Round

Epic Ales' Solar Trans Amplifier is a take on a traditional Witbier but is remixed to make a unique and invigorating beer. Instead of using wheat, the beer is brewed with rice to give it part of the unique flavor. It's then loaded up with ginger and chamomile instead of the commonly used coriander and bitter orange peel flavors. The result is a tart yet complex beer that has some similarities to a Wit, yet fits in the spiced-beer category. It can be enjoyed on its own or alongside delicate meats, such as fish.

Seattle

FREMONT BREWING COMPANY

3409 Woodland Park Ave. N., Seattle, WA 98103; (206) 420-2407; FremontBrewing.com; @FremontBrewing

Founded: 2008 **Founder:** Matt Lincecum **Brewer:** Matt Lincoln **Flagship Beer:** Universale Pale Ale **Year-Round Beers:** Universale Pale Ale, Interurban IPA, Wandering Wheat, Dark Star Imperial Oatmeal Stout **Seasonals/Special Releases:** 77 Fremont Select, Fremont Summer Ale, Harvest Ale, Abominable Winter Ale, Homefront IPA, Cowiche Canyon Organic Fresh Hop Lab, Bourbon Barrel Abominable, and many more **Tours:** No **Taproom:** Yes

Fremont Brewing Company was founded in 2008 and is perfectly situated in Fremont, one of the city's most interesting and fun neighborhoods. The tasting room, or what they call their Urban Beer Garden, is located right in the brewery—not

- **77 SELECT** SESSION IPA 4/7
- **PROLETARIAT PORTER** 4/8
- **SUPER DUPER IPA II** 4 PINT ONLY
- **NITRO: DARK STAR** 6 GOBLET ONLY
- **CASK:** ABOMB w/ CURRANT and LICORICE 4 GOBLET ONLY
- **IPA** w/ MEDJOOL DATES and GARAM MASALA 4 GOBLET ONLY

Frem
Pin

in a separate building or room, but in the actual brewery room. Multiple small tables and booths are placed right where the magic happens, giving you a feeling that you're almost a part of the process. An 18-foot community table with benches made out of old kegs provides plenty of seating for those visiting to bring big groups or make new friends. They even allow dogs if you want to grab a pint with your furry friend. A refrigerator stocked with aging beer sits among wooden barrels and allows you to buy from a small selection of Fremont beers in full growlers, cans, or 22-ounce bottles.

While their tasting room is a fun experience on its own, Fremont's beer is the main reason to seek them out. In true Northwest style, they focus on using local

Beer Lover's Pick

Bourbon Barrel Abominable
Style: Strong Ale
ABV: 9.5%
Availability: Released in Winter

Known by regulars as B-Bomb, this extremely limited release is available once a year in the winter. While their regular Abominable Winter Ale is a bit easier to find and almost as tasty, the bourbon-barrel version is well worth the wait. It has been patiently sitting in barrels for an entire year, aging and soaking in some extra bourbon, vanilla, and wood flavors. Add these to an already chocolate, caramel, and roasted malt base and you get a complex winter ale that will definitely warm you up on those cold nights.

ingredients, and when possible brews are crafted using plenty of Northwest-grown hops and malt. They offer a selection of both beautifully crafted traditional-style beers and innovative aged and sour beers. Their flagship **Universale Pale Ale** is packed with Northwest hops, making it one of their most popular offerings. Keep an eye out for their **Cowiche Canyon Organic Hop Lab,** a fresh-hop IPA brewed with organic Citra and Simcoe hops from Cowiche Canyon in the Yakima Valley. One sip and you'll taste just how fresh it is. You can find Fremont Brewing beers at many bars and restaurants around Seattle and Spokane, as well as their cans and bottles in area bottle shops.

GEORGETOWN BREWING COMPANY

5200 Denver Ave. S., Seattle, WA 98108; (206) 766-8055; GeorgetownBeer.com; @GeorgetownBeer
Founded: 2002 **Founders:** Roger Bialous and Manny Chao **Brewer:** Manny Chao
Flagship Beer: Manny's Pale Ale **Year-Round Beers:** Manny's Pale Ale, Roger's Pilsner, Chopper's Red Ale, Georgetown Porter, Lucille IPA **Seasonals/Special Releases:** Superchopp, Bob's Brown, Johnny Utah, Lisa's Chocolate Stout, Georgetown Braggot, Donkey Deux, Waldman, Sonia's, Lovely Reida, Craigalicious, Tomtoberfest, DH389, DHX
Tours: Yes, Sat; call brewery for times and reservations **Taproom:** Yes

If you visit just about any bar in Seattle, chances are they will have Georgetown Brewing Company's popular pale ale on draft. Founders Roger Bialous and Manny Chao based their aptly named Seattle brewery in the Georgetown neighborhood and quickly made a name for themselves.

While their smooth yet complex pale ale, known as **Manny's Pale Ale,** makes up the bulk of their sales, you will also find 4 other beers in their year-round lineup: the easy-drinking **Roger's Pilsner,** the hoppy **Chopper's Red Ale,** the **Georgetown Porter,** which is packed with roasted chocolate, and **Lucille IPA,** one of the state's finer IPAs, booming with floral and citrusy hops. Georgetown mixes it up throughout the year by offering a rotating selection of seasonally brewed beers. One of their most popular choices is **Superchopp,** a red ale that is available on draft most of the time, but not often enough to be added to their full-time lineup. Think of it as a hopped-up version of their Chopper's Red Ale that is sure to please most hop lovers.

Although they have been known to bottle a beer, their main focus is on draft sales. If you're interested in taking a tour, give them a call, or try your luck on the weekend, as they often lead tours of the brewery on Saturday. You can pay a visit to the industrial-looking brewery to fill up your growler or purchase a keg, but they don't have a pub or offer pints for sale.

Lucille IPA
Style: IPA
ABV: 6.8%
Availability: Year-Round

Lucille IPA, one of Georgetown's most recent additions to their year-round lineup, can be summed up in one word: balance. In the Northwest, it's tough to break into the IPA category. But when you brew a beer packed with a sweet maltiness that neatly balances bitter pine and citrus hops the way Lucille does, it's easy to see why so many people like it. Seven hop additions and three hop varieties make it loaded with bitterness that rides perfectly on the strong malt backbone.

HALE'S ALES

4301 Leary Way NW, Seattle, WA 98107; (206) 706-1544; HalesBrewery.com
Founded: 1983 **Founder:** Mike Hale **Brewer:** Lincoln Zmolek **Flagship Beer:** Hale's Pale American Ale **Year-Round Beers:** Pale American Ale, Hale's Cream Ale, H.S.B., Troll Porter, Mongoose IPA, Supergoose IPA, Red Menace Big Amber, El Jefe Weizen, Nightroll Porter, Kölsch German Style Ale **Seasonals/Special Releases:** Wee Heavy Winter Ale, Irish Style Nut Brown Ale, O'Brien's Harvest Ale, Aftermath Imperial IPA, Barrel Aged Supergoose, Rudyard's Rare Barleywine, and many more **Tours:** No **Taproom:** Yes

Hale's Ales has a long-standing history in the Northwest. They opened as one of the first craft breweries here in 1983, shortly after founder Mike Hale fell in love with the brews of England during a year of living across the pond. He realized that beers made in the US at the time were nothing like the flavorful beers of England he had been drinking, so upon his return, he opened the original brewery in Colville, Washington, and began producing his own lineup of English-style beers. Just a few short years later, a second brewery was opened in Kirkland. And by the early '90s, the Colville brewery was moved all the way east to Spokane. By 1995 the Kirkland brewery had been moved to its current location in the Fremont/Ballard district of Seattle, and the brewpub and restaurant opened shortly after. Hale's was the first brewery in the area to offer seasonal cask and nitrogen-conditioned ales. Today the brewery continues to craft a selection of 10 beers with year-round availability, along with those on rotation and specialty brews at its Seattle location.

Seattle

The flagship **Hale's Pale American Ale** was the inaugural beer from opening in 1983 and continues to be a standard by which other Northwest pale ales are judged. **Hale's Cream Ale** is a well-known smooth and creamy ale that helped put the brewery on the map. In the fall be sure to look for **O'Brien's Harvest Ale**, a hoppy seasonal that's been a tradition since 1988.

Check out the family-friendly brewpub while in Seattle and nosh some higher-end pub grub, like a truffle burger or salmon fillet. You'll also find a more traditional spread of sandwiches, seafood, and burgers. While you're there, pick up a keg, grab some bottles, or fill up your growler. While they do not offer formal tours, there are informational placards for a self-guided tour, and the friendly brewers are around as well.

Beer Lover's Pick

Supergoose IPA
Style: IPA
ABV: 7.50%
Availability: Year-Round

Although Hale's modestly considers Supergoose an IPA, you could easily classify it as an imperial IPA. They've taken their Mongoose IPA and added in even more Amarillo, Centennial, and Simcoe hops along with a larger grain bill. The result is an intense Northwest-style IPA that holds its own with the best in the state. The massive malt backbone keeps this brew grounded and tames the citrus hops into a costarring role. On the bottle you'll find a mongoose with a superhero cape, charging you to give this bold brew a try.

HILLIARD'S BEER

1550 NW 49th St., Seattle, WA 98107; (206) 915-3303; HilliardsBeer.com; @HilliardsBeer
Founded: 2011 **Founders:** Ryan Hilliard and Adam Merkl **Brewer:** Todd Garrett
Flagship Beers: Saison and Amber **Year-Round Beers:** Amber, Saison, Blonde, Pils,
Extra Special Belgian **Seasonals/Special Releases:** Chrome Satan, Murdered Out Stout,
Nautical Reference Pale Ale, Unobtanium IPA, Dry Irish Stout, Black Light Ale, and many
more **Tours:** No **Taproom:** Yes

Hilliard's Beer, located in Seattle's Ballard neighborhood, is quickly distinguish-ing itself in a state packed with some really good breweries. The brewery was started in 2011 by homebrewer Ryan Hilliard and business partner Adam Merkl, and

Hilliard's Saison
Style: Saison
ABV: 6.6%
Availability: Year-Round

It's not often you find a saison avail-able in a can. Going along with their theme of canning beers, Hilliard's thumbs their nose at tradition and decided to make their Saison one of the first to be distributed in a retro-looking can. Though it's easily porta-ble, it's best to pour this sessionable beer in a proper glass to experience its full beauty. Hazy golden in color, this traditional saison has plenty of lemon, white pepper, and bread in both nose and flavor. Pairing this versatile beer is simple. Try it with barbecue, sausage, or most spicy dishes, as the bold flavors will com-plement each other.

focuses on bringing canned craft beer to a bottle-dominated marketplace. While most other new breweries stay away from cans at the start because of high upfront costs, Hilliard's bases their brand on distributing beer in 16-ounce tallboy aluminum cans. Cans block out light and allow in less air, which keeps the beer fresh and helps maintain the flavor longer. All of their canned beers have a similar design and colors, but each style has a slightly different herringbone pattern on the bottom, making them recognizable to customers.

Along with their **Amber, Blonde,** and **Pils,** Hilliard's offers their approachable **Saison** in a can. Very few breweries in the world offer a saison-style beer in a can. The majority are bottled in 750ml cork and wire-caged bottles, but Hilliard's wanted to create a beer you could keep in your fridge for pretty much any occasion. Along with their selection of canned beer, you can find a range of beers available in their taproom or scattered throughout town on draft. One year-round brew is available only on draft: the **Extra Special Belgian.** Brewed as a typical ESB-style beer, it is fermented with saison yeast, giving it a touch of spicy notes and finishing dry and bitter.

The taproom in Ballard offers canned beers, growlers, kegs, and pints of the usual lineup along with on-site-only beers. If you're hungry, you can bring food along with you, or you may be lucky enough to visit on a day when a food truck is parked outside. Both dogs and kids are welcome to come along as well.

LANTERN BREWING

938 N. 95th St., Seattle, WA 98103; (206) 729-5350; LanternBrewing.com; @LanternBrewing
Founded: 2010 **Founder:** Chris Engdahl **Brewer:** Chris Engdahl **Flagship Beer:** Tripel
Year-Round Beers: Tripel, Dubbel, Witbier, Stout, Pale Ale **Seasonals/Special Releases:** Lucienne Sour Pale, SOS Stout, Fresh Hop Ale, Pumpkin SXS Stout, Blanche de Cerise, Blanche de Cassis, Blanche de Cannberge, and many more **Tours:** No **Taproom:** No

When it comes to brewing beer, the size of your brew kettle has nothing to do with the quality of beer you create. For Seattle-based Lantern Brewing, the 30-gallon brew kettle that owner Chris Engdahl started with has produced some unique and excellent beer. Located in the Phinney-Greenwood neighborhood, Lantern crafts small-batch Belgian-style ales that are distributed in hand-bottled 22-ounce bombers. By focusing on more Belgian-style beers, they set themselves apart from the heavy-hop trend most Northwest breweries follow. Along with using a yeast strain that originated in a Trappist monastery, each of the beers is bottle conditioned. The Belgians are famous for this technique that gives their beers a distinct, elegant finish.

Beer Lover's Pick

Tripel
Style: Tripel
ABV: 8%
Availability: Year-Round
As far as Tripels go, Lantern Brewing's Abbey-style Tripel hits it right on the head. You will find this Belgian beauty both on draft and in 22-ounce bottles sporting a yellow label, like most other Lantern Brewing beers. Watch out: This ale goes down a little too easily. Pouring a hazy golden color with a majestic white head, this brew sends a subtle aroma of bread, fruit, and Belgian yeast wafting from the glass. Your first sip will transport you to a picnic in the Belgian countryside, where you'll taste the local bread, fruit, and honey that dominate the complex flavor. This beer starts sweet but finishes fairly dry, with some alcohol present.

Because they produce on such a small brewing system, it can be difficult to find Lantern Brewing beers around the city. But if you're willing to hunt at beer festivals, farmers' markets, and a handful of area bottle shops, you'll surely find your tasty reward. Year-round they brew a **Tripel, Dubbel, Witbier, Stout,** and Belgian-influenced **Pale Ale.** In addition to the regular lineup, they offer multiple seasonal beers infused with fruits and other ingredients that are often grown in the state.

MACHINE HOUSE BREWERY
5840 Airport Way S., Ste. 121, Seattle, WA 98108; (206) 402-6025; MachineHouseBrewery.com; @machinehouse
Founded: 2012 **Founders:** Bill Arnott and Alex Brenner **Brewer:** Bill Arnott **Flagship Beer:** None **Year-Round Beers:** Mild, Gold, Bitter **Seasonals/Special Releases:** None yet **Tours:** No **Taproom:** Yes

Machine House Brewery may be one of the newest breweries in Seattle, but their beer is a bit old-school. The brewery and tasting room are located in Georgetown in the same building that once was home to the Seattle Brewing & Malting Company and Rainier. The brewery was founded by Bill Arnott, a native

Mild

Style: English Mild Ale

ABV: 3.6%

Availability: Year-Round

Machine House Brewery's Mild is a traditional English mild ale, uncommon for the hoppy state of Washington. However, don't let the lack of hop presence keep you from giving it a try. With its only 3.6% ABV, you might assume it will be watery, but the dark-brewed ale is loaded with malt flavors that will have you coming back, sip after tasty sip. The low ABV, along with its malty taste, adds to its appeal and pushes it toward being one of the best session beers in the state. At the brewery, Mild is served from a cask that gives it perfect carbonation for enjoying one after another while you catch a Sounders game.

of England, and Alex Brenner, and focuses on brewing English-style session ales. Their goal is to create easy-drinking beers with plenty of flavors that won't leave you bogged down after a night of drinking. In fact, of the 3 beers from the original standard lineup, their **Gold** boasts the highest ABV, at 4.4%. A brewery focusing on English-style session ales is uncommon in the Northwest and is a unique concept for a region known for high-alcohol styles.

Along with the aforementioned Gold, a golden ale, they also offer **Bitter** and **Mild.** Surprise! Each beer tastes as its name implies. The Mild, which comes in at 3.6% ABV, is an English mild ale with a nice brown color and a very light body that makes it easy to knock back all night long. Besides these 3 beers, you'll be able to find more sessionable beers in their taproom in the near future. Each taproom beer is served in true British "real ale" style and is poured from a cask through 3 authentic hand pumps at their custom-made bar. Stop by and belly up to that bar for a drink, kick back on the couch, or meet up with friends around tables with keg stools. Don't worry, they soften the seats up with a cushion so you can stay and have another round. Or two. As Machine House Brewery grows, they plan to distribute their beer throughout the area.

MARITIME PACIFIC BREWING COMPANY

1111 NW Ballard Way, Seattle, WA 98107; (206) 782-6181; MaritimeBrewery.com; @MaritimePacific

Founded: 1990 **Founders:** George and Jane Hancock **Brewer:** Matthew Schumacher **Flagship Beer:** Jolly Roger Christmas Ale **Year-Round Beers:** Flagship Red Alt Ale, Islander Pale Ale, Islander Pale Ale Dry-Hopped, Nightwatch Dark Amber Ale, Bosun's Black Porter, Imperial Pale Ale, Portage Bay Pilsener, Old Seattle Lager **Seasonals/Special Releases:** Jolly Roger Christmas Ale, Decompression Ale, Salmon Bay ESB, Oatmeal Pale Ale, Xtra Pale Ale, Windfest, Maibock, Summer Wheat, Old Tacoma Lager, Clipper Gold Hefeweizen, and many more **Tours:** No **Taproom:** Yes

In the Ballard district of Seattle, you can head over to Jolly Roger Taproom at the Maritime Pacific Brewing Company and have your pick of 13 beers on tap. While you're there, pull out this bit of brewery trivia to impress your friends: On the surface, the number of taps doesn't seem significant, but it was purposely chosen because they were the 13th licensed brewery in the state back in 1990. They were also the first brewery to set up shop in Ballard, which has since become one of the most beer-centric areas of the city.

The Jolly Roger taproom was added in 1997, and later moved along with the brewery to provide more space for growth. This place was packed most evenings. It's no surprise that Maritime Pacific has had such a successful business, as they are truly masters at brewing and innovation.

Over the years they have broken ground with both beer and food in innovative ways that have now become mainstream. For example, their **Jolly Roger Christmas Ale** was one of the first seasonal beers any craft brewery offered for the holiday. To this day it is still an industry standard holiday ale that has people flocking to the taproom or scouring bottle shops for a chance to drink its hefty nectar. Their **Old Seattle Lager,** originally named Skull Creek, was one of the first light lagers offered by a craft brewery in the Northwest and offers plenty of flavor in a light and easy-drinking brew.

Along with a lineup of year-round beers, Maritime Pacific also brews a rotation of seasonal and specialty beers and offers a range of cask-conditioned ales in the taproom. You can find a changing menu of eats to pair with your beers, but make sure to try the onion rings, the beer-battered bacon, or the original sliders, Lil' Jollys.

Islander Pale Ale
Style: Pale Ale
ABV: 5%
Availability: Year-Round
On the label of Maritime Pacific Islander Pale Ale you'll read the slogan "Brewed in the Northwest with Imagination." More than just your average Washington-brewed pale ale, Islander is brewed with both Yakima- and Czech Republic–grown hops, which adds to the unique flavor. Along with the pleasant hoppy bitterness, a caramel malt balances out the flavor. With an addition of malted wheat, this easy-drinking pale has plenty of body and complexities, yet is perfect as an everyday beer to be enjoyed with or without food.

NAKED CITY BREWERY & TAPHOUSE
8564 Greenwood Ave. N., Seattle, WA 98103; (206) 838-6299; NakedCityBrewing.com; @NakedCityBeer

Founded: 2008 **Founders:** Don Webb and Donald Averill **Brewer:** Don Webb **Flagship Beer:** None **Year-Round Beers:** Sad Eyed Lady of the Lowlands, Betsy's Mountain, Screening Room Red, Pinkerton Porter, Brute Force IPA **Seasonals/Special Releases:** Black Maria, Saison de La Vigne, Beyond the Pale IPA, Bindlestiff, The Knowledge, Rauchbier, The Kentucky Dude, Duplicity, The Big Lebrewski, Hoptrocity, Podunk IPA, Yankee Drifter, Bing, Fleur d'Elise, and many more **Tours:** By appointment **Taproom:** Yes

While their name might sound a bit like a strip club or invoke images that would make your mama blush, the name Naked City is actually taken from a 1948 film noir about the search for a killer in the murder of a beautiful New York

The Kentucky Dude
Style: Imperial Stout
ABV: 11%
Availability: Special Release
Brewed as Naked City's fourth-anniversary beer, The Kentucky Dude might strike a chord for fans of the movie The Big Lebowski. In fact, it's a special-brewed incarnation of The Big Lebrewski, a white Russian imperial stout that has been aged in two different Heaven Hills Kentucky bourbon barrels for 10 months before being blended together. The result is a dark-as-night beer full of booze, Kahlua, chocolate, oak, and dark fruits. It's a huge beer at 11% and should be considered a "strike" if you can find it.

woman. Although the movie is a bit dark, the brewery is anything but that. Founded in 2008 and officially serving beer in 2009, the Greenwood-based brewery and bar is a beacon of light for beer lovers in the area. Unselfishly they have chosen to serve many beers from other breweries alongside their own creations.

In 2012 Naked City was recognized as one of the top 100 beer bars by *Draft Magazine,* but all their success doesn't hinder them from staying progressive and continuing to produce well-crafted beers. Naked City has brewed over 85 beers and counting as they push the boundaries of brewing. Because they are constantly scheming up new creations, they offer just a handful of year-round beers and don't consider any of them their flagship. Instead they prefer to be known for the element of surprise. Some popular choices to look for are **The Big Lebrewski,** an imperial cream stout aged on Kahlua-soaked oak, and **Bing,** an English-style old ale brewed with Lyles Black Treacle Syrup, Bing cherries, cinnamon, star anise, and cloves.

As the brewery has grown, they have been able to offer their own kegs to local bars and restaurants throughout the Puget Sound area. However, if you can make it to the taproom, do yourself a favor: Come hungry and plan to stay awhile. Along with those 24 beers on tap, they offer an incredibly delicious food menu of various salads or burgers and a handful of entrees. If you're itching for a tour, call ahead and ask for an appointment, or seek out friendly brewer Don Webb, who will be happy to chat.

NORTHWEST PEAKS BREWERY

4912 17th Ave. NW, Ste. B, Seattle, WA 98107; (206) 853-0525; NWPeaksBrewery.com; @NWPeaksBrewery

Founded: 2010 **Founder:** Kevin Klein **Brewer:** Kevin Klein **Flagship Beer:** None
Year-Round Beers: None **Seasonals/Special Releases:** Redoubt Red, Eldorado Pale, Snowfield, Easy Peak-an Nut Brown, Blewett Smokey Scottish Ale, Enchantment Ale, Cloudy Weissen, White Chuck Ale, Ingalls Ginger, Vesper Bitter, Magic Brown, NW Peaks Black Blonde, Hannegan Red, Stuart Stout, Picket Porter, Sahale Pale Ale, and many more
Tours: No **Taproom:** Yes

Seattle's Ballard neighborhood is known as one of the most beer-loving areas in the city. With several successful breweries located within just a few miles of one another, this has proven to be an ideal place to open up a brewery. Like many other breweries in the neighborhood, Northwest Peaks Brewery has found success, although the nanobrewery operates a bit differently.

Because a smaller brew system offers flexibility, the brewery can easily experiment with a lot of different styles of beers. In fact, they have thrown out the notion that a brewery needs a flagship line of beers and instead put out a new lineup each month. While a few beers have been brewed more than once, most of them are one-hit wonders.

Redoubt Red
Style: Red Ale
ABV: 5.25%
Availability: Rotating

Like most other beers by Northwest Peaks, Redoubt Red is named for a mountain that brewer Kevin Klein has climbed. Mount Redoubt is located in northern Washington near the Canadian border and just west of Ross Lake. Though the mountain is lovely, the beer is truly something to behold. Ruby in color, this beauty has a light aroma filled with fruit and spices. In true Northwest fashion, hops are the star of the flavor as they break through a slight malty sweetness, creating an easy-drinking yet hoppy red ale.

Finding NW Peaks beer outside of Ballard is a pretty tough task. Even in the area only a handful of bars carry their beer on draft. The majority of their sales come from the NW Peak MountainBeers program. Beer drinkers can sign up for the monthly club that allows them to receive one or more growlers a month of delicious craft beer. The brewery offers 2 new beers per month and MountainBeer members just have to bring in their growler and exchange it for the next month's offering. Those who buy a year's subscription get 2 months free, and who doesn't enjoy free beer? For those far from the Ballard area who can't make a trek to the brewery each month, swing in for a visit to the taproom and get a sample of a few beers on tap. Make sure to check out their website before you head over, however, as they are open only sparingly.

ODIN BREWING COMPANY
9130 15th Place S., Ste. F, Seattle, WA 98108; (206) 762-3909; OdinBrewing.com; @OdinBrewingCo
Founded: 2009 **Founder:** Dan Lee **Brewer:** Brian Taft **Flagship Beer:** Odin's Gift
Year-Round Beers: Freya's Gold, Viking Gold, Odin's Gift, Sigrun **Seasonals/Special Releases:** Thor's Equinox, Loki, Smoky Bacon Ale, Thor's Intrigue, Thor's Fury, Pearl White Ale, Abbey Single, and many more **Tours:** No **Taproom:** No

In Seattle's South Park neighborhood lies Odin Brewing Company, a brewery that has been making a big splash both on store shelves and in restaurants throughout Washington and British Columbia. The production-only, Viking-themed brewery uses the tagline "Great Beer Designed with Great Food in Mind" even though they don't offer a brewpub or even a tasting room. Since the beginning, their lineup has completely fit into the typical Northwest-brewery mold. Many of their beers use unique ingredients, such as ginger, juniper, and angelica, to impart subtle flavors that help the beers pair well with a variety of foods. They tend to make each style less sweet than usual and a bit dry in the finish, which causes them to be very sessionable.

Their year-round lineup includes **Odin's Gift,** a unique amber ale brewed with junipers; **Freya's Gold,** a crisp and refreshing Kölsch-style ale; **Sigrun,** an approachable IPA brewed with rye malts; and **Viking Gold,** an extra-pale ale that blends Northwest-style pale ale with a slight German influence. October through March you can find **Thor's Equinox,** a dark Belgian strong ale. Named after one of the most famous Norse gods, this big beer has plenty of malt balanced with dark fruits, bananas, and a touch of woodiness. It's definitely a Belgian-influenced beer, but it drinks like a stout so thick you could slice a knife right through it.

Odin's Gift
Style: Amber Ale
ABV: 5.4% ABV
Availability: Year-Round
The name Odin's Gift comes from Norse mythology. Odin was the chief of all Norse gods who, according to legend, turned himself into an eagle and flew down to earth, where he sprinkled "magic dust" on clay vessels containing that year's grain harvest. Just add water and you have the first beer. Humankind was given the gift of fermentation. This gift is brewed with juniper berries, giving the amber ale a unique berry flavor balanced with caramel, malt, bitterness, and even a touch of chocolate.

For those seeking Odin Brewing beers, you can find them in 22-ounce bottles throughout Washington, northern Idaho, and British Columbia, as well as in multiple restaurants in kegs. With the quality of beers they have been producing, it's easy to see Odin sticking around and growing into one of the dominant breweries in the state.

PIKE BREWING COMPANY

1415 1st Ave., Seattle, WA 98101; (206) 622-6044; PikeBrewing.com; @PikeBrewing
Founded: 1989 **Founders:** Charles and Rose Ann Finkel **Brewer:** Dean Mochizuki
Flagship Beers: XXXXX Pike Extra Stout and Pike Kilt Lifter Scotch Ale **Year-Round Beers:** Pike Naughty Nellie, Pike Weisse, Pike Pale, Pike IPA, Pike Kilt Lifter, Pike Tandem, Pike Monk's Uncle, XXXXX Pike Extra Stout **Seasonals/Special Releases:** Pike Dry Wit, Pike Double IPA Double, Pike Auld Acquaintance, Pike Old Bawdy, Pike Entire, Cerveza Rosanna, and many more **Tours:** Yes, 2 p.m. Tues through Sat **Taproom:** Yes

In the 1980s, very few decent beers were on the market. The majority of American beers were filled with corn syrup and rice filler, giving the beer very little flavor. At that time, craft-beer pioneers Charles and Rose Ann Finkel had fallen in love with some of the classic beers from Europe and soon founded their own import company. It wasn't too long after that they decided to open their own brewery, known as Pike Place Brewery, in the La Salle Hotel under Seattle's famous Pike Place Public Market.

Since opening day, they aspired to brew a variety of tasty beers that paired well with food. With a loyal following quickly developing because of their beers bursting with flavor, Pike became a leader in the craft-beer revolution and helped forge the way for a solid beer culture in the state. By 1995 the demand for Pike beer had grown enough that the company moved to a new location, offered a brewpub, and changed the name to Pike Brewing Company. Not too far from the original location,

Beer Event

Pike ChocoFest

Since 2008 Pike Brewing has organized ChocoFest, an annual event to celebrate the natural harmony of chocolate and beer. Held each year conveniently around Valentine's Day, the event has grown considerably over the years. Expanding from just beer, they now invite local wineries, distilleries, meaderies, local restaurants, and food producers, as well as other local breweries, to participate. There is always an abundance of delicious chocolate, chocolate-based beers, and other drinks along with those that pair well with chocolate. Happy Valentine's Day!

XXXXX Stout
Style: Export Stout
ABV: 7.0%
Availability: Year-Round
Brewed to pair well with dreary Northwest days, XXXXX Stout is a hefty yet surprisingly approachable stout. It pours dark black with a thick tan head that sticks around for a while. Coffee and dark chocolate dominate the nose, yet the flavor is a fine marriage of dark chocolate and somewhat spicy hops with enough bitterness to make you sit up and take notice. The roasted coffee flavor returns at the end, leaving you feeling as if you just drank a cup of joe. It's fantastic on its own or paired with a sweet dessert.

Seattle

the brewpub is still one of the best venues in Seattle to get a beer. Beer lovers will appreciate the microbrewery museum located in the multilevel pub.

With 8 year-round beers that are a mix of English- and Belgian-style ales, Pike offers something for just about every drinker who enjoys flavorful beer. Along with the classics, such as **Pike Pale, Pike Kilt Lifter, Pike IPA,** and **XXXXX Pike Extra Stout,** the brewery offers multiple seasonals. If you enjoy plenty of hops, give their **Double IPA** a try. Brewed originally to commemorate Seattle Beer Week, the unfiltered IPA is a well-balanced blend of floral and piney hops with smooth biscuity malts. If you like even heftier beers, **Pike Old Bawdy Barley Wine** has plenty of fruit, caramel, and booze flavors to warm you up on a rainy Seattle evening.

PYRAMID BREWERY

1201 1st Ave. S., Seattle, WA 98134; (206) 682-8322; PyramidBrew.com; @PyramidBrew
Founded: 1984 **Founder:** Beth Hartwell **Brewer:** Kim Brusco **Flagship Beer:**
Hefeweizen **Year-Round Beers:** Hefeweizen, Apricot, Thunderhead, Outburst, Wheaten
IPA Weiss Cream **Seasonals/Special Releases:** Discord, Curve Ball, Oktoberfest, Snow
Cap, Helles Smokey, Uproar, Red Wheat with Fig, Super Snow Cap, Wit, Dunkel, Pale Ale,
Maibock, Barleywine, Chai Wheat, Oatmeal Stout, and many more **Tours:** Daily at 4 p.m.
Taproom: Yes

Pyramid Brewery's beers have been gracing store shelves across the West Coast since 1984, although its image has changed a touch since the doors were first opened. Founded as Hart Brewing by Beth Hartwell in the small western Washington logging town of Kalama, the brewery became one of the first in the US to produce microbrews.

Their inaugural beer was named **Pyramid Pale Ale** and was brewed with only Cascade hops. It is still available today as a seasonal selection. In 1989 the Hartwells sold the brewery to five Seattle-based investors, who merged the company with Thomas Kemper Brewery three years later. By the mid-1990s Hart Brewing was the fourth-largest brewery in the country and opened up a second brewery in downtown Seattle near the city's major stadiums. Around the same time, their Pyramid line made up the bulk of the company's sales, so they changed their name to Pyramid Breweries Inc. As sales picked up, they also opened another brewing location in Berkeley, California. Shortly afterward, they shut down the Kalama location, leaving their headquarters in Seattle.

Today they operate multiple alehouses along the West Coast and distribute their beers all over the country. With a focus on wheat beers, Pyramid is well-known for their **Hefeweizen** as well as their **Apricot Ale,** the most popular wheat beer, made with fresh apricots. You can also find 4 other beers in their year-round lineup that includes **Thunderhead IPA, Outburst Imperial IPA, Weiss Cream,** and **Wheaten IPA.** Throughout the year they offer multiple seasonals and special releases, including a handful of beers available only at their pubs. In the colder months, make sure to grab a six-pack of their winter warmer, known as **Snow Cap.** The deep mahogany–colored beer is packed with big malt and sweet caramel flavors perfect for sipping on a dreary night. The Seattle Alehouse is a perfect place to stop by if you're headed to Safeco and CenturyLink Fields. Pop in before or after a game and try some pub-exclusive beers and pub-style grub.

Outburst Imperial IPA
Style: Imperial IPA
ABV: 8.5%
Availability: Year-Round
It's no secret that northwesterners love hops. With that in mind, Pyramid created its Outburst Imperial IPA. In the beginning, Outburst was available only in the summer, but the hopheads spoke and it soon became a standard in the brewery's lineup. Big hop aromas come from the beer, dry hopped with Falconer's Flight and Zythos hops. Although the beer boasts 80 IBUs, the sweet malt flavors tame the citrus and pine bitterness, creating a well-balanced and easy-drinking imperial IPA. Pair it with spicy foods or drink it on its own; it's perfect either way.

Seattle

REUBEN'S BREWS
1406 NW 53rd St., Ste. 1A, Seattle, WA 98107; (206) 753-9583; ReubensBrews.com; @ReubensBrews
Founded: 2012 **Founders:** Adam Robbings, Grace Robbings, and Mike Pfeiffer **Brewer:** Adam Robbings **Flagship Beer:** None **Year-Round Beers:** American Rye, Reuben's Roggenbier, Reuben's Imperial Rye IPA, Imperial IPA, American Brown **Seasonals/Special Releases:** Robust Porter, Red, Belgian Pale Ale, Imperial Oatmeal Stout, Mocha Stout, Balsch California Lager, Pumpkin Rye, and many more **Tours:** No **Taproom:** Yes

One of the newest breweries to pop up in Seattle's Ballard neighborhood is Reuben's Brews, a small brewery founded in 2012 by Adam and Grace Robbings. The name comes from their son Reuben, who was born around the same time Grace

Roggenbier
Style: Roggenbier
ABV: 5.3%
Availability: Rotating

You could easily choose just about any beer from Reuben's Brews and fall in love with it. However, their Roggenbier is a must-try since this style rarely shows up around the Northwest. Roggenbiers originate from Germany and use lots of rye, which gives the beer both spicy and sour notes. Reuben's Brews' version is about as spot-on as you can find in the Northwest, with banana, clove, sweet malt, and plenty of that rye spiciness in the flavor. This is an incredibly easy-drinking beer that stands apart from most beers brewed in the US.

bought Adam the homebrewing kit that eventually led him to start the brewery. After years of homebrewing along with schooling through the UC-Davis intensive brewing program, Adam had the brewery up and cranking out some incredible beers. In fact, in their first year the small brewery won three medals at the World Beer Championships, including a gold medal for their **American Brown.**

Outside of Ballard it might be difficult to find Reuben's Brews on draft; however, they are occasionally popping up around the area. This is mainly due to the fact that they are focusing on selling their beer through their tasting room, which is currently located smack-dab in the middle of the brewery. For the hopheads out there you have to try their **Imperial Rye IPA.** At 8.4% ABV the bitter yet citrusy beer has a unique flavor from the rye and can easily be ranked as one of the best imperial IPAs in the state.

Make sure to check the hours of the tasting room on the website before heading down to try out their selection of great beers. Make sure to bring a growler or two, as you'll want to take some beer home. The tasting room doesn't offer food, so come ready to consume your daily caloric intake with tasty beer.

SCHOONER EXACT BREWING COMPANY

3901 1st Ave. S., Seattle, WA 98134; (206) 432-9734; SchoonerExact.com;
@SchoonerExact

Founded: 2007 **Founders:** Marcus Connery, Matt McClung, and Heather McClung
Brewer: Matt McClung **Flagship Beer:** 3 Grid IPA **Year-Round Beers:** 3 Grid IPA,
Regrade Pale Ale, Profanity Hill Porter, King St. Brown, Gateway Golden Ale, Gallant
Maiden Hefeweizen **Seasonals/Special Releases:** Puget Soundian Dark Ale, The
Imperial Project, Hoppy Holidays, Hoppy the Woodsman, Seamstress Union, Gutter
Punk'n Ale, Midnight Union, and many more **Tours:** Brewers accessible in afternoons
Taproom: Yes

While many homebrewers dream of the day they can pursue their dreams of opening up their own brewery, founders of Schooner Exact Brewing Company

Beer Lover's Pick

3 Grid IPA
Style: IPA
ABV: 6.7%
Availability: Year-Round
Named after the three grids of traffic
in Seattle that resulted from a land
dispute between three of the city's
founding fathers, Schooner Exact's 3
Grid IPA is a Northwest-style IPA that
is meant to go down easy. The golden-
looking IPA is billowing with citrus
and tropical aromas coming from multiple varieties of Yakima-grown hops.
Although the citrus hoppiness domi-
nates, the slightly caramel and bready
malt flavor give it balance, creating
an incredibly delicious IPA with a dry
finish that makes it fairly sessionable
despite the high ABV.

Matt and Heather McClung, along with their former business partner Marcus Connery, took the plunge while keeping their day jobs. Both Matt and Heather were teachers by day and worked the small brewery by night for the first few years. Working on a half-barrel system, they were able to brew only one keg at a time, which limited early growth. Their hard work paid off, though, and they have grown into a much larger brewing system in a new location, added a taproom and restaurant, and are quickly growing into one of the city's most beloved breweries.

The name Schooner Exact comes from a little history from the West Seattle neighborhood not too far from the brewery. In 1851 members of the Denny party founded Seattle when their schooner, named *Exact,* dropped anchor in present-day West Seattle. Along with several limited releases and seasonals, Schooner Exact offers 6 beers in their year-round lineup that includes their flagship **3 Grid IPA, Regrade Pale Ale, King Street Brown, Gateway Golden Ale, Gallant Maiden Hefeweizen,** and **Profanity Hill Porter,** a delicious porter brewed with 7 different malts, giving it flavors of chocolate, walnuts, and fruit. Outside of their restaurant, you can find their beer both in bottles and on draft mainly up and down the I-5 corridor in Washington.

TWO BEERS BREWING COMPANY

4700 Ohio Ave. S., Seattle, WA 98134; (206) 762-0490; TwoBeersBrewery.com; @TwoBeersBrewing

Founded: 2007 **Founder:** Joel VandenBrink **Brewer:** Joel VandenBrink **Flagship Beer:** Evolutionary IPA **Year-Round Beers:** Evolutionary IPA, 20:20 Blonde Ale, Immersion Amber, Persnickety Pale, SoDo Brown **Seasonals/Special Releases:** Crooked Belgian Wit, Fresh Hop, Jive Espresso Stout, Panorama Wheat, Pumpkin Spice Ale, Trailhead ISA, Heart of Darkness Imperial CDA **Tours:** No **Taproom:** Yes

The name of Joel VandenBrink's brewery stems from a disagreement he had with a friend. After a trip to a local pub to talk it out, they were able to have an honest conversation after each drinking two beers. Shortly afterward, the Seattle-based brewery was up and operating out of a 170-square-foot space. Just a few years and many batches of quality beers later, Two Beers is located in a 4,800-square-foot space complete with a dedicated tasting room and plenty of space to expand.

In 2011 Two Beers Brewing became the first Washington craft brewery to distribute their beer in 12-ounce cans. They also offer many of their beers in 22-ounce bottles, which are currently available in Washington, Oregon, Idaho, and Alaska. Each of their 5 year-round and 7 regular seasonal beers is created using all Washington-sourced ingredients. In the Northwest, many breweries are judged based on their

IPA. **Evolutionary IPA** doesn't disappoint. Along with the huge citrus and pine aroma and flavor, the caramel background keeps the beer grounded and incredibly drinkable. Another beer you'll definitely want to try is their special release **Fresh Hop IPA.** Their crew makes a trek to Yakima Valley to pick up just-harvested hops to add the same day. It creates a refreshingly clean and hoppy brew.

Their tasting room, known as The Woods, should be on your must-visit list for Seattle. With 12 tap handles filled with their in-house beers as well as a selection of guest taps, it's the best place to experience just how tasty their brews are. Make sure to bring a growler or two; their beer is mighty tasty.

Beer Lover's Pick

Heart of Darkness CDA
Style: Black IPA
ABV: 8.4%
Availability: Year-Round
With a name like Heart of Darkness, you expect a beer that's incredibly dark. Two Beers Brewing doesn't let you down with their Cascadian dark ale that truly is as dark as night. With delicious roasted malts and citrus in the aroma, it draws you in and you can't help but dive into the darkness. Coffee, chocolate, and roasted malts with citrus and piney hops make up well-balanced flavor packed with a noticeable bitterness. Be careful, though; the 8.4% ABV barely makes itself known and will sneak up on you like a mugger under the cover of night.

Brewpubs

BIG TIME BREWERY & ALEHOUSE

4133 University Way NE, Seattle, WA 98105; (206) 545-4509; BigTimeBrewery.com;
@BigTimeBrewery

Founded: 1988 **Founder:** Reid Martin **Brewer:** Drew Cluley **Flagship Beers:** Bhagwan's Best IPA, Scarlet Fire IPA **Year-Round Beers:** Prime Time Pale Ale, Atlas Amber Ale, Coal Creek Porter, Bhagwan's Best IPA **Seasonals/Special Releases:** Old Wooly, Scarlet Fire IPA, Whiny the Complainer, Icculus IPA, Breakfast Cereal Killer Stout, Dark Days, Hopgoblin Pumpkin Ale, Miss Figgy, Millennium Falconer, and many more

Serving the University of Washington community since 1988, Big Time Brewery & Alehouse touts itself as an "old guard of the American craft beer movement." With their 14-barrel JV Northwest system, this classic American alehouse has earned a king's ransom in medals from the Great American Beer Festival. Not just your run-of-the-mill brewpub, Big Time transports its visitors back to "yesterbeer" with an extensive collection of bottles and cans, turn-of-the-20th-century Brunswick bar, loads of old beer signs and trays, as well as various historical brewery photographs.

Although brewery-related memorabilia is great, when it comes to brewpubs it is all about the beer and the food. Usually Big Time has about 10 ales on tap, while Thursday and Friday feature a cask-conditioned "real ale" on their hand pump. Their **Prime Time Pale Ale** has won three gold medals in previous Great American Beer Festivals. Balanced hops and subtle malts make this brew a crowd-pleaser regardless of one's beer knowledge.

With their pizzas, sandwiches, salads, pomme frites with dipping sauces, nachos, and baked potatoes, as well as specials changing daily, pairing your brew with delicious food won't be a difficult task. Feel free to bring the kids in for a PB&J or a toasted cheese, as kids are permitted until 8 p.m.

ELLIOTT BAY BREWING COMPANY

4720 California Ave. SW, Seattle, WA 98116; (206) 932-8695; ElliottBayBrewing.com;
@ElliotBay_Beer

Founded: 1997 **Founders:** Todd Carden and Brent Norton **Brewer:** Doug Hindman
Flagship Beer: Alembic Pale Ale **Year-Round Beers:** Alembic Pale Ale, B-town Brown,
Highline IPA, Hop von Boorian, Luna Weizen, No Doubt Stout, Pilot Light **Seasonals/
Special Releases:** Mashing Pumpkin Ale, Noale Holiday Ale, Noir von Boorian, Riot Ale,
Unintention Ale, Vanilla No Doubt Stout, Coffee Stout, Demolition Ale, and many more

Located in the historic "Junction" of West Seattle, Elliott Bay Brewing is the
product of a shared dream of Todd Carden and Brent Norton. Since they opened
in 1997, Elliott Bay Brewing has been a role model of sustainability and philan-
thropic support in the community. With one of the largest selections of organic ales
in Washington, the brewers have used 100% organic barley for the base malt of all
of the house beers.

While you are there, try an **Alembic Pale Ale.** Brewed exclusively with Cascade
hops, this former gold medal winner at the Great American Beer Festival is consistently Elliott Bay Brewing's number-one-selling brew. If you're in the mood for a
darker beer, the **No Doubt Stout** may be the ticket. The darkest of the year-round
beers at Elliott Bay, this stout has a dark coffee-brown color and a chocolaty sweet
aroma. With a light mouthfeel, a molasses-like sweetness, and chocolate notes, this
is a robust brew. As with most brewpubs, Elliott Bay Brewing both sells growlers and
will fill your own growler with their delicious brews. In fact, on Monday they will
even do it for half price at the California Avenue location.

The food menu at Elliott Bay is filled to the brim with delicious delicacies to
accompany your eco-friendly brew. Sustainability also plays a large part in the operation of the kitchens at all Elliott Bay locations. Even the waste oil from the kitchen
is picked up by a local biodiesel company and recycled into biofuel.

GORDON BIERSCH BREWERY RESTAURANT

600 Pine St., Ste. 401, Seattle, WA 98101; (206) 405-4205; GordonBiersch.com;
@GBBrewingCo

Founded: 1988 **Founders:** Dan Gordon and Dean Biersch **Brewer:** Drew Colpitts
Flagship Beer: Märzen **Year-Round Beers:** Golden Export, Hefeweizen, Blonde Bock,
Czech Pilsner, Märzen, Schwarzbier **Seasonals/Special Releases:** Maibock, WinterBock,
Festbier, SommerBrau, IPB, Dunkelweizen, and many more

With establishments from coast to coast as well as stretching across the Pacific
in Taiwan and Hawaii, Gordon Biersch opened the doors of their first brewpub on July 6, 1988, in Palo Alto, California. With most of the restaurants featuring

on-site breweries, patrons can be assured of a fresh-tasting pint. Featuring German lagers and ales, Gordon Biersch's commitment to delivering the freshest possible beer to their customers has led to a fair share of awards at the World Beer Cup as well as the Great American Beer Festival.

The Seattle location, although situated in a mall, has outdoor seating along with glass ceilings. With an exposed kitchen and open seating area, the black-and-white-striped booths are a great place for patrons to watch the goings-on in the kitchen. Gordon Biersch's most popular beer, the **Märzen,** is an extremely smooth Bavarian lager with quite a malty flavor. Overall it is a great sessionable beer for Oktoberfest. Order a pint of this brew to go with GB's Märzen barbecue chicken sandwich, which is topped with smoked bacon, cheddar cheese, and the house Märzen barbecue sauce.

Looking for something a little lighter? Bitter with spicy, signature Saaz hops from the Czech Republic, Gordon Biersch's **Czech Pilsner** is a classic Bohemian-style pilsner that has an herbal and floral aroma. This refreshing, crisp beer has a clean malt taste with hints of apple. If you're just looking for an appetizer, pair this Pilsner with the much-talked-about Gordon Biersch garlic fries.

MCMENAMINS
300 E. Pike St. Seattle, WA 98122; (206) 223-1698; McMenamins.com; @CaptainNeon
Founded: 1995 (McMenamins as a company 1983) **Founders:** Mike and Brian McMenamin **Brewer:** Kyle Jungck **Flagship Beer:** Hammerhead **Year-Round Beers:** Hammerhead, Terminator Stout, Ruby, Evergreen IPA, Porter, Wheat, Gold, Purple Haze **Seasonals/Special Releases:** Nut Brown, Kris Kringle, Nitro ESB, and many more

The McMenamins name is synonymous with beer in the state of Washington. In 1974 Mike McMenamin opened up his first tavern. Since then Mike and his brother Brian have opened up over 60 locations throughout Oregon and Washington. With brewpubs, hotels, concert venues, and multiple theater pubs, McMenamins has branched out to many other avenues for the imbiber of craft beer to enjoy. Beer, wine, distilled spirits, and even coffee now don the McMenamin name in their extensive line of products and offerings.

Of the eight locations in Washington, three are historical properties. The Six Arms brewpub in Seattle is decked out with floor-to-ceiling windows and was originally a showroom that showcased the newest automotive technology of the day. Cars and car-related businesses filled the Six Arms building from the early 1900s until 1995, when the McMenamins brothers became the custodians of the building's rich history.

Made with kiln-baked specialty grains, the **Terminator Stout** from McMenamins has a strong roasted-malt aroma with flavors of coffee and chocolate. This dark brew works well to assist in washing down a Wild Wil's Jumbo Deluxe burger, which has Tillamook cheddar cheese, bacon, and a fried egg. If you're looking for a beer on the lighter side, a pint of **Ruby** may fit the bill. An unfiltered American-style fruit pale ale, this beer uses a hint of raspberries to provide a pinkish color. Crisp and a little tangy, the refreshing carbonation and the raspberry tartness combine to create a very refreshing beer. Combining this with the Brewer's Salad, which has blue cheese crumbles, roasted hazelnuts, marinated red onions, and raspberry–Ruby ale vinaigrette, makes for a light, delicious lunch.

OUTLANDER BREWERY & PUB

225 N. 36th St., Seattle, WA 98103; (206) 486-4088; OutlanderBrewing.com;
@OutlanderBrew
Founded: 2012 **Founders:** Dragan Radulovic and Nigel Lassiter **Brewer:** Nigel Lassiter
Flagship Beer: None **Year-Round Beers:** None **Seasonals/Special Releases:** That's What's Up, Braggot, The Oatmeal Stout, Rauch n' Maple, Outlander Hop Bomb, Costas Ooppaa!, Not a Beer (gluten free), Cherry Belgian, Graham Cracker, Goats N Roses, Coffee Stout, Munich Barleywine, Peanut Butter Stout, and many more

The Fremont-based Outlander Brewery & Pub could actually be referred to as a nano-brewpub. Opened in 2012, the small pub located in an old blue house built in 1900 is brewing a whole range of experimental and nontypical beers on a tiny

one-barrel system (enough to fill up two kegs each time they brew). While the size of their system isn't typical of most brewpubs, it works very well for their business model. Stepping inside the quaint pub you almost get a feeling you're visiting a friend's house for a few beers. However, this is one friend who has taken his brewing to the next level and always has something new and exciting to try.

Within just a few months of opening, they had already brewed quite a range of beers with the thought of never brewing a beer more than twice unless it was requested. Their selection is partly determined by their customers, with monthly polls helping them decide what they'll brew next. Beers such as their **Peanut Butter Stout, Graham Cracker Ale, Chili Amber, Monster Mash Raisin Pumpkin, Honey Basil Ale,** or **Strawberry Wheat** give you a glimpse into what types of creations they come up with. With such a rotation of new beers, it can often be tough to find a place to sit in the pub, as regulars keep coming back to imbibe the unique creations.

Along with a rotation of new beers, you can find a small menu consisting of cheese and meat plates, meat and veggie pies, quiches, and a handful of other snacks. In the summer you can sit out on the patio, where they grill up beer sausages and listen to records on their old phonograph.

RAM RESTAURANT & BREWERY

2650 NE University Village St., Seattle, WA 98105; (206) 522-3565; TheRam.com
Founded: 1971 **Founders:** Jeff Iverson and Cal Chandler **Brewer:** Dave Leonard
Flagship Beer: Buttface Amber **Year-Round Beers:** Big Horn Blonde, Big Horn
Hefeweizen, Big Red Ale, Buttface Amber Ale, Total Disorder Porter **Seasonals/Special
Releases:** S'no Angel, Maibock Spring Bier, Oktoberfest, Washington Blonde, and many
more

Although technically born in 1971, the Ram Restaurant in-house brewery known as Big Horn Brewing Company did not come into fruition until 1995. Big Horn Brewing Company is one of the largest brewpub companies in the country and has won over 15 medals for their various beers at the Indiana Brewers' Cup, North American Beer Awards, and the Great American Beer Festival.

In Seattle the Ram offers two locations: one at University Village just north of downtown and the other at the Northgate Mall. Outside of Seattle they also offer eight other locations in the state. Stop in for a **Buttface Amber Ale.** Made with 5 different malts and 4 different hop varieties, the Buttface is the most complex beer of the Ram lineup. With a high malt character and hints of sweet caramel and toffee, this beer has a great mouthfeel for the style, as well as having low bitterness.

If you fancy satisfying your sweet tooth instead, perhaps go for the **Total Disorder Porter.** A silver-medal winner at the Great American Beer Festival, this two-row barley base along with chocolate and carastan malts culminate in a brew that is heavy on the coffee and malt notes. With a light mouthfeel and a touch of brown sugar sweetness on the finish, this beer finishes with chocolaty notes. Pair it with a dentist-cringing dessert of Colossal Sizzling Bread Pudding. Topped with vanilla ice cream and caramel sauce, this house-made bread pudding with custard, nutmeg, cinnamon, and vanilla comes served on a hot skillet.

ROCK BOTTOM BREWERY

1333 5th Ave., Seattle, WA 98101; (206) 623-3070; RockBottom.com/Seattle
Founded: 1991 (company), 1996 (Seattle location) **Founder:** Frank Day **Brewer:** Josh
Dalton **Flagship Beer:** Hop Bomb **Year-Round Beers:** Kölsch, White Ale, Red Ale,
IPA, Special Dark **Seasonals/Special Releases:** Daylight, Faller Wheat, Hop Bomb IPA,
Peashooter Pale Ale, Rain City Red, Flying Salmon Stout, and many more

Just blocks away from Seattle's famous Pike Street Market lies an amalgam brewery of sorts in the form of Rock Bottom Brewery. Although it is technically a chain restaurant and owned by a corporation, each location has its very own brewmaster, who is allowed to apply both his brewing knowledge as well as his creativity to create new recipes for the particular location. Josh Dalton, the head brewer here, was awarded large-brewpub brewer of the year at the Great American Beer Festival in 2008.

Steaks, burgers, sandwiches, pizzas, salads, desserts—you name it and this place delivers. This kid-friendly establishment also offers a kids' menu with the usual favorites for the wee ones. Even the most finicky of eaters would be hard-pressed to not find a tasty treat that requires washing down with a pint. (Not the kids, of course, but they might like the house-brewed root beer!) Be on the lookout for their **Faller Wheat** seasonal beer. This unfiltered, light-bodied session ale was a 2005 silver-medal winner at the Great American Beer Festival in the Hefeweizen category.

Don't be fooled by the "chain" element of this brewery. Let the accolades and the beer "bling" this brewery has earned speak for themselves.

URBAN FAMILY PUBLIC HOUSE

5329 Ballard Ave. NW, Seattle, WA 98107; (206) 861-6769; UrbanFamilyPublicHouse.com; @UrbanFamBrewing
Founded: 2012 **Founders:** Sean Bowman, Timothy Czarnetzki, and David Powell
Brewer: Justin Quinlan **Flagship Beer:** None **Year-Round Beers:** None **Seasonals/Special Releases:** Red Derby Porter, Saison des Feux, La Vagabond, Lee Road Pale Ale, Le Cercle Rouge

Located in the heart of Ballard, this brewpub got its name from when the now three owners of the brewpub all lived in a shared house in Washington, DC. People called them a "modern urban family" and that sentiment carried over into the naming of this brewpub. With over 20 taps at the ready, a handful being brewed by Urban Family, there is plenty of beer to choose from. On menus labeled "Ours" and "Theirs," figuring out which beers they brew won't be a challenge.

The menu consists of small plates and burgers, Belgian frites, and poutines. Pick a brew and pair it with a Bacon Blue burger, which is topped with onion chutney, Oregon blue cheese, and house-made bacon jam . . . repeat, bacon jam. Try this burger with a **Lunar Caustic IPA,** which has a strong malt presence, along with notes of lemon zest and bitter orange. If IPAs aren't your thing, try the **Saison des Feux.** With tropical fruit and light smokiness, the flavor profiles in this brew will align nicely with the bacon jam.

Beer Bars

BEVERIDGE PLACE PUB

6413 California Ave. SW, Seattle, WA 98136; (206) 932-9906; BeveridgePlacePub.com; @BPPub

Draft Beers: 36 **Bottled/Canned Beers:** Over 150

One must-visit watering hole in West Seattle is Beveridge Place Pub. Known throughout the country, Beveridge Place Pub has been named as one of the 100 best beer bars in America by *Draft Magazine* and best pub on the West Coast in 2011 by *Beer West Magazine*. In 2008 the pub moved to its current location and has continued serving both beer geeks and casual beer drinkers alike. Outside, the building has an old-time-saloon type of feel that carries over a bit into the interior. With eclectic wooden furniture, couches, and vintage decor throughout, you will feel immediately welcome. The front room is filled with antique beer signs and houses the bar, which is complete with a bowling-lane bartop. Behind the bar is the pub's centerpiece, a beautifully crafted barback built in 1907 and made with cherry-stained tiger maple. To the right of the pub you can enter the game room to watch some sports or play pool, foosball, or a handful of other games.

What makes Beveridge Place Pub so special is the beer selection. With 36 beers on draft, most of which constantly rotate from Washington breweries, there is always something new to try. Along with a well-planned tap selection, the fridges in the back hold over 150 bottles, with beer from Belgium, Germany, Great Britain, Japan, and all over the world. For those who aren't into beer, they offer an excellent selection of wines by the glass, meads, ciders, and sake. Aside from a few snacks such as nuts and popcorn, they don't offer any food themselves, but they do have a solid list of nearby restaurants that deliver a wide variety of food you can bring in to enjoy with your brews.

Brouwer's Hard Liver Barleywine Festival

For those who enjoy a good barleywine, it doesn't get much better than Brouwer's Hard Liver Barleywine Festival (hardliver.com). With over 60 aged barleywines pouring from years past, you get to sample some of the best and biggest beers around. Most fall in the range of 8–12% ABV, so good luck attempting to try them all. A tip you should take into consideration: Look at the list before arriving so you know what beers you want to try, and order those first. It can get incredibly packed inside and people will start lining up hours before the doors open, so get there early.

BROUWER'S CAFE
400 N. 35th St., Seattle, WA 98103; (206) 267-2437; BrouwersCafe.com; @Brouwerscafe
Draft Beers: 64 **Bottled/Canned Beers:** Over 300

When you enter Brouwer's Cafe, you'll quickly feel as if you've been transported to a modern Belgian beer hall. Walk in a little farther and you'll have the choice of heading up the wooden staircase to the second floor or into the beautifully designed and cavernous main area. Wooden tables and booths offer plenty of seating, while the two bars offer additional areas to imbibe. The massive skylight lets plenty of light in during the day and the openness of the U-shaped second floor makes the space feel gigantic.

For those in the mood for scotch, the bar in the back carries over 60 varieties, while the main bar has 64 beers on draft and over 300 bottles. To say they take their beer seriously is an understatement. With a top-notch selection, you can come pretty much every day of the year and still find something you haven't tried from all over the world. Beers are always poured in a proper glass that gets a good rinsing right before it's filled, and the head of the beer is then shaved off with a knife. The tap lines are replaced with new tubing each time a new keg is put on to make sure no other beer has run through the lines.

Seattle

Along with an outstanding beer selection, you'll find a selection of Belgian-inspired foods on the menu, such as mussels and frites and *stoofvlees,* a traditional Belgian stew. Brouwer's Cafe does tend to get pretty busy on the weekends, so plan accordingly based on your preferences.

CHUCK'S HOP SHOP

656 NW 85th St., Seattle, WA 98117; (206) 297-6212; Chucks85th.com; @Chucks85th
Draft Beers: 38 **Bottled/Canned Beers:** 1,000

To call Chuck's a beer bar is a little misleading. Started as Chuck's 85th St. Market in the Greenwood neighborhood, the store was simply a convenience store with an incredible beer selection as well as beer on draft. Over the years, however, the store has grown into much more than just your typical quickie mart. Sure, there are

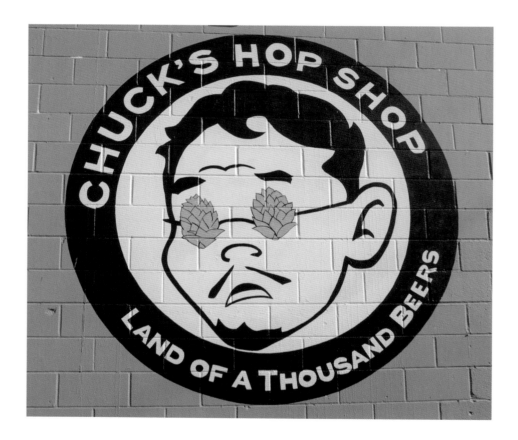

still aisles of chips, candy, and your typical market offerings, but locals will more likely describe it as one of Seattle's best places to get a growler filled or drink a few pints of some of the most incredible beers in the city. With 38 beers on draft and an impressive selection of over 1,000 bottled brews available in the coolers, this is one local market that every beer lover would be happy to have in their neighborhood.

Out front you'll find a small patio to enjoy your brews on nicer days, while inside you can walk past the food aisles and find more seating and tables to kick back and enjoy some good brew. You'll also notice a large TV displaying their current draft list and a few facts about each beer. The atmosphere is relaxed and has an everyday neighborhood feel where everyone is invited. You can order half pints if you want to explore multiple beers on your trip, thus making your decision a bit easier when trying to decide from a selection of 38 well-chosen beers.

Aside from the convenience-store food and coolers filled with ice cream, you'll frequently find a rotation of food trucks parked outside offering a variety of foods to pair with your beer. Parking can be tight, as their lot is small, so look for street parking on any of the nearby side streets.

THE NOBLE FIR

5316 Ballard Ave. NW, Seattle, WA 98107; (206) 420-7425; TheNobleFir.com; @TheNobleFir
Draft Beers: 16 **Bottled/Canned Beers:** About 30

You'll feel immediately connected to the outdoors upon entering The Noble Fir, located in the Ballard neighborhood conveniently on Ballard Avenue. High ceilings with plenty of natural light give the space a cheerful and welcoming vibe. Throughout the clean and well-organized bar is wooden furniture made with Douglas fir and western hemlock, hiking maps, and outdoor scenes hanging on the walls—all of which play to the outdoor theme. You can also peruse the large selection of hiking maps and travel books while enjoying a vast selection of beverages. Under the bar they even have carabiner coat hooks to hang your jacket.

While the atmosphere is comfortable, the drink selection is really what sets The Noble Fir apart. It's not so much the quantity they offer, although you will find 16 beers on draft, but their selection of beers should get most beer geeks to make the trek into Ballard regularly. The rotating taps come from breweries all over the world, with many being hard-to-find seasonal and limited-release ales and lagers not found in many other places throughout the city. Their bottle selection is equally impressive, with beers not typically found at your local supermarket. Aside from beer, they also specialize in ciders, with a hefty selection in bottles, and generally two or three on draft, as well as a small selection of wine. While you will find a small food selection of specialty meats, cheeses, and breads, don't expect to fill up. Their kitchen produces some delicious small plates that are best enjoyed with good friends.

THE PINE BOX
1600 Melrose Ave., Seattle, WA 98122; (206) 588-0375; PineBoxBar.com; @PineBox
Draft Beers: 33 **Bottled/Canned Beers:** Around 5

Located conveniently on the corner of Pine Street and Melrose Avenue, The Pine Box opened in 2012 to serve the beer-loving neighborhood of Capitol Hill. The bar is located in what was once a funeral home that was the site of action superstar Bruce Lee's funeral. Inside the beautiful old building you almost get a feeling that you're in church, with the high ceilings, crown molding, church-pew seating, and even a choir loft that has plenty of extra tables to enjoy your drinks upstairs.

You'll find a full bar with a massive whiskey selection along with 32 beers on draft and one on cask. Although it's highly unlikely there won't be something that sounds good to drink on the beer menu, just wait a little bit and it will change fairly quickly. So quickly, in fact, that they don't print menus, but instead offer their beer selection on two TVs up front, or you can view an updated draft list right on your

Hops & Props

Seattle has a long tradition of aviation. Hops & Props combines that love of aviation with good craft beer to create a fund-raiser every year for the Museum of Flight, the largest nonprofit air and space museum in the world. The one-day event offers beer from more than 50 breweries. Since it is a fund-raiser, it doesn't attract your typical beer-geek fans, but it's a great excuse to drink beer and look at some pretty cool planes. For more information, check out the event website at museumofflight.org/hops-and-props.

smart phone. Their selections range from many West Coast–brewed beers, to those around the US and world. One of the most interesting features they offer that sends beer geeks flocking to order a pint is the Randall they have installed directly to their tap lines. The Randall is a device developed by Dogfish Head Brewing that acts as a chamber, filled with hops, cocoa nibs, fruit, coffee, or anything else imaginable. Beer is then passed through the device on its way out of the keg while infusing the beer with unique flavors. It's not something you see every day, but it makes for a unique experience.

Come hungry to The Pine Box, as they offer a selection of salads, pizza, sandwiches, and other entrees to pair with your beer. You'll also want to keep an eye out for their many events, such as the Pine Box Can Derby where anyone can build a race car out of beer cans and race them just like Cub Scouts.

STUMBLING MONK
1635 E. Olive Way, Seattle, WA 98122; (206) 860-0916
Draft Beers: 12 **Bottled/Canned Beers:** About 50

Stumbling Monk in Capitol Hill isn't your typical neighborhood bar. You won't find food, music, fancy decor, or even a close parking spot unless you're lucky. What you will find, however, is an incredible selection of mainly Belgian-style beers at great prices. Upon entering you'll feel like you're in a dive bar mixed with a coffee shop. A couple of booths mixed with tables and a few seats at the bar take up the majority of this fairly small and almost run-down space. The lights tend to be dim, creating a cozy atmosphere perfect for a date or just relaxing with a couple friends. Aside from a decent selection of board games, there is very little entertainment to be had other than the company of your friends and fellow beer drinkers. Despite all of its quirks, the Stumbling Monk is still one of the best bars in the city due mainly to their beer selection.

You'll be able to find a rotating draft list consisting mainly of beers from Belgium as well as American-brewed Belgian-style beers. A handful of other styles, such as IPAs and stouts, balance out the taps along with a well-crafted bottle list of some rare and vintage brews, creating a drink selection that should please most beer drinkers. They don't offer food other than a few bags of chips, so make your visit a pre- or post-dinner experience, or you can order food from an assortment of nearby restaurants that deliver. You'll also want to make sure not to come too early, as they don't open until 6 p.m. However, with the small space and high-end beer selection, it does get packed fairly regularly on weekends.

TAP HOUSE GRILL

1506 6th Ave., Seattle, WA 98101; (206) 816-3314; TapHouseGrill.com; @TapHouseGrill
Draft Beers: 160 **Bottled/Canned Beers:** None

In the Northwest, if there was an award for the sheer number of beers on draft, Tap House Grill would take the gold. Known for having 160 beers on tap at both their Seattle and Bellevue locations, the restaurant and bar offers so many drink choices it will take you some time to decide what to order. Each location has a similar beer menu consisting of ambers, Belgian beer, IPAs, pale ales, stouts, porters, fruit beers, and everything in between. Their selection is a nice blend of Northwest brews along with plenty of choices from all over the world, including a decent amount of seasonal beers. Looking at the bar with all the taps will overwhelm just about anyone, but don't worry, they offer beer samplers where you can try 4 beers in 6-ounce glasses.

The Seattle location is right in the heart of downtown on 6th Avenue, so it attracts a lot of travelers. Walking in the doors, you immediately head downstairs into the restaurant, where a modern world of beer awaits. Since it's underground it's a bit dark, yet you'll feel as if you've stepped into a restaurant in a nice Las Vegas casino. Bellevue's original location is surrounded by windows, so it has a lighter and more inviting feel.

Inside both locations are plenty of TVs to watch games, along with 2 pool tables at their Seattle location. Almost as numerous as the beer selection is the food selection, with steak, ribs, sushi, pasta, seafood, sandwiches, and plenty of appetizers on the menu that pair well with beer. The full bar is perfect if you're taking along a friend who doesn't like beer, as they offer a large menu of cocktails and wine.

ÜBER TAVERN

7517 Aurora Ave. N., Seattle, WA 98103; (206) 782-2337; UberBier.com; @UberTavern
Draft Beers: 17 **Bottled/Canned Beers:** Over 125

Just north of Green Lake on Aurora Avenue lies a small, red, nondescript building. Inside it's a cozy space that might make a few claustrophobic customers squirm, but suck it up—the beer selection is amazing. With a circle fireplace table in the middle surrounded by a few other tables and a bar that seats about 10, it's not the largest place in the city to go. On nicer days there is a row of seats out front so you can sip on your brews while watching the traffic drive by. Behind the bar you'll notice a few beer coolers stocked with an assortment of over 125 bottles and cans that will have any beer lover salivating. Up above you'll also see multiple TV screens broadcasting the current tap list. All 17 of the beers on draft are some of the best you'll find in the city. While many are from the West Coast, they specialize in getting the best beers they can, and you'll usually find beers from all over the world as well as the US. If you can't decide what to drink, don't worry; they offer 4-ounce samples of their beers at some decent prices.

While there, you can fill up growlers or order from a huge selection of kegs to go. You can also order any of the bottles to take home if you don't want to drink it there. They don't offer food, yet you can feel free to bring in any food or order from a plethora of nearby places that deliver. Since the tavern is fairly small, it does fill up rather quickly, especially on weekend nights, but it's worth the crowds.

The Eastside

N

BREWERIES

Bellevue Brewing Company	13
Black Raven Brewing Company	10
Brickyard Brewing	3
Dirty Bucket Brewing Co.	5
Duvall Springs Brewing	8
Foggy Noggin Brewing	2
Herbert B. Friendly Brewing	18
Issaquah Brewhouse	15
Mac & Jack's Brewery	12
192 Brewing Company	1
Redhook Ale Brewery	9
Snoqualmie Brewery & Taproom	16
Triplehorn Brewing Company	4
Twelve Bar Brews	7

BARS

The Collective on Tap	6
Dog & Pony Alehouse	17
Malt & Vine	11
Pine Lake Ale House	14

0   2.5   5 miles

The Eastside

For the suburban cities situated east of Seattle the craft-beer scene has been picking up over the past few years. In the past, the Eastside suburbs had Redhook in Woodinville, Mac & Jack's in Redmond, Issaquah Brewhouse in Issaquah, and Snoqualmie Brewing out in Snoqualmie. Had you been reading this around 2005, this most likely would have been the shortest chapter in the book. Fortunately, a new wave of brewers has been popping up in cities like Woodinville, Kenmore, Renton, Redmond, and Bellevue, all of which are producing some incredible beers to serve their respective cities.

Even though Seattle has some amazing breweries, the Eastside is producing beer that is just as good. Award-winning breweries such as Black Raven Brewing and Foggy Noggin Brewing are crafting unique beers outside the traditional Northwest lineup. It's exciting to watch the growth in the area and it's only getting better. So if you find yourself in the suburbs, have no fear, good beer is here.

Breweries

BELLEVUE BREWING COMPANY

1820 130th Ave. NE, #2, Bellevue, WA 98005; (425) 497-8686; BellevueBrewing.com; @BellevueBrewing

Founded: 2012 **Founders:** John Robertson and Scott Hansen **Brewer:** Tony Powell
Flagship Beers: ESB, Oatmeal Stout, IPA, Scotch Ale, Pale Ale **Year-Round Beers:** ESB, Oatmeal Stout, IPA, Scotch Ale, Pale Ale **Seasonals/Special Releases:** Cascadian Dark Ale **Tours:** No **Taproom:** Yes

In December 2012 the town of Bellevue received its first local brewery when Bellevue Brewing Company opened its doors. Within the first month of business their beers started showing up around the area in places on draft outside of their own pub. Upon launching the brewery, they started off with a lineup that includes a slightly bitter yet fruity **ESB,** a bold citrus and piney **IPA,** a full-bodied **Scotch Ale,** a smooth **Pale Ale,** and an **Oatmeal Stout** that could very easily replace your dessert. At the time of this writing they've released only these five beers but will be offering a range of seasonals and other releases in the near future.

Beer Lover's Pick

Oatmeal Stout
Style: Oatmeal Stout
ABV: 5.8%
Availability: Year-Round

As one of Bellevue Brewing Company's first launched beers, their simply named Oatmeal Stout is like a chocolate breakfast in your mouth. The dark brown beer has a subtle granola-like aroma mixed with sweet chocolate, roasted coffee, and dark cherries. A medium body gets you feeling like you want to chew through it, especially when you taste the cocoa nibs, coffee, and breakfast-like maltiness. In the pub you can order their fudge brownie salted caramel ice cream, which is made with the Oatmeal Stout and limited to those over 21. One word: yum!

While you can start to find their beer on draft around the Bellevue area, their taproom is the best venue for tasting their beer as well as eating some incredible food. The cavernous room is huge, with seating for up to 300 people. It's all tables and a bar, giving the dining room a cafeteria-like feel. Brightly painted walls add to the ambience, but it's not fancy. "Comfortable" would be a better way to describe it. The big space also makes it a perfect location to watch games on the big projector.

Outside of their beer, there are plenty of options for other beverages, such as wine, soda, and coffee. A selection of salads, sandwiches, and pizzas fill the menu along with plenty of kids' options that are all served on a Frisbee. Make sure to try the BBC nachos with your choice of pork, beef, turkey, or even lamb, a perfect pairing with their IPA.

BLACK RAVEN BREWING COMPANY

14679 NE 95th St., Redmond, WA 98052; (425) 881-3020; BlackRavenBrewing.com; @BlackRavenBrew

Founded: 2009 **Founder:** Beaux Bowman **Brewer:** Beaux Bowman **Flagship Beer:** Trickster IPA **Year-Round Beers:** Trickster IPA, Totem Northwest Pale, Sunthief Kristallweizen, Tamerland Brown Porter, Morrighan Stout, Second Sight Strong Scotch Ale **Seasonals/Special Releases:** Wisdom Seeker Double IPA, Grandfather Raven, Old Birdbrain, Splinters, Pour Les Oiseaux, La Petite Mort, Coco Jones, Possum Claus, and more **Tours:** No **Taproom:** Yes

In 2009 Black Raven Brewing Company opened its doors in a nondescript business park in Redmond and the Washington beer scene hasn't been quite the same since. Focusing on creating interesting beers, the Redmond production brewery is creating some of the best beer in the state and distributing it on draft as well as in a few bottles, although these can be hard to come by.

Year-round they offer a lineup of beers that have all won awards at various competitions. One example is their **Trickster IPA,** which offers a beautiful blend of citrus and bitter hops with plenty of sweet caramel. Another in the year-round repertoire is the **Sunthief Kristallweizen,** a German wheat style that is not often brewed in the state. Aside from the year-round lineup they are constantly brewing one-off, seasonal, and special-release beers. While you pretty much can't go wrong with any of their limited-release brews, make sure to look for their hefty **Grandfather Raven Imperial Stout,** packed with a plethora of flavors, or their **Old Birdbrain Barleywine** that's been aged in rye-whiskey barrels.

Make sure to stop by the tasting room at the brewery to grab a pint or some tasters, especially since they offer beers you can't find elsewhere. The warm-feeling

Wisdom Seeker
Style: Double IPA
ABV: 9%
Availability: Brewed Quarterly

Black Raven's Wisdom Seeker is a hop lover's dream come true. In an area of great hoppy beers, it has to be considered one of the best double IPAs coming out of the West Coast. Brewed with 7 hop varieties, it's meant to satisfy the true beer geek. Massive citrus, pine, and tropical fruits in the nose are followed by a similar flavor with a solid caramel malt backbone giving a sweet flavor to cut the bitterness. It's available in very limited 22-ounce bottles and on draft; seek this beer out.

tasting room is a relaxed atmosphere to grab a pint and talk beer with fellow neighborhood drinkers. No food is available, but Flying Saucer Pizza is nearby and will deliver right to your table. They also have food carts that rotate in the parking lot throughout the week. One word of warning is to watch where you park, as some of the neighboring businesses are quick to tow your car.

BRICKYARD BREWING

5817 238th St. SE, Ste. 3, Woodinville, WA 98072; (425) 483-2337; BrickyardBrewing.com
Founded: 2012 **Founders:** Joe Montero and Ean Forgette **Brewer:** Ean Forgette
Flagship Beer: Masonry Oatmeal Stout **Year-Round Beers:** Brickyard IPA, Masonry Oatmeal Stout, Concrete Blonde, Stones Throw Pale **Seasonals/Special Releases:** Kiln Warmer Winter Ale, Brickyard Pumpkin Ale **Tours:** Contact the brewery and they'll show you around **Taproom:** Yes

In 2012 a host of breweries opened up shop across the state. One of the few that opened in Woodinville was Brickyard Brewing, a small yet neighborhood-friendly brewery that is becoming one of the many great spots in the city to drink good beer. The name Brickyard comes from the nickname of a local road (SR 522) that connected Seattle to the area that was once called the Red Brick Road. They use the Brickyard theme when naming their beers, such as their year-round lineup of **Brickyard IPA, Masonry Oatmeal Stout, Concrete Blonde,** and **Stones Throw Pale.** Along with their year-round lineup, they brew up a few seasonals along with a few limited-release beers. For example, they've done a very limited-release chocolate version of their Masonry Oatmeal Stout around Valentine's Day, and a chipotle pepper version of the Concrete Blonde Ale. Look for their beer at area bars and restaurants, along with a limited supply of bottles. It's best, though, to make a trip to their tasting room.

Located in a warehouse, the tasting room doesn't strike you as anything fancy. It's just a relaxing and laid-back spot to enjoy their beer and possibly play a game of backgammon at the bar. While it's not a restaurant, they often have taco nights and slider nights where they offer food. Along with that, you have to give their Real Beer Float a try. Using their Masonry Stout, they add a scoop of Snoqualmie Gourmet Ice Cream that is a perfect dessert just about anyone will enjoy, even if you're not a stout fan. Feel free to bring the kids to the tasting room, and dogs are permitted as well.

Masonry Oatmeal Stout

Style: Oatmeal Stout

ABV: 6.8%

Availability: Year-Round

Going along with the Brickyard theme, Masonry Oatmeal Stout is crafted as beautifully as a talented brick mason would build a small castle. Huge layers of chocolate up front give way to a roasted and incredibly smooth finish. It's a big stout but drinks a bit lighter than you might expect, allowing your palate to enjoy multiple pints. This is a beer that was pretty much made to turn into a beer float. Just add a scoop or two of quality vanilla ice cream and enjoy an almost perfect desert.

DIRTY BUCKET BREWING CO.

19151 144th Ave. NE, Ste. 101, Woodinville, WA 98072; (206) 819-1570; DirtyBucketBrewery.com; @TheDirtyBucket

Founded: 2012 **Founders:** Steve Acord, Chris Acord, and Sharon Wagner-Acord **Brewer:** Steve Acord **Flagship Beer:** Dirty Amber Ale **Year-Round Beers:** Dirty Amber Ale, Filthy Hoppn' IPA, Bedraggled Irish Red **Seasonals/Special Releases:** Ruski Porridge, XXX-Tra Filthy IPA, Black Lab Stout, Dirty Blonde Ale, Full Nelson India Black Ale, Rusty Pail Ale, Dirty Jack, Hefen' Pineapple, and many more **Tours:** Just ask if they aren't too busy **Taproom:** Yes

Woodinville-based Dirty Bucket Brewing Co. might not have a name that exactly makes you salivate for a good craft beer, but don't let that fool you. Founded by brothers Chris and Steve Acord along with Steve's wife, Sharon, in 2012, the brewery actually got its name from their days of brewing in their garage using buckets. In the first year of their existence, they brewed on a Sabco Brew-Magic system, a small half-barrel system most notably used by Sam Calagione of Dogfish Head Craft Brewery when he was just starting out. The system allowed Dirty Bucket to brew a lot of different beers, but they needed to expand to keep up with demand. Their location is just down the street from Triplehorn Brewing in Woodinville's warehouse district in a small, yet ideally located warehouse with easy street access. Their beer is distributed in kegs around the area, but most of it pours through the tap

lines in the tasting room. While it can get packed during peak hours, on nice days they roll up the garage door, allowing you to take your beer outside in the roped-off parking lot area. You can see the brewery on the other half of the wall, which makes you feel as if you are part of the company.

Throughout the year they produce a wide range of beers, although you can generally find their flagship **Dirty Amber Ale** on draft. A solid amber ale, it's light-bodied with well-balanced caramel and piney hops. Also make sure to check out their **Full Nelson India Black Ale,** which should make most IPA fans happy. Brewed with just Nelson Sauvin hops, it's an interesting beer with plenty of fruit flavors that duel it out with the roasted malts.

Filthy Hoppn' IPA

Style: India Pale Ale

ABV: 6.4%

Availability: Year-Round

In the Northwest pretty much every brewery has an IPA, but not all are created equal. For Dirty Bucket Brewing, their Filthy Hoppin' IPA is one of the easiest-drinking in the state. Just like the name implies, it's "filthy" with a hazy amber color and "hoppin'" with plenty of Willamette, Chinook, and Cascade hops that provide plenty of piney aromas and flavor. Mild bitterness is balanced against a caramel malt body, creating one smooth IPA that is worth seeking out.

DUVALL SPRINGS BREWING

18028 288th Ave. NE, Duvall, WA 98019; (425) 269-1281; DuvallSpringsBrewing.com; @duvallsprings

Founded: 2012 **Founders:** Chris Lagerstad, Jake Siebert, and Brady Hoyle **Brewers:** Chris Lagerstad, Jake Siebert, and Brady Hoyle **Flagship Beer:** Burn Ban Porter **Year-Round Beers:** Burn Ban Porter, Bos Bruut Belgian Strong Ale **Seasonals/Special Releases:** Red Beast Tripel, Breakfast of Champions Oatmeal Stout, Blue-eyed Brunette, Red Door Raspberry Hef, Forgiveness Pale **Tours:** No **Taproom:** No

In Duvall, three friends came together to open the small town's first brewery in 2012. Duvall Springs Brewing, a nanobrewery, produces beer in a shed out in a rural area outside of town. With no tasting room, their beer is showing up around the Eastside and Seattle on draft and can be tough to come by. However, the ambitious owners are looking to grow the brewery and have their eyes set on opening a tasting room in the very near future.

They offer a range of both Belgian-inspired and American-influenced beers with their **Burn Ban Porter** and **Bos Bruut Belgian Strong Ale,** two of their most popular beers. Translated into English, Bos Bruut means "Forest Monster." Since they brew out in the forest and have heard strange noises in the night, they figured they'd brew a big Belgian-style beer to help ease their fear. Bos Bruut should ease just about anyone's fear, as the 10.5% ABV will have you feeling incredibly relaxed. It also helps that the alcohol flavor is present but not very vocal. As they continue to grow, they will be brewing up a lot of different styles and can be found pouring their brews at local festivals, such as Belgianfest in Seattle.

Burn Ban Porter
Style: Smoked Porter
ABV: 6%
Availability: Year-Round

The name alone of the Burn Ban Porter should stir up images of big smoky fires billowing up into the forest sky. Just as the name implies, this is one big smoked porter with a bit of ash in the flavor. They smoke the grains over fruit woods to give it a unique flavor not found in many other porters. It does drink a little lighter than the "black as motor oil" color might have you guessing. Duvall Springs Brewing suggests you drink this with a hefty New York strip steak, which might just be the ultimate pairing.

FOGGY NOGGIN BREWING

22329 53rd Ave. SE, Bothell, WA 98021; (206) 553-9223; FoggyNogginBrewing.com; @FogNog
Founded: 2008 **Founder:** Jim Jamison **Brewer:** Jim Jamison **Flagship Beers:** Bit O' Beaver, Christmas Duck **Year-Round Beers:** Bit O' Beaver, Christmas Duck **Seasonals/Special Releases:** Rufus, Big Chief, Spotted Owl, Oski Wow-Wow, Kastrated Dawg, Chief Lightfoot, Butch's Brew, Diablo del Sol, Anniversary Ale, MLK Alt, Wasky, and many more
Tours: No **Taproom:** Yes

To call Foggy Noggin Brewing a nanobrewery almost feels like an overstatement. In brewing, size doesn't matter when it comes to quality, and the small brewery is putting in a lot of hard work to make that statement true. Their half-barrel brewhouse, which is enough to brew just 15 gallons of beer at a time, is located in a shed behind founder Jim Jamison's residential-neighborhood house. As small as it is, he was able to turn the garage of the house into a tasting room. This allows thirsty customers to visit on most Saturdays to fill up a growler, buy a couple 22-ounce bottles, and even relax and drink a couple pints. The intimate setting gives you the feeling that you're visiting a friend that's a master of homebrewing.

Although the output is small, Foggy Noggin beers can occasionally be found at Eastside bars as well as a handful of festivals every year. With a focus on English-style ales, the small brewery produces a wide variety of beers while generally offering two beers year-round. Since Jim is an Oregon State University fan, he named one

Wasky

Style: Burton-Style Ale

ABV: 6.6%

Availability: Limited Release

Most people outside of the versed beer-geek world are unfamiliar with Burton-style ales. Burton upon Trent is a historical region in England known for the birth of the IPA. Before the IPA, though, they were brewing Burton-style ales. Foggy Noggin's Wasky gives those around the area an idea of what those ales tasted like. Much maltier and sweeter than a regular English pale ale, it's brewed with brown sugar and molasses that is noticeable in the flavor before giving way to a dry and bitter finish. They recommend it be aged for at least a year before drinking.

of the year-round offerings **Bit O' Beaver,** a beer he perfected back in his homebrewing days. An English bitter, it is a very sessionable beer with light bitterness that is a perfect accompaniment to watching the Beavers play the Ducks. They also offer **Christmas Duck,** an English porter with plenty of sweet roasted flavors that will have you feeling like Christmas all year long. You can also generally find a few other seasonals and limited releases being poured in the taproom.

HERBERT B. FRIENDLY BREWING

527 Wells Ave. S., Renton, WA 98057; (425) 243-4372; HBFBrewing.com; @DrinkHBF
Founded: 2010 **Founder:** Erik Davis **Brewer:** Erik Davis **Flagship Beers:** Make It So,
Taildragger Pale Ale **Year-Round Beers:** Make It So, Taildragger Pale Ale **Seasonals/
Special Releases:** Northwest Breakfast Stout, TBD Cream Ale, I'm Dreaming of a White
Stout **Tours:** No **Taproom:** Yes, limited hours

Although founded in 2010, it wasn't until January 2013 that Herbert B. Friendly Brewing had a grand opening and first poured its beers. A very small Renton-based nanobrewery, they specialize in brewing small-batch beers that push the boundaries of traditional styles. One question you might have is: Who exactly is Herbert B. Friendly? Owner and brewmaster Erik Davis says the name comes from the days when he and a friend would throw raves and electronic-music events. When they caught people smoking weed, they'd call them HBF, or Herb Be Friendly. The time came to name the brewery and he wrote down Herbert Benjamin Friendly as a joke, but the name stuck after shortening down Benjamin to just B. The light-heartedness in the naming goes with their philosophy of not taking themselves too seriously.

As they're a new brewery, they recently opened up the taproom for growler fills on Saturday. There are plans in the works for bottling their beers, but for now the best place to find Herbert B. Friendly beers is direct from the source. Year-round they

Beer Lover's Pick

Make It So
Style: English Ale
ABV: 5%
Availability: Year-Round

For self-proclaimed beer geeks and nerds in general, it makes sense to name a beer after the well-known catchphrase from Captain Jean-Luc Picard of *Star Trek: The Next Generation*. The label for the beer even has the Herbert B. Friendly character dressed in the captain's iconic red outfit. Make It So is an English-style ale that has been brewed with a dose of Earl Grey tea, giving it a unique flavor. Perfect for drinking just about anytime.

brew **Make It So,** an English-style ale brewed with Earl Grey tea, and **Taildragger Pale Ale,** a Northwest-style pale ale named in honor of all the hobby pilots at the Renton airfield. You can also find small-batch seasonals, such as the **Northwest Breakfast Stout,** aged on toasted oak and bourbon.

ISSAQUAH BREWHOUSE

35 W. Sunset Way, Issaquah, WA 98027; (425) 557-1911; rogue.com/locations/rogue-breweries.php; @frogales

Founded: 1994 **Founder:** Unknown (currently owned by Rogue Ales) **Brewer:** Dave Hutchinson **Flagship Beer:** White Frog **Year-Round Beers:** White Frog, Menage-a-Frog, Contraband, Frog Rye IPA **Seasonals/Special Releases:** Frosty Frog, Bullfrog Ale, Hippie Frog Chamomile Ale, Grapefruit Frog, Summer Frog Wit, Frog in the Rye, Quadruple Frog, Smoked Frog, Kilted Frog, Wicked Frog, and MacFrog Scotch Ale, and many more **Tours:** Yes, 1 p.m. weekdays **Taproom:** Yes

Out in Issaquah there is only one option if you're looking for beer that's actually brewed in the city: Issaquah Brewhouse. Opened in 1994, the brewpub was bought out by Rogue Ales in 2000. Since then, Rogue has helped the small pub grow into something special for beer lovers. After years of operating in the original location, they expanded in 2002 and then again in 2005, adding more space to the oddly shaped building. While technically a brewpub, Rogue has taken a few of their beers, such as their flagship **White Frog** and **Menage-a-Frog,** and distributed them in bottles throughout the state. While the ties are still strong, Issaquah Brewhouse has its own head brewer and brews the entire Issaquah lineup of beers on site.

One of their most popular beers is the multiple-award-winning Menage-a-Frog, which is available both on draft and in wax-dipped 750-ounce bottles. Aromas of honey, fresh bread, and spice make this Belgian-style Tripel almost as enjoyable to smell as it is to drink. Look for it in both the pub and in area bottle shops. Along with the lineup of 3 or 4 Issaquah Brewhouse beers, you can find 20 or so Rogue beers on draft in the pub, ranging from their year-round offerings to their seasonal and limited releases. Along with those, they also offer about 8 or so guest taps from area breweries, many of which are rare beers not available anywhere else in the region.

Laid-back and relaxed, the family-friendly brewpub offers a kids' food menu of pub grub served to them on a Rogue Frisbee they can take home. Adults can enjoy a wide range of food, with multiple excellent Kobe beef options, such as the Kobe bacon cheeseburger, Kobe chili, or Kobe beef tacos.

White Frog Ale

Style: Witbier

ABV: 5.2%

Availability: Year-Round

Just as you'd expect based on the name, Issaquah Brewhouse's White Frog Ale is a Belgian-style Witbier that features a white frog on the label of the 22-ounce bottles. Although it's fairly light and easy-drinking, it has a lot going on. With aromas of orange and coriander that follow through to the flavor along with notes of chamomile, banana, and subtle clove, the light mouthfeel makes it a beer you won't tire of. Try pairing it with any of their seafood, such as the salmon or even the mahimahi tacos.

MAC & JACK'S BREWERY

17825 NE 65th St., Redmond, WA 98052; (425) 558-9697; MacAndJacks.com

Founded: 1993 **Founders:** Mac Rankin and Jack Schropp **Brewer:** Mac Rankin **Flagship Beer:** African Amber **Year-Round Beers:** African Amber, Serengeti Wheat, Blackcat Porter, Two Tun IPA, Cascadian Dark Ale, C-U Lator **Seasonals/Special Releases:** Bourbon Barrel Oak Aged Porter, Mint Chocolate Porter, Hefeweizen **Tours:** Yes, Sat and Sun at 1 and 3 p.m. **Taproom:** No (they offer a retail store)

What began as two friends brewing out of a garage starting in 1993 has grown into one of the state's largest breweries. By 1997 Mac Rankin and Jack Schropp had grown enough to move their brewery out of Schropp's garage and into a former transmission shop in Redmond. From the beginning they have taken a no-frills approach to brewing by keeping their lineup of beers consistent and rarely brewing seasonal beers. Along with sticking to a selection of 6 year-round beers, they have stuck with their draft-only approach to distribution and have yet to bottle any of their beers. As one of the country's largest draft-only breweries, Mac & Jack's has consistently been ranked among the top 50 craft breweries in the nation by the Brewers Association based on sales volume.

The majority of their beer sales comes from their flagship beer, **African Amber.** A cloudy amber ale, African Amber is packed with enough hoppiness to please a predominantly Northwest fan base, yet balanced enough to be enjoyed by those who aren't hopheads. Their other beers follow the African theme with **Serengeti Wheat, Blackcat Porter, Two Tun IPA, Cascadian Dark Ale,** and **C-U Lator,** a complex barleywine with big flavor and hints of fruit. While African Amber is still the easiest of their beers to find, the rest of the lineup is distributed to restaurants and bars throughout the Northwest.

In Redmond you can visit the brewery 7 days a week, just outside of downtown; however, they don't offer a restaurant or traditional tasting room. You can buy kegs, growlers, and merchandise and even get samples, but they don't offer pints at their retail store. On the weekend you can stop by at 1 or 3 p.m. for a tour of the production brewery, get your questions answered, and see how the business runs.

African Amber
Style: Amber Ale
ABV: 5.2%
Availability: Year-Round
Created from one of brewer Mac Rankin's original homebrew recipes as a house beer for Park Pub, Mac & Jack's African Amber has become the brewery's bread and butter. Park Pub is located next to the Woodland Park Zoo, which was the inspiration for the name African Amber. Specialty malts are sandwiched between floral hop flavors in both the beginning and the finish, yet the bready malts dominate the medium-bodied brew. African Amber is available only on draft, so fill up your growlers with it when you can.

192 BREWING COMPANY

7324 NE 175th St., Kenmore, WA 98028; (425) 424-2337; 192Brewing.com
Founded: 2009 **Founder:** Derek Wyckoff **Brewer:** Derek Wyckoff **Flagship Beer:**
Shticky Blonde Ale **Year-Round Beers:** Hop'n Mad Red, Kenmore Gold **Seasonals/
Special Releases:** Shticky Blonde Ale, Sassy Granny's Apple Ale, Winter Wheat, 10 Hop
IPA, Shed Light, 'Nilla Stout, and more **Tours:** No **Taproom:** Yes

192 Brewing Company was officially licensed as Kenmore's first brewery in 2009. At the time it could have easily been considered one of Washington's smallest breweries, although with the exception of their newer Lake Trail Taproom, it's still very small. The 192 in the name refers to the actual square footage of the brewery, located in founder Derek Wyckoff's backyard shed. In addition to the brewery itself, they have since opened the Lake Trail Taproom, right next to the Burke-Gilman Trail. While the old warehouse doesn't look like much, it's a perfect location for those riding their bikes or walking along the trail to stop in to quench their thirst. Since the brewery is so small, they often run out of their few beers very quickly; however, they offer 15 taps filled mostly with beer from other breweries. In addition to offering other Washington breweries on tap, they'll also do brewers nights where you can meet brewers from other companies.

Although they don't have a ton of their own beer on draft, you'll generally find one or two. One beer they've brought to a few beer festivals is their **Sassy Granny's**

Beer Lover's Pick

Shticky Blonde Ale
Style: Blonde Ale
ABV: 6%
Availability: Year-Round
Being from such a small brewery, 192 Brewing's Shticky Blonde Ale has progressively gotten better each time it's brewed. In 2012 the recipe was tweaked slightly, creating the best version yet. With the addition of wild honey, it's an unfiltered beer that has plenty of sweetness, yet has the balance to keep you knocking back pint after pint. Be careful, though—the 6% ABV is a lot higher than you'd think this light-bodied and delicious session brew boasts.

Apple Ale. Flavors and aromas of green apples and cinnamon create a subtle apple pie–like flavor, yet it's very light and refreshing.

If you're looking to try their beer, the Lake Trail Taproom is the best place to find them, as they offer them only on draft. They often have events and plenty of live music in the beer garden, perfect for relaxing and enjoying a mug or two of beer. You can even stop in to buy homebrewing supplies while you fill up a growler.

REDHOOK ALE BREWERY

14300 NE 145th St., Woodinville, WA 98072; (425) 483-3232; Redhook.com; @Redhook _brewery
Founded: 1981 **Founders:** Paul Shipman and Gordon Bowker **Brewer:** Jen Talley
Flagship Beer: ESB **Year-Round Beers:** Long Hammer IPA, ESB, Copperhook Ale, Pilsner **Seasonals/Special Releases:** Winterhook, Wit, Nut Brown, Blueline Series, Brewery Backyard Series, and many more **Tours:** Yes, check website for times
Taproom: Yes

In the early 1980s the beer world was a much different place. The term "craft beer" didn't exist and beer was little more than a watered-down lager produced by a handful of macrobreweries. With a dream of producing beer with a little more flavor, partners Paul Shipman and Gordon Bowker launched Redhook in a former transmission shop in Seattle's Ballard neighborhood. Over 30 years later the brewery has morphed into one of the largest in the country and is now owned by Craft Brew Alliance and has a distribution agreement with Anheuser-Busch InBev. With the brewery in Woodinville and a second location built in 1996 in Portsmouth, New Hampshire, to keep up with demand, Redhook distributes all over the country.

Today Redhook carries 4 year-round beers, including their award-winning flagship **ESB, Pilsner, Copper Hook,** and **Long Hammer IPA,** one of their oldest beers that is both bottled and canned. Throughout the year they offer multiple seasonal brews, such as **Winterhook,** a winter ale that has been brewed annually since 1985. Each year it's brewed they change the recipe to give their drinkers a little variety and keep them guessing.

Their Forecasters Pub at the brewery in Woodinville offers all of their year-round and seasonal beers along with many that are exclusive to the pub. When the weather is right they have a large outdoor patio for you to enjoy their beer along with pub-style meals. You can get a tour of the brewery daily, but make sure to check the website for times, as they change based on the season. The one-hour tour consists of a walk-through of the brewery, an explanation of their brewing process, multiple samples of beer, and a souvenir tasting glass.

Double Black Stout
Style: Stout
ABV: 7%
Availability: Special Release

Brewed a handful of times over the years, Redhook's Double Black Stout is a collaboration beer crafted using coffee from an area roaster. In the past Starbucks was used, but in the 2012 release Redhook partnered up with Caffé Vita out of Portland, Oregon, to brew a beer packed with caramel and roasted malts along with enough coffee that you might forget you're actually drinking beer. There is plenty of bitterness to make this a stout that coffee lovers will absolutely enjoy, but could scare a few casual drinkers away.

SNOQUALMIE BREWERY & TAPROOM

8032 Falls Ave. SE, Snoqualmie, WA 98065; (425) 831-2357; Fallsbrew.com
Founded: 1997 **Founders:** Pat Anderson, David McKibben, Dave Eiffert, LeRoy Gmazel, and Tom Antone **Brewer:** Rande Reed **Flagship Beer:** Wildcat IPA **Year-Round Beers:** Schooner Zodiac Kölsch, Perfectly Great Amber (PGA), Haystack Hefeweizen, Copperhead Pale Ale, Wildcat IPA, Steam Train Porter, Black Frog Stout **Seasonals/Special Releases:** Summer Beer, Harvest Moon, Avalanche Winter Ale, Spring Fever Grand Cru, Brewer's Choice Series **Tours:** No **Taproom:** Yes

Snoqualmie Brewery & Taproom has become a destination for those seeking out delicious beer in the farthest corner of the Eastside. Founded in 1997, the brewery has taken many shapes over the years. Starting out, they focused on distributing

Wildcat IPA
Style: IPA
ABV: 6.6%
Availability: Year-Round
Snoqualmie Brewery's Wildcat IPA is a bit of a beast. Brewed using only Yakima-grown Columbus hops, it shows that single-hop beers can have a lot of dimension to them. Bold and bitter pine and citrusy hops dominate but are balanced by a somewhat sweet and bready malt backbone. With a medium mouthfeel and smooth carbonation, it's an easy-drinking IPA for hopheads out there looking to get their fix of hops without being blown away. Look for it on draft or in 22-ounce bottles throughout the Northwest.

The Eastside

their goods on draft throughout the area and didn't add the bottling line until 2001. In 2006 the brewery was growing and they opened up the taproom, allowing unique and seasonal beers to be brewed more often.

Of Snoqualmie's original lineup of beers, today only their bold yet approachable flagship **Wildcat IPA** remains. You can find their lineup of 5 other beers in 22-ounce bottles along with a range of seasonal beers throughout the year. In the taproom they offer a large selection of specialty-brewed beers along with their **Black Frog Stout,** which is exclusive to their pub. The stout is loaded with chocolate malt and rolled oats instead of flaked barley, giving it a smooth chocolate and espresso flavor with incredible texture.

Their taproom was remodeled in 2011, creating over three times the space and providing an excellent place to take the family. With the children's menu and the homebrewed root beer, those with kids will love it. Their regular food menu consists of appetizers, salads, sandwiches, and pizza. Come for food or head into the taproom to fill a growler or Cornelius keg to go.

TRIPLEHORN BREWING COMPANY

19510 144th Ave. NE, Woodinville, WA 98072; (425) 242-7979; TriplehornBrewingCo.com; @TriplehornBrewi
Founded: 2011 **Founders:** Rich Nesheim and Ray Nesheim **Brewer:** Ray Nesheim
Flagship Beer: Land Wink Dry Hopped IPA **Year-Round Beers:** Land Wink Dry Hopped IPA, Folkvang Irish Red, Falcon Cloak Blonde, Intervention Double IPA **Seasonals/Special Releases:** Harvest Porter, NeMeSis Milk Stout, Bitfrost Pale, Freya's Wit, Belgian Mystic, Blockhead Imperial IPA, and many more **Tours:** No **Taproom:** Yes

As the newest brewery to hit the Woodinville beer scene in 2012, Triplehorn Brewing Company is also the second-largest brewery in the city next to Redhook. Going along with a Viking theme, the production brewery and tasting room are tucked into a space at the back of a building in Woodinville's warehouse district. While not visible off the street, it's one of those breweries that is worth the quest to find. Unlike most of the other breweries in the area, their tasting room is open 7 days a week with fantastic hours to come enjoy a range of their beers. Besides just sampling the beer, the tasting room is an experience of its own. Although this is not the largest room, there is a beautifully crafted bar with a TV in the corner showing all kinds of sports and entertainment. The true beauty, however, is when you walk out toward the brewery and can stop and sit at multiple tables to enjoy watching the brewers work their magic. Aside from peanuts, they don't offer food, so make sure to come prepared to spend your time just enjoying their brews.

Available around the area in kegs, Triplehorn offers 4 beers year-round and a range of creative and delicious seasonal beers. Whatever beer you start with, you'll want to finish with the **NeMeSis Milk Stout,** especially if it's offered on nitro. The chocolate and elegant roasted-coffee flavors will make you want to get a growler to give to your valentine instead of the overly used box of chocolates come February 14. Their **Land Wink IPA** is perfect for those newer to the IPA style who aren't looking for a smack to the face of hops. While the piney, floral, and citrus hops are present, the smoothness of the bitterness makes it just a bit too easy to drink.

Folkvang Irish Red
Style: Irish Red Ale
ABV: 6%
Availability: Year Round

In Norse mythology, Folkvang is a field ruled by the goddess Freyja where half of those who die in combat go upon death, while the other half go to the god Odin. In beer, however, it's Triplehorn Brewing Company's tasty Irish red ale. The ruby-colored beer has a strong caramel base with plenty of sweetness mixed in, a touch of smoke, and a slight lingering bitterness coming from the UK hops. Get a growlerful and pair it with some rich foods, such as pizza, pasta, or meats.

TWELVE BAR BREWS

12826 NE 178th St., Ste. C, Woodinville, WA 98072; (425) 482-1188; TwelveBarBrews.com
Founded: 2011 **Founder:** Kirk Hilse **Brewer:** Kirk Hilse **Flagship Beer:** Wicked Riff IPA
Year-Round Beers: Pentatonic Pale, Turnaround Red Ale, Wicked Riff IPA, Supertonic India Black Ale **Seasonals/Special Releases:** Slow Rye'd Oaked IBA **Tours:** Yes, just ask if they aren't too busy **Taproom:** Yes

Woodinville-based Twelve Bar Brews has been popping up quickly on taps around the Seattle area. The production brewery isn't concerned with making hundreds of different crazy beers; instead they focus on brewing 4 styles and creating them very well. Founded by longtime homebrewer Kirk Hilse, the brewery is a blend of two of his passions: beer and music. As a pun on the musical term "twelve-bar blues," Hilse named the brewery Twelve Bar Brews and even included multiple instruments in the logo. To keep the theme going outside of the brewery, you can spot Twelve Bar Brews beers on draft at many local restaurants and bars with their tap handles that look like the head of a guitar.

Each of their 4 year-round beers has some kind of musical influence in the name and is brewed to be tasty enough to drink over and over. They include the dry and citrusy **Wicked Riff India Pale Ale,** the rye-infused **Pentatonic Pale,** the caramel-sweet yet piney hop–packed **Turnaround Red,** and the dark, dry, and slightly coffee-tasting **Supertonic India Black Ale.** Each of the beers is available only on draft, so find it in a bar or head down to their tasting room and fill up a growler.

Supertonic India Black Ale

Style: Cascadian Dark Ale

ABV: 6.9%

Availability: Year-Round

In music the supertonic is the scale note one step above the tonic, which is the first scale degree of a diatonic scale. With Twelve Bar Brews' Supertonic India Black Ale, you could almost say it's one step up from an IPA—not necessarily better than an IPA, just a step away. In this case, it drinks a lot like an IPA with a dark roasted-malt character that gives it a slight coffee bitterness. Both citrus and floral hops are present, but the roastiness of the malt gives this brew a unique dimension. Pair this with some big barbecued meats or perhaps a meat lover's–style pizza.

If you're doing a Woodinville beer or wine tour, make sure to stop by Twelve Bar Brews and drink a few pints in the Broken Strong Tap Room. Not incredibly large, the space is big enough for you to get in and order a pint of each of their brews, with another local brewery's beer on guest tap. As a production brewery the taproom is open only during the weekends and doesn't offer any food. If you can sneak a peek inside the brewery, you'll see their beautiful copper kettles.

Beer Bars

THE COLLECTIVE ON TAP

17802 134th Ave. NE, #6, Woodinville, WA 98072; (425) 488-2795; CollectiveOnTap.com; @CollectiveonTap

Draft Beers: 20 **Bottled/Canned Beers:** 25

Over the past few years the city of Woodinville has started growing into a town known for its breweries, even though wine is still king in the area. The problem, though, is that aside from Redhook and Triplehorn, the other breweries in the city offer limited tasting-room hours. It just made sense to open The Collective On Tap in late 2012 to provide the area with local craft beer 7 days a week. Located on the edge of downtown Woodinville, the space was formerly home of Tot Spot Cafe, an indoor playspace for kids. Kat Stremlau, owner of the kids' cafe, decided to partner up with friend Jan Newton to turn the space into a playspace for craft-beer lovers. With a love of good beer, the two women have created a space for everyone to come and enjoy some of the best beer in the area and dine on an array of good food.

Inside you'll immediately feel comfortable. With free Wi-Fi and plenty of outlets around, you could bypass your trip to Starbucks and bring your laptop in to work with a beer in hand. You'll find 20 beers on draft with most from local breweries and a handful brought in from other states. The tastefully selected beers cover a spectrum of styles, and plenty of seasonal and special-release beers make their way on the menu.

They also have a food menu that is meant to pair with food. Their philosophy is to keep their menu changing, but they specialize in small plates and grazers. You'll find food such as spiced candy bacon, pizza, and soup. Brewers nights are common, where you can come meet brewers from different breweries, try their beer, and geek out on all the beer talk.

DOG & PONY ALEHOUSE

351 Park Ave. N., Renton, WA 98057; (425) 254-8080; TheDogAndPony.com

Draft Beers: 32 **Bottled/Canned Beers:** About 30

Local beer-loving residents of Renton know just where to go to kick back and drink great beer. For years Dog & Pony Alehouse has been hard at work changing out their 32 beers on draft to quench the thirst of those who walk through their door. Inside it has the feel of a local watering hole with an eclectic mix of signs and

Keep Current on Washington Beer

With so much beer culture around the state, over 150 breweries, and count-less beer bars, what's a beer geek to do to stay up-to-date on the Washington beer scene? Don't worry; there are plenty of great websites out there reporting on what's new and what's going on around the state. Here are a few great resources:

BlogAboutBeer.com

Okay, this is a selfless plug for my own site. While not technically focused on just Washington, it covers all kinds of interesting beer shenanigans in the Northwest and afar.

BrewDad.com

Mike, aka BrewDad, blogs about all kinds of news and trips, and gives beer reviews from all over the Northwest. If a beer is brewed in the Northwest, most likely BrewDad has drunk it and rated it on the website RateBeer.com.

SeattleBeerNews.com

For those in and around the Puget Sound area, *Seattle Beer News* keeps you informed on area news. The site also features an events section so you can keep up-to-date with special events around Seattle.

WashingtonBeer.com

The website of the Washington Beer Commission is all about supporting the state's breweries. Along with putting on multiple events throughout the year, they keep their site up-to-date with what's going on around the state.

WashingtonBeerBlog.com

When changes happen, such as new breweries or beer bars open, special beers are released, or the unfortunate event of breweries closing, chances are Kendall Jones is ready to report it. The blog covers the entire state and does it well.

furniture scattered about, as if the decor is letting you know it's all right to relax and have a good time. Those who are looking for a good time are covered: The ale-house offers a pool table, a couple of TVs, an outdoor beer garden, great food, and plenty of beer that is anything but boring. The green chalkboard near the bar shows what's on tap, with Northwest beers being a heavy favorite of the draft lines. If you can't find a beer you like out of the 32 well-chosen beers they offer, come back in a week or two and you'll be met with an almost completely different beer menu featuring a few hard-to-find beers generally added to the mix.

The food selection is very much your typical pub-style fare, with sandwiches, burgers, salads, and a few entrees, such as fish and chips and a sausage platter. If you're into sports, their TVs usually have games going on, so head in and order a few beers during a game. If you're going with multiple people, try to carpool, as parking can be tough at times.

MALT & VINE

16851 Redmond Way, Redmond, WA 98052; (425) 881-6461; MaltAndVine.com; @MaltAndVine
Draft Beers: 20 **Bottled/Canned Beers:** Over 900

Malt & Vine is the ultimate suburban bottle shop. Situated in a strip mall in Redmond, the shop doesn't offer much in terms of beauty or exciting atmosphere. The selection of both beer and wine, however, turns the shop into a shining beacon of fermentation, making it a perfect place to shop and drink, for both locals

and those on a beverage hunt. Walking in, you're met with multiple tables where you can kick back and enjoy a selection of 20 draft beers, or a bottle of over 900 beers, wines, and mead. On both sides of the tables are fridges packed with beer selections from all over the world, yet the selection is still heavily Northwest influenced. The tap list changes frequently with a selection of rotating styles, so you'll never get bored. If you're also into wine, their boutique wines are in the back and will definitely satisfy the wine lovers you bring with you.

Go ahead and go shopping in the bottle shop or just go to have a couple pints. You can even bring your laptop and get a little work done with their free Wi-Fi. While they don't offer food, they encourage you to bring in your own food. Plenty of restaurants are nearby, including a great gyros place next door, so you don't need to go hungry while drinking some of the state's best beers. On top of providing a great selection of beverages regularly, you can also stop by for one of their many beer tasting events and cask pours.

PINE LAKE ALE HOUSE

640 228th Ave. NE, Sammamish, WA 98074; (425) 898-9099; PineLakeAleHouse.com; @PLAH_OnTap
Draft Beers: 20 **Bottled/Canned Beers:** Fewer than 10 (mostly big-brand domestics)

If you find yourself in the city of Sammamish, have no fear; there is excellent beer in the suburbs. Just head over to the Pine Lake Ale House and you'll find some delicious beers running through the tap lines. From the outside it doesn't look like much. Nestled in a suburban strip mall anchored by Safeway, the alehouse could easily be passed off as a boring restaurant in the 'burbs. Step inside, though, and you'll notice the large chalkboard with their beer selection and immediately be glad you came. You'll find many Washington breweries on draft, such as Georgetown, American Brewing, Black Raven, Mac & Jack's, Snoqualmie, and many others. You can also find a great selection from surrounding states as well as those from across the country and the world. If you're lucky enough, you might even show up when they tap Russian River's Pliny the Younger. Fans of hops will appreciate their rather large selection of IPAs, but they make sure their selection has options for everyone.

Take the family or head out with friends and sit at the bar to watch some games. Make sure to come hungry, though, as they offer a big selection of burgers, pastas, Mexican food, sandwiches, salads, and seafood. Go with their Monte Cristo sandwich. It's packed with Bavarian ham, roasted turkey, cream cheese, and swiss cheese served between bread that's been dipped in egg and then tossed on the grill.

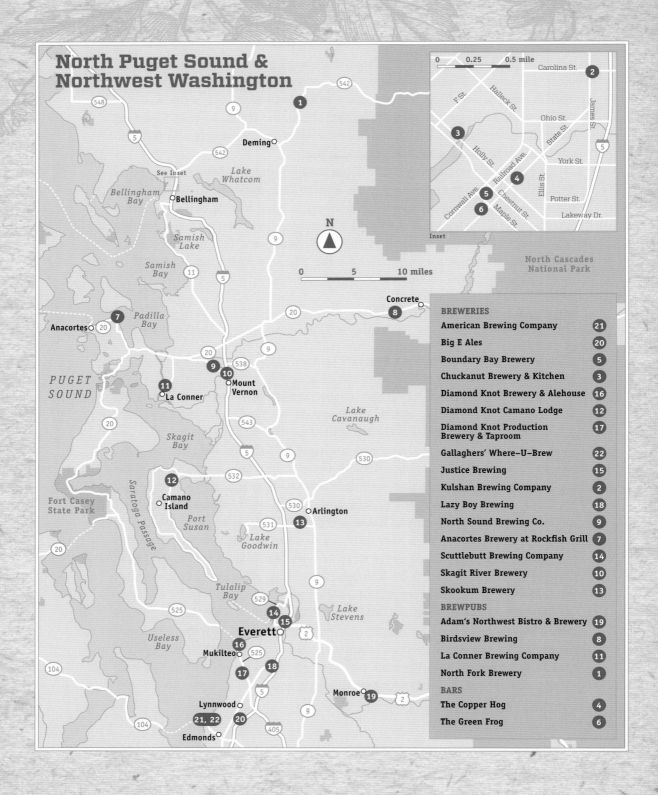

North Puget Sound & Northwest Washington

From Lynnwood on up north to Bellingham, the northwest section of Washington is a unique area in the state for craft beer. The area is grounded on some of the state's most well-known brewpubs, such as Boundary Bay Brewery and Chuckanut Brewery in Bellingham, Diamond Knot Brewing Company in Mukilteo, Skagit River Brewery in Mount Vernon, Big E Ales in Lynnwood, and Anacortes Brewery in Anacortes. The spacious area is also home to many newer and exciting production breweries, such as the American Brewing Company, Kulshan Brewing Company, Lazy Boy Brewing Company, and North Sound Brewing Company.

With so many well-crafted beers being produced in the area, locals don't need to look to Seattle to get their beer. However, if they do want to change things up and find beers produced from their neighbors to the south, they don't have to look far. Restaurants and craft-beer bars that understand good beer and help thirsty consumers connect with unique and local brews are popping up all over the area. Pair that with the fact that the area is one of the most scenic parts of the state, and you quickly realize you might need to schedule northwest Washington for your next beercation.

Breweries

AMERICAN BREWING COMPANY

180 W. Dayton St., Warehouse 102, Edmonds, WA 98020; (425) 774-1717; AmericanBrewing.com; @AmericanBrewing
Founded: 2011 **Founder:** Neil Fallon **Brewer:** Skip Madsen **Flagship Beer:** Breakaway IPA **Year-Round Beers:** Breakaway IPA, American Blonde, Caboose Oatmeal Stout **Seasonals/Special Releases:** Winter Classic, Brave American, Ed's Red, Piper's Scotch Ale, High Stick Imperial Red, Power Play, Big Pucker, Captain Munson's IPA, Baltic Porter, and many more **Tours:** No **Taproom:** Yes

Founded in 2011 in Edmonds, American Brewing Company has quickly made a splash in the Northwest beer scene. Although founder Neil Fallon didn't have experience in the beer industry, he was able to bring one of the area's great brewers, Skip Madsen, on board. With many years of brewing experience under his belt, Skip took the reins and brewed a lineup that has put the brewery on the map. Their beer is headed up by their flagship **Breakaway IPA,** a hefty 7.2% ABV balanced brew with generous amounts of both malt and citrusy hops that finishes fairly dry. Interestingly enough, the label on their 22-ounce bottles features a hockey player colored with red, white, and blue. While hockey might not be the most American sport, Breakaway IPA is about as American as you can get.

Aside from the IPA, they also offer their **Caboose Oatmeal Stout** and **American Blonde** in 22-ounce bottles and on draft throughout the state. In Edmonds it's worth a trip to visit their warehouse brewery. The taproom, named Breakaway Room, isn't visible from the street, but yellow mugs painted in the parking lot lead you to the side door to enter. Inside you can try multiple beers on draft while peering through the window to watch the crew brewing up beers. Multiple TVs and shuffleboard provide entertainment while you sample their range of year-round and seasonally brewed beers. You can also find live music often, so make sure to keep up with their Facebook page if that's your thing. They don't offer food other than popcorn and nuts, but encourage you to bring in your own or order from one of the nearby take-out restaurants. Make sure to bring a growler since you'll definitely want to take home some beer.

Beer Lover's Pick

Caboose Oatmeal Stout
Style: Oatmeal Stout
ABV: 7.0%
Availability: Year-Round
When a brewery creates a beer to style that looks, smells, and tastes exactly the way it should, it is a beautiful thing to appreciate. American Brewing Company crafted its Caboose Oatmeal Stout just about as accurately to style as you can get. Almost black in color with a fluffy mocha-color head, it looks fantastic. Though you could stare at its beauty, the aroma draws you in with a blend of rich chocolate, oats, and plenty of coffee. Creamy flavors of coffee, roasted malts, and dark chocolate weave themselves into a slightly bitter yet smooth finish, all of which do a perfect job of masking the 7% ABV.

ANACORTES BREWERY

320 Commercial Ave., Anacortes, WA 98221; (360) 588-1720; AnacortesRockfish.com; @Rockfish_Grill
Founded: 1994 **Founders:** Allen Rhoades, Paul Wasik, and Rick Star **Brewer:** Kevin Pierce **Flagship Beer:** IPA **Year-Round Beers:** IPA, Red, Helles Festival Lager, Amber, Honey Cream Ale **Seasonals/Special Releases:** Noel Winter Ale, Old Sebastes Barleywine, Broadsword Scottish, Pilsner, Märzen, Aviator Dopplebock, Vienna, Pale, Mai Oh Maibock, Brown, Hefeweizen, Oatmeal Stout, Locomotive Breath Imperial Stout, Oktoberfest, ESB, Klosterbier, Belgian Dubbel, Belgian Trippel, and many more **Tours:** Yes; on demand based on workload of the brewery staff **Taproom:** Yes

Situated on the north end of Fidalgo Island is the city of Anacortes, most known for its ferry terminal serving Lopez Island, Shaw Island, Orcas Island, San Juan Island, and Victoria, British Columbia. What better way to wait for your ferry than with a nice meal and some craft beer. Anacortes Brewery has been serving the town its selection of beers since 1994. Located at the Rockfish Grill, the brewery focuses most of its attention on serving at the pub, but you can find their beers on draft at over 50 establishments around the Puget Sound. Operating on a seven-barrel system, they brew over 25 kinds of ales and lagers to make sure everyone will find something they like. From traditional IPAs and red ales to more unusual beers aged in bourbon barrels, nothing is off-limits in what they brew.

Some standbys include their award-winning lightly bitter Northwest-style **IPA,** their American-influenced **ESB,** and their intense **Locomotive Breath Imperial Stout.** Occasionally they will brew **Klosterbier,** a beer originally brewed with the help of a brewmaster visiting from Kalt Loch Brewery in Bavaria. Modeled after a beer they brewed for Engelberg Monastery, the dark lager has some slight chocolate and roasted malts and a faint touch of smoke, yet is easily sessionable.

Each time you visit the Rockfish Grill you'll find a wide range of beers being served. On Friday starting around 3 p.m. a beer on cask is usually offered. Along with food, the grill serves a range of Northwest-inspired food including seafood, steak, wood-fired pizza, burgers, sandwiches, and a wide variety of desserts. Kids eat free on Tuesday, so make sure to bring them along for dinner. They also offer dinner and a movie every Monday, where you can buy a discounted movie ticket for the Anacortes Cinema across the street when you order any food item.

Old Sebastes Barleywine
Style: Barleywine
ABV: 9.9%
Availability: Seasonal

Released once a year, Anacortes Brewery's Old Sebastes Barleywine is one of those beers you have to try every year. Each year's batch ages differently and you'll find different flavors and nuances from year to year. If you're lucky enough, you'll be able to try multiple years side by side to see how it ages. It's brewed as a traditional English barleywine that booms with aroma and flavor. If you consider yourself a beer geek, take your time sipping on this one, as you most likely will be analyzing its intricacies all night.

BIG E ALES (ELLERSICK BREWING CO.)

5030 208th St. SW, Ste. A, Lynnwood, WA 98036; (425) 672-7051; BigEAles.com;
@BigEAlesBrewPub

Founded: 1997 **Founder:** Rick Ellersick **Brewer:** Rick Ellersick **Flagship Beers:** Hoppy
Red Head and Scotch Ale **Year-Round Beers:** Lawnmower Lager, Golden Ale, Honey
Wheat, Copper Ale, Blackberry Ale, Scotch Ale, Hoppy Redhead, IPA, 2-Pt IPA **Seasonals/
Special Releases:** Märzen, Raspberry Sour, Summer Creamsicle, Oktoberfest, Porter,
Holiday Spice **Tours:** No **Taproom:** Yes

Big E Ales has a similar story to many breweries in the state, such as when home-brewer Rick Ellersick decided to get licensed and sell beer that he created in his garage. However, when he did it, no one else was running a brewery out of their garage. It didn't take long for him to need to expand, so he moved the brewery into its current industrial park location and added the brewpub. From the outside, the location doesn't look like much other than the grain silo to the left of the building. Inside, however, the pub has a contemporary and clean feel, along with obvious signs that they are very much a part of the local community. Their selection of food is hefty, with plenty of burgers, sandwiches, wings, and fries on the menu.

Big E Ales are generally brewed to style, but Ellersick is very creative in his brewing and loves to use fruit and other goodies in his beers. With 11 beers on draft and a root beer at any given time, you'll always be able to try something new. The award-winning **Blackberry Ale** is one of the most popular beers they offer

Hoppy Redhead
Style: Extra Special Bitter
ABV: 6.5%
Availability: Year-Round

Big E Ales' Hoppy Redhead is a traditionally brewed ESB, yet possesses a few characteristics of an amber. Glowing red and copper in color, the beer has an aroma that is all about the fresh citrus and floral hops. The flavor, however, is dominated by caramel and sweet maltiness before the earthy hops kick in, giving a slight bittering finish. The malt flavor is big enough to stand up to multiple styles of food, but try it with their barbecue ribs if eating in their pub.

year-round and is a must-try when visiting. Also look for their unique **Holiday Spice** ale, brewed with pumpkin, orange peel, coriander, cinnamon, and nutmeg for a very warming brew. Outside of the pub, you can find their beer on draft at multiple bars in North King County and Snohomish County. You can also find their **Scotch Ale, Hoppy Redhead,** and **Lawnmower Lager** available in 16-ounce cans throughout the same region. At the pub their growler prices are fantastic, or you can opt to get a party pig, a 2.25-gallon vessel with a push-button tap that makes dispensing beer a lot of fun.

BOUNDARY BAY BREWERY

1107 Railroad Ave., Bellingham, WA 98225; (360) 647-5593; BBayBrewery.com; @BoundaryBay

Founded: 1995 **Founder:** Ed Bennett **Brewer:** Aaron Jacob Smith **Flagship Beer:** IPA **Year-Round Beers:** Blonde Ale, ESB, Amber Ale, Scotch Ale, IPA, Oatmeal Stout, Dry Irish Stout **Seasonals/Special Releases:** Imperial IPA, Old Bounder, Single Hop, Cascadia Dark Ale, Belgian Tripel, Porter, Ginger Peach Blonde Ale, Cabin Fever, Dunkles Bock, Maibock, Lightner Beer, Ski to Sea ESB, Pilsner, Traverse Ale, Harvest Ale, and more **Tours:** Call ahead **Taproom:** Yes

Opened in 1995, Boundary Bay Brewery is one of the most loved brewpubs not just in Bellingham or Washington, but in the entire country. Having earned over 70 awards on both a national and an international level at some of the largest competitions for breweries, they let their beer speak for itself. Fortunately for those in the surrounding areas of Washington, their distribution has grown and now you can find their beer in 22-ounce bottles as well as on draft at multiple bars and restaurants.

Named after Boundary Bay, a bay north of Bellingham that is part Canadian and part American territory, the brewery has a distinct feel for the city it's from. Inside the 1920s warehouse that houses the brewery and pub, you're met with old wooden furniture and floors, 2 main eating areas, and a view of the brewery through a few windows to the left of the bar. If you look up, you'll see all of their medals dangling from the ceiling. The pub, which they call the bistro, offers a full pub menu complete with a kids' menu packed with tasty options.

Their beers are generally big and bold and are heavily focused around Northwest styles. In the pub they offer 7 beers year-round, with their **IPA** being the most popular. Considered by some as one of the best IPAs in the state, it starts out malty before turning to citrus, pine, and lingering bitterness. Along with their regulars, you can find a good selection of rotating, small-batch, and seasonal beers. Look for **Cabin Fever** in the winter, a winter warmer that has won plenty of awards. It's thick, malty, and packed with caramel, holiday spices, and citrus hops. Bring your growlers, as they offer very reasonably priced fills in the pub.

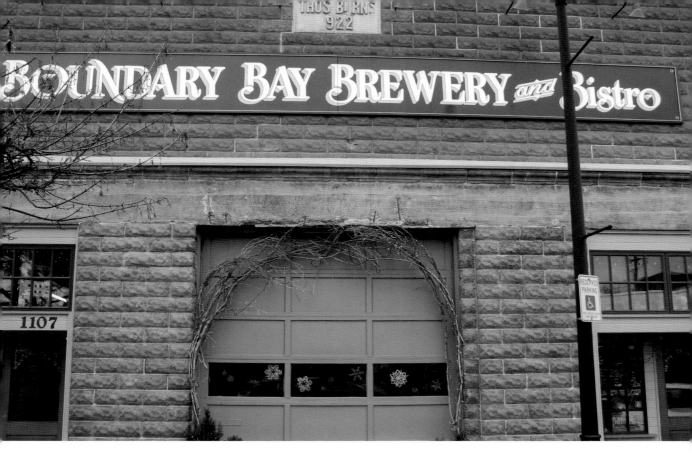

Imperial IPA
Style: Double IPA
ABV: 9.9%
Availability: Seasonal

As one of Boundary Bay's most sought-after beers, their Imperial IPA can easily be summed up in one word: hoppy. The bready and caramel malts work hard to balance out the intense citrus, pine, and floral hops that dominate both the flavor and the aroma. Although it has balance, the hops end up winning in the end with a lingering bitterness that extreme hopheads will love. It's easy to see why this beer has won multiple awards, but it isn't for the faint of heart. Look for it seasonally in 22-ounce bottles at the brewery or on draft around the state.

CHUCKANUT BREWERY & KITCHEN

601 W. Holly St., Bellingham, WA 98225; (360) 752-3377;
ChuckanutBreweryAndKitchen.com; @ChuckanutBeer
Founded: 2008 **Founders:** Mari and Will Kemper **Brewers:** Will Kemper and Bryan
Cardwell **Flagship Beers:** Chuckanut Pilsner and Chuckanut Kölsch **Year-Round Beers:**
Kölsch, Pilsner **Seasonals/Special Releases:** Vienna, Dunkel, Bock, Helles, Amber,
Brown Porter, American Dark Lager, Alt Bier, British IPA, Stout, Rauch Märzen, Märzen,
British Brown, Dortmunder Lager, British Pale Ale, Schwarzbier, Special Bitter, Sticke Alt,
Oktoberfest, and many more **Tours:** Yes **Taproom:** Yes

To call Will Kemper, founder and brewmaster at Chuckanut Brewery, an expert in the beer industry almost doesn't do justice to his experience and knowledge. Those who have been around Washington awhile might remember Thomas Kemper Brewing out of Poulsbo, Washington, in the mid-1980s. As cofounder of the brewery, Kemper helped it become a well-known brand in the area before it was eventually merged with Pyramid Breweries. After that, Kemper helped a great number of craft breweries get started all over the country as well as in Mexico and even Turkey.

He and his wife, Mari, who runs the kitchen, opened Chuckanut Brewery & Kitchen to provide locals both quality beer and food rivaled by very few. Unlike a great majority of breweries in the Northwest, Chuckanut specializes in German-style

Pilsner
Style: Pilsner
ABV: 5%
Availability: Year-Round
When you think Pilsners, many people immediately get the image of the fizzy, flavorless beers often advertised during American sporting events. However, when done right, Pilsners can pack in a lot of flavor in an easy-drinking pint that's not often achieved by many American breweries. Chuckanut Brewery's Pilsner has won multiple awards at a national level, and upon tasting it's easy to see why. A breadlike maltiness gets followed by a bold herbal hop middle and finishes dry, clean, and ready to order another. Its bitterness is perfect for cutting through spiciness in Thai or Mexican dishes, yet delicate enough to pair with most seafood.

beers with an emphasis on lagers. Although they do brew English- and American-style beers, their German beers are their bread and butter and have won them multiple awards at the Great American Beer Festival and the North American Brewers Association Awards. Their **Pilsner** and **Kölsch** are the most popular beers they sell, both of which are among the best-brewed beers in their respective styles on the West Coast. Another of their award winners is the **Vienna Lager,** a beer that has been dominating the big beer festivals just about every year. The toasted and caramelized malt character make it a perfect pairing for grilled vegetables as well as seafood such as smoked salmon or crab cakes.

Outside of the brewpub you can find their beers on draft at some of the better beer bars around the Puget Sound as far south as Tacoma. However, if you visit Bellingham, make Chuckanut Brewery & Kitchen a priority to visit. Contact them to schedule a tour of the brewery, as their brewing technology is impressive for a company of their size.

DIAMOND KNOT BREWING COMPANY

621A Front St., Mukilteo, WA 98275; (425) 355-4488; DiamondKnot.com; @DiamondKnot
Founded: 1994 **Founders:** Bob Maphet and Brian Sollenberger **Brewer:** Pat Ringe
Flagship Beer: India Pale Ale **Year-Round Beers:** India Pale Ale, Industrial IPA, Blonde Ale, Brown Ale, ESB, Steamer Glide Stout, Possession Porter, Hefeweizen
Seasonals/Special Releases: Front Street Bitter, Slane's Irish Style Red, Vienna, Golden Ale, Ho! Ho! Winter Ale, Industrial Red, Shipwreck XXXIPA, and more **Tours:** Yes, at production facility by appointment. **Taproom:** Yes

Diamond Knot Brewing founders Bob Maphet and Brian Sollenberger used to spend countless hours in their time off from their jobs at Boeing working on their brewery and were finally able to launch their first beer in 1994. Originally the brewery was located in the back of a tavern named Cheers Too!, although it operated separately from the business. Eventually the duo were able to expand enough and buy the building, which is now home to the Brewery & Alehouse. They took the name Diamond Knot from a famous ship with the same name that collided with another ship 6 miles west of Port Angeles in 1947.

Known for their incredibly clean and hop-forward flagship **IPA** and its bigger brother known as **Industrial IPA,** they offer a selection of year-round beers that are all brewed fairly true to style. If big, hoppy beers make you happy, keep an eye out for their **Shipwreck XXXIPA,** brewed seasonally. While their Industrial IPA is the big brother of the India Pale Ale, think of Shipwreck XXXIPA as the much bigger brother of both. Aside from the copious amounts of Galena and Columbus hops as well as a hefty grain bill, they take untoasted white oak chips and soak them in port wine for a few weeks before stuffing them into the kegs and letting them condition in the strong yet delicious brew.

Along with the Brewery & Alehouse, located right by the ferry terminal in Mukilteo, Diamond Knot also operates their Pizza House in Mukilteo, the Camano Lodge, which is located on Camano Island, and their production facility with a small tasting room in Mukilteo.

Beer Lover's Pick

Industrial IPA
Style: IPA
ABV: 7.9%
Availability: Year-Round
Diamond Knot Brewing Company's Industrial IPA features a clean label with an apparently hand-drawn old-time diver on the label. This hazy orange beer features aromas of grapefruit, lemon, and grass jumping out of the glass. With a sweet yet slightly bitter flavor, the balance of both citrusy hops and caramel malts creates a smooth IPA that is far from being the hop bomb often found in Northwest-style IPAs. It's perfect for drinking pretty much anytime—even non–IPA fans are likely to enjoy it.

GALLAGHERS' WHERE-U-BREW

180 W. Dayton St. Ste. 105, Edmonds, WA 98020; (425) 776-4209; WhereUBrew.com
Founded: 1995 **Founder:** Dennis Gallagher **Brewer:** Dennis Gallagher **Flagship Beer:**
Galley Mac Amber **Year-Round Beers:** Galley Mac Amber **Seasonals/Special Releases:**
Down Under IPA, Cut Your Grass Blonde, The Monk, Bearded Cannonball Stout, Topaz Pale,
Faceplant Winter Ale, And We Win! IPA, White Knuckle IPA, 5th Avenue Wheat, Broken
Stones IPA, Nuthouse Brown Ale, Hals Celebration IPA, Eddy Hop IPA, and many more
Tours: Yes **Taproom:** Yes

Gallaghers' Where-U-Brew is unlike any other brewery in the state. It's also unlike any other homebrewing shop. Think of it more like a combination brewery and homebrew shop, except you're the brewmaster. Located in the same building in Edmonds as the American Brewing Company, Gallaghers' is unique, to say the least. Inside the shop they have multiple brew kettles, bottling stations, and a whole range of ingredients. You come in, choose a recipe, brew it yourself with the help of the on-site brew crew, and then return two weeks later to bottle your brew and take it home. What's unique is that they are also a licensed brewery and generally have a range of 7 beers created on the same equipment they allow their customers to brew on. In fact, the recipes you can choose to brew yourself come from a list of over 50 beers they've brewed and have on draft in the pub. If you're not sure what to brew, just grab a taster and see which beers you like best.

Beer Lover's Pick

The Monk
Style: Tripel
ABV: 8.5%
Availability: Limited Release

As a beer that pops up from time to time at festivals such as Belgianfest and the Washington Brewers Festival, The Monk is often a favorite of festivalgoers. If you can drink it with a monk's robe on, the experience is that much better. This unique Belgian beer is smooth and boasts plenty of fruit and coriander. It's dry hopped with orange peels to add to the intense citrus aroma and flavors that are balanced with a Bavarian style of yeast that provides the unique flavor.

With so many beers to choose from, there is pretty much something for everyone. Their tap list usually contains multiple IPAs but they offer a range of American, German, and English styles. Most popular is the **Galley Mac Amber,** a beer that is comparable to Mac & Jack's African Amber. While you'll have to visit to try their beer, you can also find it at a handful of brew festivals around the area, including the Washington Brewers Festival.

JUSTICE BREWING
2414 Chestnut St., Everett, WA 98201; (425) 835-2337; JusticeBrewing.com; @JusticeBrewing
Founded: 2012 **Founder:** Nate McLaughlin **Brewer:** Nate McLaughlin **Flagship Beer:** White & Nerdy **Year-Round Beers:** White & Nerdy, Whiter & Nerdier IPA, 13 Questions Single Hop Pale Ale **Seasonals/Special Releases:** Stout Hearted Belgian Stout, Berliner Weiss, Duplex Belgian Dubbel, Belgian Pumpkin Beer **Tours:** By appointment only **Taproom:** No

As the number of nanobreweries in the state rises, beer lovers are being rewarded by being able to find new and creative beers outside the typical Northwest lineup of IPAs, pale ales, stouts, and porters. Everett-based Justice Brewing has started off small but it is doing big things. Founder and brewer Nate McLaughlin was able to get the brewery licensed in 2012 and quickly started distributing their lineup of Belgian-style beers around the area on draft as well as select 22-ounce bottles. The brewery itself is located in an unattached garage in a residential neighborhood of Everett. Due to city laws, there can't be any signage outside or retail sales, but you can make an appointment to pick up growlers or bottles by contacting the brewery itself. Your other option for finding their beer is to visit their website, which features a map of where the beer is distributed in bottles and available on draft around the area.

The Belgian-style beers are headlined by **White & Nerdy,** a Belgian white with an American twist. It's brewed with sweet orange peel, Pilsner malt, wheat, traditional Belgian yeast, and plenty of Citra hops. Unlike traditional beers in the style, the Northwest twist of adding extra hops gives it a unique yet refreshing character. They also offer **Whiter & Nerdier,** which is the big brother of White & Nerdy brewed with an even heftier ingredient list to create a fuller-bodied beer. For stout fans, they have a dry stout that's fermented with a Belgian yeast strain, creating a very interesting and tasty brew.

Berliner Weiss
Style: Berliner Weissbier
ABV: 4.5%
Availability: Rotating

If you've had a Berliner Weissbier, you probably already know
whether you'll love it or hate it.
While the style isn't for everyone, it should be on everyone's
radar to give it a try. Justice
Brewing does a fantastic job
with their version of this style,
not commonly brewed in the
Northwest.. Using a 60-hour
mash allows wild bacteria to help
give this beer its unique taste.
The cloudy sour and tart wheat
brew has no hop bitterness, yet
there is noticeable lemon in the
tart finish.

KULSHAN BREWING COMPANY

2238 James St., Bellingham, WA 98225; (360) 389-5348; KulshanBrewingCompany.com;
@KulshanBrewing
Founded: 2012 **Founder:** Dave Vitt **Brewer:** Dave Vitt **Flagship Beer:** Bastard Kat IPA
Year-Round Beers: Dude Man Wheat Ale, Good Ol' Boy Pale Ale, Red Cap Red, Bastard
Kat IPA, Trans-Porter, Midnight CDA **Seasonals/Special Releases:** Horseman's Head
Pumpkin Ale, Royal Tenenbaum Christmas Ale, Kitten Mittens Winter Warmer, Double Brother
Double IPA, Full 90 IPA, Saison du Kulshan, and many more **Tours:** No **Taproom:** Yes

Setting up shop in Bellingham's Sunnyland neighborhood in 2012, Kulshan
Brewing Company has quickly gotten the attention of beer fans in the area.
Taking a building that once was a Pro Tools store, they have transformed it into a

very inviting brewery that fits perfectly into the relaxed Bellingham atmosphere. Owner and brewer Dave Vitt was a homebrewer who learned how to brew while in Bellingham. He spent a few years down in Olympia working at Fish Brewing to learn the craft before returning and opening the Kulshan Brewing Company. The brewhouse itself features a seven-barrel system that was once part of Dick's Brewing in Centralia. Although it's just on loan from its current owner, they have set up the brewery to be able to grow and expand when the times comes to upgrade the system.

Most of their beer is served in the rather large taproom, while it can also be found on draft at multiple area restaurants and bars. Most of their beers tend to focus on Northwest styles with plenty of American-grown hops. **Bastard Kat IPA,** their most popular beer, is a West Coast–style IPA packed with plenty of citrus and a strong bitterness. While it is a mainstay, they also often have multiple other IPAs in the taproom at the same time to give IPA fans a wide selection.

Kulshan's tasting room is rather large considering they don't offer food. With multiple areas to sit and enjoy your beverage, the welcoming environment creates a community feeling. They often have food carts outside or you can walk down to Coconut Kenny's just a few buildings away and get some pizza to bring in.

Royal Tenenbaum Christmas Ale
Style: Herbed/Spiced Beer
ABV: 8.62%
Availability: Seasonal
Have you ever wondered what it would be like to drink a Christmas tree? Though this probably is not a thought in most people's minds, Kulshan Brewing set out to find out in this very festive seasonal ale. Columbus and Cascade hops add to the piney flavor, although the Douglas fir branches in the boil kettle and spruce tips loaded in the hopback provide most of the flavor. A bready and toasted malt backbone gives a sweetness to keep the Christmas flavor from being too overwhelming while doing a great job at hiding the alcohol.

LAZY BOY BREWING

715 100th St. SE, Ste. A-1, Everett, WA 98208; (425) 423-7700; LazyBoyBrewing.com; @LazyBoyBrewing

Founded: 2006 **Founder:** Shawn Loring **Brewer:** Shawn Loring **Flagship Beer:** IPA
Year-Round Beers: IPA, Hefeweizen, Porter, Amber, Lager **Seasonals/Special Releases:** Mistletoe Bliss, Belgian Golden Strong Ale, Elvis the Pelvis, Oatmeal Stout, Belgian Dubbel, Oktoberfest, Summer Rye, Dumb Luck Special Winter Porter, and many more **Tours:** No **Taproom:** Yes

For brewer Shawn Loring, the name Lazy Boy was just the right name for his company. When opening up the brewery in 2006, Loring was no newcomer to the brewing industry after spending time at multiple other breweries throughout the US, such as Pike Brewing in Seattle and his own brewpub in Cheyenne, Wyoming.

Beer Lover's Pick

Lazy Boy IPA
Style: IPA
ABV: 6.2%
Availability: Year-Round
Lazy Boy Brewing's simply named IPA can be classified as a slightly maltier Northwest-style IPA. With the signature fat guy on the label with the beer name written across a shirt that's a bit too small, you'll want to drink this while kicking back and being lazy. The beer pours a beautiful copper color with minimal head along with an orange, citrus, and caramel aroma billowing out of the glass. With 75 IBUs, the bitterness is present, yet the caramel malt does a great job of not letting the hops dominate.

Knowing he needed a catchy name, he reached back to the early '90s, when he had a group of guys he homebrewed with who called themselves "The Lazy Boys," referring to how they took their time during the brewing process. Since the brewery opened, the name, the logo of a fat guy on all the bottles, and the quality of beer have catapulted it to success.

Today you can find 22-ounce bottles of their year-round and seasonal beers throughout Washington and Oregon, with their recognizable logo that tempts people to give their beers a try. Along with the flagship Northwest-style **IPA,** year-round Lazy Boy offers a German-style **Hefeweizen,** a crisp sessionable **Lager,** an **Amber** brewed with English hops, and a light yet chocolaty **Porter.** One of their most notable seasonal brews is the **Belgian Golden Strong Ale.** Having won a gold medal at the North American Beer Awards, the 9.5% ABV strong ale has plenty of sweet honey, hay, and Belgian yeast to keep your taste buds zinging. The brewery in Everett features a tasting room with a great view of the brewing operations where you can watch the brewers in action while sipping on one of the 9 beers on draft. Like those of a lot of breweries in the area, the taproom doesn't have a kitchen, but a nearby Round Table Pizza will deliver. You can also bring the kids or your dog to the tasting room.

NORTH SOUND BREWING CO.

17406 SR 536, Unit A, Mount Vernon, WA 98273; (360) 982-2057; NorthSoundBrewing.com; @NorthSoundBrew

Founded: 2010 **Founder:** Kurt Ahrens **Brewer:** Kurt Ahrens **Flagship Beer:** Hop Chops IPA **Year-Round Beers:** Hop Chops IPA, Goosetown Brown Ale, Bitter Rain ESB, Big Bend Blonde Ale, Mystery Wheat Ale, and Slainte Stout **Seasonals/Special Releases:** Big R Imperial Red Ale, Baffing Spoon Scottish Ale, 101 Imperial IPA, Pearl's Pale Ale, Hop Saw IPA, Succulous Imperial Porter, Creepy Monkey Barrel–Aged Double Brown, Hopsolute IPA, and many more **Tours:** By appointment only **Taproom:** Yes

Over on the west side of Mount Vernon, just off Memorial Highway in what was once a used car lot, lies North Sound Brewing Co. As the second brewery in the city, North Sound has been doing its part to help transform Mount Vernon into an excellent little beer city. Founded by homebrewer Kurt Ahrens in 2010, the company brews up a range of bold and interesting unfiltered beers. In the tasting room they offer 9 beers on draft at a time, while you can also find their beers on tap around the north Puget Sound area.

Most hopheads will enjoy their delicious citrusy and bitter light-bodied **Hop Chops IPA.** For those seeking a little more kick, the **101 Imperial IPA** is bound to smack you in the face with hops. It's called 101 because it's 10.1% ABV, 101 IBUs, and it costs them $101 for the hops used to dry hop each batch. To see how well your

Creepy Monkey Barrel–Aged Double Brown
Style: Imperial Brown Ale
ABV: 12%
Availability: Limited Release

North Sound's Goosetown Brown is one of their most popular beers. It's a solid brown ale, yet they wanted to crank it up a few notches. So what's a brewer to do? Add twice as much malt and hops in half as much water, of course. They didn't stop there and decided to age it in three kinds of whiskey barrels before blending it all back together. The end result is a huge 12% ABV that is packed with so much complexity you'll taste something new with just about every sip. Let's just hope this one will return.

taste buds can detect flavors, try the **Mystery Wheat Ale.** Each time they brew it they add different fruit juice, so you can take your best guess at figuring out what the flavor is in the particular batch you're drinking.

Their taproom is all about the beer. Other than a selection of chips, nuts, and pepperoni sticks, you'll have to bring your own food in unless it's a Monday, when they get pizzas delivered and sell pieces by the slice. On nice days the beer garden is a perfect setting to eat, drink, and enjoy the company of others. For locals or those just passing through, make sure to stop in on Wednesday with your growlers ready to be filled, as they have some amazing deals. On Thursday they offer a new beer on cask at the bar, which is the perfect condition to drink their **Slainte Stout.**

SCUTTLEBUTT BREWING COMPANY

1205 Craftsman Way, Ste. 101, Everett, WA 98201; (425) 257-9316; ScuttlebuttBrewing.com; @ScuttlebuttBrew
Founded: 1996 **Founders:** Phil and Cynthia Barrett **Brewer:** Matt Stromberg **Flagship Beer:** Amber Ale **Year-Round Beers:** Homeport Blonde, Hefe Weizen, Amber Ale, Tell Tale Red, Gale Force IPA, Porter **Seasonals/Special Releases:** Weizenbock, Tripel 7, 10° Below, Bombshell Blonde, Mateo Loco Imperial Red Ale, Black Pilsner, Mai Bock, Golden Mariner, Old No. 1 Barley Wine, Hoptopia, Nut Brown, Scotch Ale, Commodore's Pale, Belgian Winter, and many more **Tours:** By appointment **Taproom:** Yes

With a name like Scuttlebutt Brewing Company, one of the first things people want to know is what the heck it means. While scuttlebutt is a term used for a cask of drinking water on sailing ships, the brewery actually gets its

name from co-owner Cynthia Barrett. Before she was born her father nicknamed her Scuttlebutt, a name that stuck with her until she asked him to stop using it when she was 13. Years later when her husband, Phil, decided they should take his homebrewing hobby and open a brewery, the name Scuttlebutt stuck. Opened since 1996, the Everett-based brewery has focused on brewing a wide range of beers ranging from typical styles found in the Northwest to an array of seasonal and rare style beers. Year-round they offer a handful of beers including their most popular, **Amber Ale,** a balanced brew with plenty of caramel flavor. Another popular staple is their unfiltered **Gale Force IPA,** which is packed with plenty of Northwest hops and finishes with a lingering bitterness.

Along with their growing production facility that produces beer in both kegs and bottles, Scuttlebutt also runs a restaurant under the same Scuttlebutt Brewing name near Everett's waterfront. With plenty of seating and a beautiful wood bar, it should be on your list of restaurants to visit if you find yourself in or near Everett. Come hungry, as they offer a wide range of seafood, sandwiches, burgers, and steaks. The fish and chips are generally a smart choice, especially when paired with their Amber Ale and **Nut Brown** beers.

As Scuttlebutt has grown over the years, so has its distribution. You can find 12-ounce and 22-ounce bottles in Washington and Idaho, as well as multiple other states throughout the US.

Hoptopia
Style: Imperial IPA
ABV: 8%
Availability: Rotating

With a name like Hoptopia and a pirate on the label, you'd expect a certain bite from this imperial IPA. Scuttlebutt doesn't let you down, although the bite isn't as tough as the 8% ABV might lead you to believe. Citrus and pine fill out the aroma and both punch you a bit in the face upon drinking, with a strong grapefruit bitterness. With a subtle sweetness, the malt backbone does its job well of not letting the bitterness get out of control, while the alcohol makes its presence known.

SKAGIT RIVER BREWERY

404 S. 3rd St., Mount Vernon, WA 98273; (360) 336-2884; SkagitBrew.com; @SkagitBeer
Founded: 1995 **Founder:** Charlie Sullivan **Brewer:** Mike Armstrong **Flagship Beer:**
Sculler's IPA **Year-Round Beers:** Sculler's IPA, Gospel IPA, Skagit Brown Ale, Del Rio
Lager, Hefeweizen, Farm to Market ESB, Helmet Pale Ale, Highwater Porter **Seasonals/**
Special Releases: Trumpeter Stout, Jenny's Scottish Ale, Yellowjacket Pale Ale, Blackjack
Lager, Dutch Girl Lager, and many more **Tours:** No **Taproom:** Yes

As one of the older brewpubs in the north Puget Sound area, Skagit River Brewery has been brewing beer since 1995 in downtown Mount Vernon. A 1929 warehouse once owned by the Pacific Fruit and Produce Company, the large building next to train tracks was converted to a brewery and pub that has been quenching

Beer Lover's Pick

Trumpeter Imperial Stout
Style: Imperial Stout
ABV: 10%
Availability: Winter

The trumpeter swan is known to be
the heaviest bird native to North
America as well as the largest
waterfowl species still in existence
on earth. It's huge. So if Skagit
River Brewery named its beer and
labeled it with a trumpeter on the
bottle, you know it's got to be
huge. With 10% ABV it is a massive
imperial stout packed with plenty
of caramel, chocolate, roast, and
smoke that ends with a subtle hop
bitterness and licorice in the finish.
Available in the winter, this a delicious beer that is sure to warm you
up on those cold nights.

 is the beer bottle photograph.

the thirst of area residents ever since. If you walk into the pub you can head straight back and peer through the windows of the production brewery. Along with serving those in the pub, Skagit River Brewery distributes their ales and lagers around the area in kegs as well as 22-ounce bottles.

With a commitment to using local ingredients in their beers, Skagit River uses predominantly Yakima Valley hops and Northwest-grown barley and wheat. Like many breweries in the area they are best known for one of their IPAs, a Northwest-style citrusy IPA known simply as **Sculler's IPA.** The rest of the year-round lineup is what you'd expect to find in most brewpubs in the area with a brown ale, pale ale, ESB, Hefeweizen, and lager. Throughout the year they release a few seasonals and special releases such as their true-to-style **Jenny's Scottish Ale** and the rich and hefty **Trumpeter Imperial Stout.**

Food options range from Northwest-style pub fare to barbecue, seafood, and pasta. Their mac and cheese is loaded with 5 cheeses and tossed in a creamy garlic sauce. Try it paired with their **Skagit Brown Ale,** a beer robust enough to stand up next to the rich sauce without overwhelming the flavor. Bring a growler or buy one there; they'll fill them up before you leave.

SKOOKUM BREWERY

17925A 59th Ave. NE, Arlington, WA 98223; (360) 403-7094; SkookumBrewing.com; @SkookumBrewery
Founded: 2007 **Founders:** Ron Walcher and Jackie Jenkins **Brewer:** Ron Walcher
Flagship Beer: None **Year-Round Beers:** Jackass IPA, Olde Tom, Hooskal Stout, Mule, Brown & Hairy, Gone Monk, Amber's Hot Friend, Sorrel Ale **Seasonals/Special Releases:** Woody's Oak, Murder of Crows, Solitary Confinement, Mammoth Jack, Figgy Chile Stout, Effen Heffen, Angel's Ale, and many more **Tours:** No **Taproom:** Yes

Husband-and-wife team Ron Walcher and Jackie Jenkins originally started Skookum Brewery on their residential property out in the woods. The tasting room had a wooden-lodge look with beautiful river rock and wood, creating a feel that you were drinking beer on a ranch. Customers would drive down an old gravel road and just when they felt like they were lost, they'd spot the building. As word spread, more and more people learned of both their beer and the tasting room, and pretty soon a steady stream of cars were visiting on weekends. The neighbors weren't so fond of the lost peace and quiet, even if they did still enjoy their beer. Understandably Skookum set out to find a new location and settled in at their new location near the Arlington Airport.

Amber's Hot Friend
Style: Amber Ale
ABV: 5.2%
Availability: Year-Round

With a name like Amber's Hot Friend, you expect a beer to have a little feistiness to it. Don't worry, this friend of Amber's is as gorgeous as she is feisty. Technically an amber ale, she packs in plenty of hops, causing her to drink a little more like a pale ale. A beautiful toasted nut and caramel malt body gives her plenty of curves while keeping her grounded and not letting the citrus and floral hops take over. The pleasant hoppy finish, though, is prevalent enough for you to take notice when she walks into the room.

With the Northwest rich in Native American history, the brewery took the term "skookum" for their name, a word that has two meanings in Chinook jargon. One meaning is a monster similar to Sasquatch; the other meaning has a very positive connotation. If you've tried their beer, you'll understand both of the meanings. Both beastlike and positively delicious, **Jackass IPA** is a hopped-up Northwest-style IPA with enough bitterness to justify its bold name. Stout lovers will appreciate **Murder of Crows Bourbon Barrel Aged Stout.** With just a touch of bourbon and wood in the flavor, you get quite a bit of dark chocolate and roasted coffee, making it go down a little too easy.

Brewpubs

ADAM'S NORTHWEST BISTRO & BREWERY (TWIN RIVERS BREWING)

104 N. Lewis St., Monroe, WA 98272; (360) 794-4056; AdamsNWBistro.com; @AdamsNWBistro

Founded: 1994 (brewery), 2011 (bistro) **Founder:** Adam Hoffman **Brewers:** Adam Hoffman and Glen Parker **Flagship Beer:** Nut Brown Ale **Year-Round Beers:** IPA, NW Pale Ale, Nut Brown Ale, and a Stout on Nitro **Seasonals/Special Releases:** Saison, Märzen, Kölsch, Amber, Black IPA, Winter Spice Ale **Tours:** Yes **Taproom:** Yes

With over 25 years of experience in the kitchen and a background in home-brewing, Adam Hoffman found a way to enjoy both worlds. Adam's Northwest Bistro & Brewery (the brewery is Twin Rivers Brewing) combines Northwest cuisine and fine ales brewed on a locally made brewing system. (Rumor has it the system was built by inmates from the prison in Monroe, but you'll have to bend Adam's ear about that!)

Proud to have the only brewery in Monroe, the brewers of Twin Rivers have experimented with many beer styles, from traditional to seasonal. And as Twin Rivers continues to grow and cement itself in the craft-beer world, Adam Hoffman seems committed to providing the customer with what he or she wants. So while you enjoy a pint, talk about it with your server.

The Northwest is sort of IPA country, with hop-forward beers taking center stage at many venues. Bucking this stereotype, Twin Rivers lets an old friend share the spotlight. With an affinity for brown ales, the team at Twin Rivers is proud of the **Nut Brown Ale.** Used as an ingredient in their beer and onion soup, this unofficial flagship beer seems capable of anchoring both a meal and an enjoyable beverage at the same time.

BIRDSVIEW BREWING

38302 SR 20, Concrete, WA 98237; (360) 826-3406; BirdsviewBrewingCompany.com

Founded: 2006 **Founders:** Bill and Kris Voigt **Brewer:** Bill Voigt and Julie Voigt **Flagship Beer:** Screaming Eagle IPA **Year-Round Beers:** IPA, Pail Ale, Amber Lushus, Sweet Brown Molly, Ditsy Blonde, Pilsner **Seasonals/Special Releases:** Mayanara Imperial Stout, It's Da Porter, Ditsy Blonde, and more **Tours:** Yes **Taproom:** Yes

Originally intended to be a tasting room only, this family-owned and -operated place soon turned into a full-blown brewery with a small deli. With a seven-barrel system, brewmaster Bill Voigt works hard to maintain all 10 of Birdsview's brews on tap. It is a good thing Voigt has his youngest daughter, Julie, helping him out. Kris Voigt, affectionately referred to as "Deli Queen," is in charge of whipping up delicious treats in the kitchen for the patrons. Although the website says the deli is a very small operation, the menu is quite impressive, with loads of exciting items to choose from while imbibing the proverbial fruits of the Voigt family's labors.

Birdsview's Pail Ale (which the menu says it is spelled right as it refers to 19th-century England, where the beer was carried in pails) is an ESB brewed with caramel and pale malt. With a light sweet malt aroma and faint floral hops, this brew finishes with light fruit notes and light bitterness. Pair it with a blue cheese and bacon dog, which is topped with crumbled bacon and blue cheese bits. If blue cheese on a hot dog is too wild, try a Julie's Special: turkey, bacon, and swiss cheese with mayonnaise on a toasted ciabatta bun. Pair it with a **Screaming Eagle IPA,** which is a malt-forward IPA with earthy hop tones, toffee malt, and brown sugar on the finish.

LA CONNER BREWING COMPANY

117 S. 1st St., La Conner, WA 98257; (360) 466-1415; LaConnerBrewery.com
Founded: 1995 **Founder:** Scott Abrahamson **Brewer:** Doug Alvord **Flagship Beer:** IPA
Year-Round Beers: Pilsner, Wheat, IPA, Brown, Pale, ESB **Seasonals/Special Releases:** Porter, Stout, Doppelbock, "Olde Curmudgeon" Barley Wine, Vienna-Style Lager, Oktoberfest, Tannenbaum, Belgian **Tours:** No **Taproom:** Yes

Having won awards at the Great American Beer Festival, US Beer Tasting Championships, and the World Beer Cup, La Conner Brewing is definitely worth checking out. With 6 beers always on tap and 8 others on a seasonal rotation, this tourist-town brewpub offers a fair share of brews that can be enjoyed by the fireplace or in the garden terrace.

Their menu is heavy on upscale pub fare, emphasizing wood-fired pizzas. But the menu is far from limited to just pizzas, with an extensive menu of appetizers, soups, salads, paninis, burgers, quesadillas, and tacos, as well as a children's menu for this family-friendly establishment.

Growler fills are available and as many as 4 La Conner beers come in six-packs to go. Wash down that wood-fired pizza with a pint of **La Conner IPA.** This Northwest-style India Pale Ale features Yakima Valley–grown hops and pours a blond-yellow color. With the aroma and taste being dominated by grapefruit, this beer is refreshing with a low level of bitterness for the style. Lucky patrons will be there when La Conner has its **Sour Ale** on tap. Featuring local raspberries, this beer is a Great American Beer Festival winner. With aromas of cherries and sour apples, it's quite tart but has a nice clean finish.

NORTH FORK BREWERY

6186 Mt. Baker Hwy., Deming, WA 98244; (360) 599-2337; NorthForkBrewery.com
Founded: 1997 **Founders:** Sandy and Vicki Savage **Brewer:** Eric Jorgensen **Flagship Beer:** India Pale Ale **Year-Round Beers:** India Pale Ale, Barleywine **Seasonals/Special Releases:** American Wheat Ale, Son of Frog, Lighter Shade of Pale, Strong Scotch Ale, Mild Brown, Avalanche Amber, Porter, Special Bitter, Dry Stout, Extra Special Bitter, and many more **Tours:** No **Taproom:** Yes

In the foothills of Mount Baker you will find North Fork Brewery. With a rustic atmosphere and a distinguished menu, North Fork is one of the smaller breweries in the area. They produce only 109 gallons per batch (3.5 barrels). Since 1997 North Fork has been supplying Deming with fine ales and gourmet pizzas. With a commitment to the time-intensive style of British ales, North Fork has an extensive list on offer.

North Fork also has an impressive pizzeria menu featuring mouthwatering choices to choose from. Lovers of unconventional pizzas can add garlic-roasted chicken breast or smoked salmon to a pie for an extra cost. Appetizers, salads, sandwiches, lasagna, and calzones grace the pages of this delicious menu as well. While waiting for your smoked salmon pizza to hit the table, try a pint of North Fork's best-selling **IPA.** With restrained hoppiness for the style, this IPA has light, fresh malt notes, mild fruity hops, and hints of buttery sweetness. While you're savoring the soft citrus profile of this brew, order the kids some of North Fork's homemade root beer.

A rather unique feature to the North Fork Brewery is that they perform weddings and holy unions in their wedding chapel. North Fork has an ordained minister on site legally appointed to perform your nuptials, holy union, or commitment ceremony.

Beer Bars

THE COPPER HOG

1327 N. State St., Bellingham, WA 98225; (360) 927-7888; TheCopperHog.com;
@TheCopperHog
Draft Beers: 18 **Bottled/Canned Beers:** About 50

You could call it a touch of Europe just south of the border. Located in downtown Bellingham, The Copper Hog is a European-inspired gastropub that should make both beer lovers and their non–beer loving friends very happy. Multiple windows provide the space with plenty of light during the day, which helps add to the European-style decor. Throughout you'll notice soccer paraphernalia, so if that's your sport, you'll feel right at home. Multiple TVs show soccer as well as other sports, or you can choose to play your own game of darts to keep yourself entertained.

Eighteen taps offer a rotating selection of local beers as well as quite a few from around the world. While you'll find more popular beers, such as Guinness and Heineken, they also offer multiple local beers you won't likely find elsewhere around Whatcom County. The bar also offers an extensive whiskey selection along with an assortment of upscale cocktails, so anyone who is thirsty will be well taken care of. An upscale pub-fare menu gives you plenty of options to eat. If for some reason you don't like the menu, just come back a few months later, as it is constantly changing. Sure, they offer traditional options such as fish and chips, shepherd's pie, and bangers and mash, but they aren't generally created the same way you might be used to. Their well-created food menu isn't huge, but all of the options pair well with the beers on draft. Make sure to check out their happy hour, as you'll find some deals on a range of tasty foods.

THE GREEN FROG

1015 N. State St., Bellingham, WA 98225; (360) 961-1438; AcousticTavern.com;
@AcousticTavern

Draft Beers: 30 **Bottled/Canned Beers:** 2

First opening its doors in 2005, The Green Frog as it stands today is the newer and larger version of what it once was. The name was originally The Green Frog Cafe Acoustic Tavern. Owners James Hardesty and Nate Carlson are fans of 1970s Texas folk music and took a line from the song "Desperados Waiting for a Train," by Guy Clark. The song talked about a beer joint named the Green Frog Cafe, hence the name. The Washington State Liquor Control Board didn't like the name, as it was said to confuse people that it wasn't a cafe, so they ended up adding Acoustic Tavern to the name. Today the Bellingham beer bar is known simply as The Green Frog.

Inside the space you'll notice a stage setup on the right, which is used frequently for live shows. The walls are lined with corrugated metal and plenty of guitars hanging around. Out back is a large deck with lots of room to enjoy with a group of friends. In the back of the building is the bar with stools made of repurposed tractor seats, allowing you to take a seat and spend some considerable time working the beer menu. With 30 beers on draft you just might be there awhile. The majority of the beers you'll find come from Washington breweries along with a few local ciders. They've turned an old bookshelf into a barback stocked with a growing selection of whiskey and other liquors. Along with a range of drinks, they have an interesting selection of grilled cheese sandwiches, each served with your choice of tomato soup or salad. If you're looking for something interesting, try The Elvis, a cheddar, bacon, and peanut butter sandwich.

Beer Event

April Brews Day

Each year over 35 breweries pack into downtown Bellingham to celebrate April Brews Day. The event is a fund-raiser for the Max Higbee Center, a nonprofit organization that provides recreation programs for teens and adults with developmental disabilities. Along with supporting a great cause, you can try special beers from a wide range of Northwest breweries. For more information, check out the event website at maxhigbee.org/april-brews-day.html.

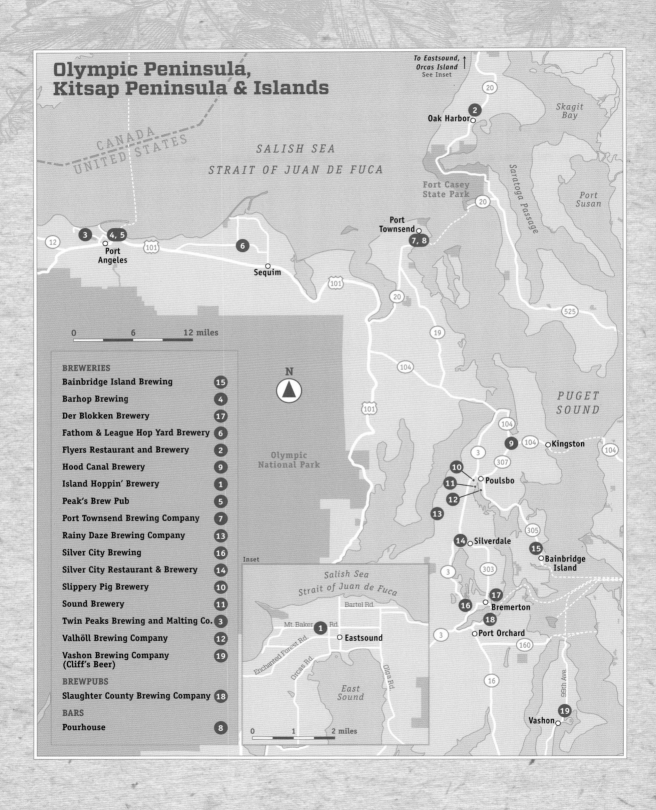

Olympic Peninsula, Kitsap Peninsula & Islands

To Eastsound,
Orcas Island
See Inset

CANADA
UNITED STATES

SALISH SEA
STRAIT OF JUAN DE FUCA

Skagit Bay

Oak Harbor

Fort Casey State Park

Saratoga Passage

Port Susan

Port Townsend

Port Angeles

Sequim

Olympic National Park

PUGET SOUND

Kingston

Poulsbo

Silverdale

Bainbridge Island

Bremerton

Port Orchard

Vashon

BREWERIES

Bainbridge Island Brewing	15
Barhop Brewing	4
Der Blokken Brewery	17
Fathom & League Hop Yard Brewery	6
Flyers Restaurant and Brewery	2
Hood Canal Brewery	9
Island Hoppin' Brewery	1
Peak's Brew Pub	5
Port Townsend Brewing Company	7
Rainy Daze Brewing Company	13
Silver City Brewing	16
Silver City Restaurant & Brewery	14
Slippery Pig Brewery	10
Sound Brewery	11
Twin Peaks Brewing and Malting Co.	3
Valhöll Brewing Company	12
Vashon Brewing Company (Cliff's Beer)	19

BREWPUBS

Slaughter County Brewing Company	18

BARS

Pourhouse	8

0   6   12 miles

N

Inset

Salish Sea
Strait of Juan de Fuca

Bartel Rd.

Mt. Baker Rd.

Eastsound

Enchanted Forest Rd.

Orcas Rd.

Olga Rd.

East Sound

0   1   2 miles

Olympic Peninsula, Kitsap Peninsula & Islands

In the northwest portion of the state, the Olympic Peninsula, Kitsap Peninsula, and islands provide a scenic and laid-back lifestyle compared to the bigger cities along the I-5 corridor. Plenty of parks and outdoor activities make the area booming with those either seeking adventure or looking for a relaxing getaway. Whether you're visiting or you call the area home, you don't have to hop on the ferry to Seattle to find quality beer.

For years there weren't many options in the area for fresh beer. Port Townsend Brewing Company and Silver City Brewery were two of the main options. Today, however, things are much different. Bainbridge Island and Orcas Island each have their own breweries, so both locals and those visiting the islands can support the local economies. Over in the Poulsbo area, newer breweries Valhöll Brewing Company, Sound Brewery, and Slippery Pig Brewery have made the town into a must-visit destination for craft-beer lovers. With the way things are trending, it won't be any surprise if we see many new and exciting breweries open their doors in the area over the next few years.

Breweries

BAINBRIDGE ISLAND BREWING

9415 Coppertop Loop, Ste. 103-104, Bainbridge Island, WA 98110; (206) 451-4646;
BainbridgeBeer.com; @BainbridgeBeer
Founded: 2012 **Founders:** Russell Everett and Chuck Everett **Brewer:** Russell Everett
Flagship Beers: Eagle Harbor IPA and Kommuter Kölsch **Year-Round Beers:** Kommuter
Kölsch, Eagle Harbor IPA, Bainbridge Bitter Pale Ale, Blakely Brown Ale, Battle Point
Stout **Seasonals/Special Releases:** Sol Patch Pumpkin Ale, Puget Sound Giant
Hoptopus, Winslow Wheat, Arrow Point Amber, Wing Point Winter Ale, Battle Point Stout,
Landfall Pale Ale, Point White Wit, Sand Spit Saison, Whiskey Jack, and many more
Tours: Yes **Taproom:** Yes

Up until Bainbridge Island Brewing opened in 2012, the island was lacking its own brewery. Sure, you could find some decent beer around the island, but having the pride of a locally produced beer made the grand opening that much more special. Started by father and son Chuck and Russell Everett, the brewery is run mainly by family. Russell, an award-winning homebrewer, decided to change directions as a lawyer specializing in alcoholic beverage law and turn his hobby into a business. Many of their beers so far have been recipes from his homebrewing days.

For those who aren't familiar with Bainbridge Island, life revolves around the ferry terminal, as it ships passengers back and forth from Seattle. The brewery and taproom itself are located roughly 2.5 miles from the ferry terminal. If it's your first time at the taproom, it would be in your interest to try a sampler. The year-round lineup includes an **IPA, Pale Ale, Brown Ale, Stout** and their malt-forward **Kommuter Kölsch.** While all solid beers, their seasonal brews is where the creativity really is. Using whiskey barrels from nearby Bainbridge Organic Distillery, they've crafted some tasty beers, such as **Battle Point Stout 2** and **Whiskey Jack.** You can find their beer outside the island on draft at some of the better beer bars around the Puget Sound.

Whiskey Jack
Style: Pumpkin Ale
ABV: 6.5%
Availability: Seasonal

What would make a pumpkin ale even better? Whiskey, of course. As its name implies, Whiskey Jack is a beer Bainbridge Island Brewing created using its Sol Patch Pumpkin Ale and aged it in wheat whiskey barrels from Bainbridge Organic Distillers. The result is a beer with plenty of pumpkin spice, pumpkin, and bourbon flavors with just a hint of vanilla. It finishes dry, keeping your palate from getting wrecked and allowing you to easily sip on a few pints. If they brew this again, make sure to get a growlerful or you just might regret it when it's gone.

BARHOP BREWING

124 W. Railroad, Port Angeles, WA 98362; (360) 460-5155; BarhopBrewing.com
Founded: 2010 **Founder:** Tom Curry **Brewer:** Tom Curry **Flagship Beer:** FnA IPA
Year-Round Beers: FnA IPA, PA 7, Judge Porter, Redneck Logger **Seasonals/Special Releases:** Gluten Freedom Ale, Catcher Rye, Predecessor ESB, Loser Dog Brown, Gone Dam Pale Ale, Winterhop Stout, Bud the Wiser, and many more **Tours:** No **Taproom:** Yes

Barhop Brewing has seen a lot of growth in the short time it's been open. Originally the brewery was located behind the Harbinger Winery, with which the brewery shared close ties. Not too long after the tiny production brewery opened, their taproom was opened not too far from the ferry terminal taking people between Port Angeles and Victoria, British Columbia. After just over a year, it was time to expand again and bring the brewery and taproom into one brewery. At the end of 2012, Barhop Brewing moved into its current location on the waterfront, just a short walk from the old taproom. The new location is a 7,000-square-foot warehouse with half dedicated to the brewery, while the other half is the tasting room.

Brewmaster and owner Tom Curry creates a range of Northwest-inspired beers that make both locals and tourists very happy. The bold and extremely flavorful **FnA IPA** is their top seller. It packs a bitter citrus and piney bite from the use of Chinook, Centennial, and Amarillo hops that's balanced out by a nice malt foundation. You'll also want to try the scarily drinkable **PA 7**, a 7% ABV pale ale. It's a beer that doesn't

Judge Porter
Style: Porter
ABV: 6.1%
Availability: Year-Round
Barhop's Judge Porter is one of those beers that hopheads need to judge for themselves. Brewed with a healthy dose of Nugget, Willamette, and Tettnanger hops, it packs a strong dark-coffee bitterness. A sweet chocolate and caramel malt base balances out the flavor, creating an incredibly drinkable porter that ends with a nice little hop kick. Look for this porter year-round. Don't let its darkness scare you even if it's summertime. It's roasty but can easily be enjoyed all year long.

taste like your typical pale ale, with a malty and honey flavor with a touch of spice and hops that goes down well.

The newer taproom has plenty of space for you to visit and sample their beers. They even offer guest beers on draft, so you can always find something to quench your thirst no matter what mood you're in. You'll find a small selection of food, but they also allow you to bring in food. If you're heading up to Victoria, make sure to stop in and have a few beers while you're waiting for the ferry.

DER BLOKKEN BREWERY
1100 Perry Ave., Bremerton, WA 98310; (360) 377-2344; DerBlokken.com; @DerBlokken
Founded: 2010 **Founders:** Andy and Jessica Husted **Brewer:** Andy Husted **Flagship Beer:** Black **Year-Round Beers:** Sacred Hop **Seasonals/Special Releases:** Black, Castover, Russet, Pactolian, Mutha' Hefe, Ginga, Autumn Scotch, Double Black, VIPA, Mexican Chocolate Stout **Tours:** No **Taproom:** Yes

Bremerton's Manette neighborhood is home to the growing brewpub Der Blokken Brewery. Founded by Andy and Jessica Husted, owners of Fritz European Fry House, the small pub has gone from just serving their beer in house to distribution around the area in kegs and 22-ounce bottles. The name "Der Blokken" is a made-up Dutch word for black, in reference to the color of Andy's first beers and a black Lab Jessica once loved. Going along with that theme, their flagship beer is called **Black.** The full-bodied dark brew is what they call a porter/stout, as it falls right between the two styles with hints of dark chocolate and coffee. Outside of Black they have a

Sacred Hop
Style: Double IPA
ABV: 8%
Availability: Year-Round

One of the best parts about the Northwest for hopheads is the abundance of big IPAs. It's not just the amount, but the quality of IPAs that are crafted by a number of breweries, and Der Blokken's Sacred Hop double IPA fits right in. The label on the 22-ounce bottle shows a hop cone with wings as if to say this is one angelic beer. Perfectly balanced, the malts take the stage early before giving way to a crisp, dry, and florally bitter finish that has some notable booziness.

rotation of a handful of beers that make their appearance throughout the year, such as **Ginga,** a somewhat spicy Irish red ale; **Mutha' Hefe,** their Hefeweizen brewed with Belgian yeast that imparts a banana flavor; and **Sacred Hop,** their double IPA with plenty of flavor and a dry, bitter finish.

Their beautiful bar is located right next to a roll-up door that is opened on nicer days, making it feel almost like a beer garden. Behind the bar is 12 taps, with as many as 8 of them serving guest taps from breweries all over the country that you won't find anywhere else in the area. At the pub you can choose between a taster flight of Der Blokken beers and an alternative flight of any beers and ciders they have on draft. A beautiful piece of bottle-cap art hangs on the wall, showing the old Manette Bridge. The mural was created by local artist Dave Ryan, who nailed 7,000 bottle caps to a sheet of plywood to create the mural.

FATHOM & LEAGUE HOP YARD BREWERY

360 Grandview Dr., Sequim, WA 98382; (360) 286-0278; FathomAndLeagueBrewery.com
Founded: 2009 **Founders:** Tom and Lisa Martin **Brewer:** Tom Martin **Flagship Beer:** Discovery Stout **Year-Round Beer:** Olympic Peninsula Ale **Seasonals/Special Releases:** Krabben Kölsch, Mastodon Scotch Ale, Discovery Stout, Raingold Pilsner, Four Leaf Irish-Style Stout, Dungeness Dunkle Weizen, Alder Wood Smoked Oat Stout
Tours: No **Taproom:** No

Fathom & League Hop Yard Brewery may be one of the smallest breweries in the state, but that doesn't stop founder and brewer Tom Martin from making some

Alder Wood Smoked Oat Stout
Style: Oatmeal Stout
ABV: 5.4%
Availability: Seasonal
The name for Alder Wood Smoked Oat Stout, brewed in collaboration with Gabriel Schuenemann, co-owner and chef of Sequim-based Alder Wood Bistro, has dual meanings, as it was brewed first to serve in the restaurant. Using rolled oats from a local farm that have been smoked with fresh alder wood, the beer has a touch of smoke and a smoothness from the oats. It also contains anise and vanilla, creating a sweet aroma with plenty of rich chocolate and sweet flavors. This is a beer that could easily replace your holiday treats.

unique beers. Tom used the name Fathom & League as a nod to the intrepid mariner-brewers of 1792. On May 5 of that year, Captain George Vancouver sent his crew ashore at Diamond Point to brew the very first batch of beer in the Pacific Northwest. They also spent time surveying the coast and made their measurements in fathoms and leagues. Tim acquired his business license on May 5, 2009, to commemorate the day.

The brewery itself is housed in a 240-square-foot detached garage next to the Martin residence. Because the brewing system is small as well, it can be tough to find their beer on draft, even in Sequim. However, multiple area restaurants carry it in kegs, and they do occasionally bottle some batches. As much as they can, they tend to use local ingredients. Many of the hops come straight from the backyard, while most of the malts come from Canada.

In the winter months you'll find maltier brews, such as the **Four Leaf Irish Stout, Alder Wood Smoked Oak Stout,** or the popular **Discovery Stout,** packed with malt, hops, and even honey. In the spring and summer months they release **Krabben Kölsch, Mastodon Scotch Ale,** and **Raingold Pils** to help quench the thirst from warmer weather. The well-balanced **Olympic Peninsula Ale** is the only year-round beer they offer. They don't have a tasting room, so your best bet is to look up their Facebook page for the latest listings of where it's being poured around the Peninsula.

FLYERS RESTAURANT AND BREWERY

32295 SR 20, Oak Harbor, WA 98277; (360) 675-5858; EatAtFlyers.com; @FlyersBrew
Founded: 2005 **Founders:** Jason Tritt, Tony Savoy, and Greg and Rosa Tritt **Brewer:**
Tony Savoy **Flagship Beer:** Pacemaker Porter **Year-Round Beers:** Humbles Blonde
Ale, Heat Seeker Hefe', Afterburner IPA, First Flight Amber Ale, Barnstormer Brown Ale,
Pacemaker Porter **Seasonals/Special Releases:** Spitfire Best Bitter, Jet Fuel Coffee
Porter, Proptoberfest, Crash and Burn Smoked Stout, Copper Hog Red Ale, Daybreak
Breakfast Stout, Sick Duck Imperial Stout, Low Vis White IPA, and more **Tours:** Yes;
contact brewery for details **Taproom:** Yes

Established in 2005, Flyers Restaurant and Brewery has been winning awards
for its beers ever since. Its aviation theme comes from owners who have had
multiple generations serving in the military. The Naval Air Station Whidbey Island

Beer Lover's Pick

Pacemaker Porter
Style: Porter
ABV: 5.5%
Availability: Year-Round
Like many brewpubs do, Flyers figured
they'd add a porter to their lineup. Little
did they know that the robust porter
named Pacemaker would quickly become
one of their top sellers and win multiple
national awards. It's a thing of beauty
to see it poured into a glass: deep black
in color with a thin tan head that makes
the beer look thick. Coffee, chocolate,
and roasted malts come together in both
the aroma and flavor to create a well-
balanced, drinkable, yet bold porter. Its
smoothness shines throughout the entire
22-ounce bottle while the very little bitterness makes it a tasty treat.

is just a couple of miles away, so the theme just made sense when a lot of their customers work at the base. The theme extends from the airplane propellers on the sign outside and their tap handles to their logo, beer names, and decor inside the restaurant.

Distribution of their beer extends all over the state as well as in Oregon and Idaho, but it can be tough to find. Their core lineup of beers can often be found in 22-ounce bottles. Their year-round roster of offerings contains beers that have won awards, such as the **Barnstormer Brown Ale, Pacemaker Porter,** and **First Flight Amber.** While these are all solid beers, their real creativity shines with the seasonals and special-release beers that show up from time to time. Many of their special releases are brewed for specific bars or events around the area, such as **Kentucky Überwine,** which is brewed for Über Tavern in Seattle, and **Bottleworks VIII** (140 Schilling Strong Scotch Ale), brewed for Bottleworks in Seattle. Brewmaster Tony Savoy knows what he's doing in the brewhouse, so you can't go wrong with pretty much any of their beers.

Their restaurant and brewery on Whidbey Island is the best spot to sample all of their beers. They offer an extensive food selection containing sandwiches, burgers, wraps, salads, steaks, ribs, seafood, pizza, and all kinds of other entrees.

HOOD CANAL BREWERY
26499 Bond Rd. NE, Kingston, WA 98346; (360) 297-8316; HoodCanalBrewery.com; @HoodCanalBeer
Founded: 1996 **Founder:** Don Wyatt **Brewer:** Don Wyatt **Flagship Beer:** None **Year-Round Beers:** Dosewallips Special Ale, Bywater Bay ESB, Dabob Bay IPA, Agate Pass Amber, Big Beef Stout. Breidablik Barley Wine **Seasonals/Special Releases:** Mt. Walker Wheat, Southpoint Porter, Lilliwaup Doppelbock, Termination Pt. Imperial IPA, Zelatched Point **Tours:** No **Taproom:** Yes

As the first craft brewery to open up in North Kitsap, Hood Canal Brewery has been serving locals a range of good beer since 1996. Founder Don Wyatt was a homebrewer who also had spent some time working at Thomas Kemper Brewery before it closed. When he opened Hood Canal Brewery, it was strictly a production brewery housed in an 800-square-foot pole building outside his home just north of Poulsbo. Today the brewery is located off Bond Road right between Kingston and Poulsbo in a warehouse that also contains a tasting room. The tasting room itself isn't anything fancy other than a great spot to try out their beers and munch on a few small snacks they have for sale. Inside you sit right in the brewery, so if you like a raw brewery experience, this is the place to go. They do have free Wi-Fi in case

Breidablik Barley Wine
Style: Barleywine
ABV: 8.7%
Availability: Year-Round
In Norse mythology, Breidablik is home to Baldr, the god of love and beauty. In North Kitsap County, it is the name of a rural area as well as the name of Hood Canal Brewery's barleywine. It's a complex brew with aromas of dark fruits, toffee, tobacco, and sherry billowing out of the glass. Any hoppiness is bullied out by a huge malt complexity that switches from tobacco and biscuit notes to a caramel sweetness that heats a bit with alcohol. This is a beer you'd pour into a snifter and sip while cozied up next to a warm fire.

you want to hang out for some time and get a little work done while trying a taster of their beers.

Their lineup is available in both bottles and on draft around the area. Each is named after a nearby landmark, such as their **Agate Pass Amber,** after Agate Passage in the Puget Sound, or their **Dosewallips Special Ale,** after a river on the Olympic Peninsula. Make sure to try their **Dabob IPA,** a slightly sweet IPA that finishes with citrus, or the light and refreshing Dosewallips Special Ale.

ISLAND HOPPIN' BREWERY
33 Hope Ln., Eastsound, WA 98245; (360) 376-7069; IslandHoppinBrewery.com
Founded: 2012 **Founders:** Becca Gray, Jim Parker, and Nate Schons **Brewer:** Nate Schons **Flagship Beer:** Old Madrona **Year-Round Beers:** Island Hoppin' IPA, White Cap American Wit, Rip Tide Porter, Old Madrona, Old Salts Brown Ale, Parker's Reef Pilsner, Lime Kiln Lager, Spearfisherman Imperial Pale, K Pod Kölsch, Indian Summer Golden Ale, Copper Hog IPA, A Street Wheat, Oaty Stout **Seasonals/Special Releases:** Orctoberfest, Snow Line Winter Ale **Tours:** No **Taproom:** Yes

The largest of Washington's San Juan Islands, Orcas Island is home to beautiful shorelines; the 5,252-acre Moran State Park; Mount Constitution, the highest point in all the islands boasting spectacular views; and the village of Eastsound. With plenty of restaurants, art galleries, and boutique shops, it's a tourist haven and

one of the best places to visit in the state. It is also home to Island Hoppin' Brewery, the only brewery on Orcas Island. Head brewer Nate Schons fell in love with the craft while living in New Zealand for a short time. When he came back to the States, he got his start by working at the Cashmere Brewery in Cashmere doing everything from cleaning kegs to mopping the floors. He also learned how to brew professionally, which has helped the young brewery create some well-designed beers.

With their specialization in small-batch brewing, you'll find a wide variety of styles being produced in the brewery. In the taproom they offer 6 taps that constantly rotate beers with everything from standards, such as their **Island Hoppin' IPA** and **Rip Tide Porter,** to seasonals, such as **Orctoberfest** and **Snow Line Winter Ale.** Outside the brewery you can find their beer on draft around the islands, with distribution starting to grow broader.

Beer Lover's Pick

Old Madrona
Style: Imperial Red
ABV: 8.2%
Availability: Year-Round
The greatness of Old Madrona starts off with the label. A tree on the front is a Pacific madrona, a common tree along Washington's coastal areas that has a rich red bark. Just like the tree, Old Madrona is what they call a double red, basically an amped-up red ale. Earthy malts lay the foundation while the citrus hops power their presence into the aroma and flavor. It finishes with a lingering bitterness that's as smooth as it is intense.

The beautifully crafted taproom offers a small selection of snacks, but packs in some great values for beer. If it's your first time, definitely order a flight for only $6, which comes with four of their beers poured into half-pint glasses. They offer a heated patio to enjoy your beers outside, and dogs are always welcome out there.

PORT TOWNSEND BREWING COMPANY
330 10th St., #C, Port Townsend, WA 98368; (360) 385-9967; PortTownsendBrewing.com; @PTBrewing
Founded: 1997 **Founders:** Guy and Kim Sands **Brewer:** Carter Camp **Flagship Beer:** Hop Diggidy IPA **Year-Round Beers:** Bitter End IPA, Port Townsend Pale Ale, Boatyard Bitter, Brown Porter, Chet's Golden Ale, Reel Amber Ale, Hop Diggidy IPA, Peeping Peater Scotch Ale, Straight Stout, Barley Wine **Seasonals/Special Releases:** Winter Ale, Santa Kisser, Beast Mode Imperial IPA, Dead Sea Imperial IPA, Pumpky Brewster Stout, Luciferous Bourbon Barrel Sour Ale, Yoda's Green Tea Gold, Mad Sailor Imperial Sour Brown, and many more **Tours:** No **Taproom:** Yes

The original Port Townsend Brewing Company was founded back in 1905. Over the next 15 years it quickly grew into one of the largest and longest operating breweries at the time. Unfortunately, Prohibition began in January 1916 and got the best of even them, after they tried to stay afloat by producing nonalcoholic beverages. In 1997 Guy and Kim Sands decided to take the leap and open a new incarnation of the Port Townsend Brewing Company. When they first opened they offered just two beers. Over time they've expanded and now brew quite a few year-round beers as well as seasonals.

The tasting room is a pretty no-frills place where the focus is on the beer. Other than beer and a small selection of wine, the only other thing they serve is peanuts, but that's not a problem. Inside you'll find a unique mix of people ranging from workers in the boating industry getting off work to locals and tourists alike, all there to enjoy beer and relax. In the summertime you can sit in the beer garden and listen to live music while sipping from a selection of over 10 beers on draft. It is the place to be when the weather is warm; they have plenty of chairs and you'll generally find a very friendly crowd to mingle with.

For those who can't make it up to Port Townsend, you can find their wide range of beers on draft and 22-ounce bottles around the Puget Sound. A few of their regular beers to look for is the English-style **Barley Wine** with flavors of dark fruit and molasses, their classic Northwest-style **Hop Diggidy IPA,** or their peat-smoked **Peeping Peater Scotch Ale.**

Beer Lover's Pick

Peeping Peater Scotch Ale
Style: Scotch Ale
ABV: 6.6%
Availability: Year-Round
Port Townsend's Peeping Peater Scotch Ale is its year-round scotch ale brewed with peat-smoked barley, hence the name Peeping Peater. The beer is dark amber in color, with aromas of caramel, peat, and toasted malt gently filling the air, enticing you to take a sip. Its flavor follows the nose with some slight toffee and brown sugar in the finish. A medium body and a low level of carbonation help add to its drinkability. Try pairing it with some smoked salmon or smoked cheeses.

RAINY DAZE BREWING COMPANY

14974 Olympic View Loop Rd. NW, Silverdale, WA 98383 (may have to move soon); (360) 509-9005; RainyDazeBrewing.com; @RainyDazeBrewer

Founded: 2012 **Founders:** Michael Painter and Mike Montoney **Brewer:** Mike Montoney **Flagship Beer:** None **Year-Round Beers:** Belgian Bastard, Rainy Rye, English Pale, Silver Lining CDA, Red Sunset RIPA, Empire Porter **Seasonals/Special Releases:** Jack Got Baked, Holiday Bazaar, Stash Box, Tropic Thunder, Winter Daze, Stu's Wood Stout, Santa's Teabag, Alt, and many more **Tours:** No **Taproom:** No

There are plenty of rainy days in Washington. The rain inspired the name and logo of one of the newest breweries in the state, Rainy Daze Brewing Company, based in Silverdale. After working for years at his own auto shop and spending a lot of time homebrewing, cofounder Mike Montoney decided it was time to change direction and turn his hobby into a career. He and friend Michael Painter set out to bring their range of well-crafted beers to the public. When Poulsbo-based Battenkill Brewing announced they were going out of business, Mike jumped at the chance to buy their 1.5-barrel brewing system to open Rainy Daze.

The brewery itself is currently housed in a residential neighborhood. When they first opened they had a taproom at the same location, but the county stepped in and stopped that. At the time of this writing they're looking for a new location to house the brewery and taproom, so be sure to check out their Facebook page for the most up-to-date information on where they're located.

Beer Lover's Pick

Stash Box Pale Ale
Style: Pale Ale
ABV: 6%
Availability: Rotating
What happens when you use some saved-up Simcoe hops to create a beer? If you're Rainy Daze Brewing, you create one amazing pale ale. The amber-looking beer has plenty of pine and citrus in both the flavor and the aroma to impart a subtle but not distracting bitterness. Its bitterness is strong enough, however, to hold up to fried or spicy seafood, such as clams, crab cakes, shrimp, or fried fish.

Their small size allows them to create a variety of small-batch ales ranging from seasonals, such as their well-balanced pumpkin porter named **Jack Got Baked,** to their regular line with beers such as the hoppy and delicious **Silver Lining CDA.**

SILVER CITY BREWERY

2799 NW Myhre Rd., Silverdale, WA 98383; (360) 698-5879; SilverCityBrewery.com; @SilverCityBrew

Founded: 1996 **Founders:** Scott Houmes and Steve Houmes **Brewer:** Don Spencer **Flagship Beer:** Ridgetop Red **Year-Round Beers:** Ridgetop Red, Bavarian-Style Hefeweizen, Clear Creek Pale Ale, Panther Lake Porter, Fat Scotch Ale, Saint Florian India Pale Ale, Whoop Pass Double IPA **Seasonals/Special Releases:** Deluxe Spring Lager, Oktoberfest, Ziggy Zoggy, Winter Bock, Fat Woody Scotch, Old Scrooge Christmas Ale, Imperial Stout, and many more **Tours:** Yes, 4 p.m. Wed–Sat **Taproom:** Yes

Silver City Brewery has been brewing up award-winning beers since 1996. From the beginning, founders Scott and Steve Houmes set out to create a brewpub in the West Sound that was world-class. It didn't take long for locals to take notice that the pub was crafting a wide range of tasty beers along with a menu of delicious foods. As the demand for their beer spread outside of Silverdale, the company decided to open up their production facility in nearby Bremerton, allowing them to distribute their beer throughout the state in both bottles and kegs. Although brewing moved to the new facility, the flagship brewpub in Silverdale is still considered one of the best brewpubs in the state and has been recognized on a national level.

What has spurred the brewery's continued growth has been the quality of their beer. Their 7 year-round beers, which have all been brewed fairly close to style, each have racked up multiple national awards. While all are well crafted, favorites include their flagship **Ridgetop Red, Fat Scotch Ale,** and a hoppy beast of a beer known as **Whoop Pass Double IPA.** Look for their limited-release **Fat Woody Scotch Ale.** They take their Fat Scotch Ale and age it on American white oak for a month, creating a unique beer with vanilla character.

In Silverdale you'll want to pay a visit to their brewpub. Remodeled in 2010, the pub is pretty massive with plenty of seating and room at the bar to enjoy their lineup of beers while eating some of their pub grub. The kids even have an option to try their handcrafted root beer or ginger ale. Along with their pub, the production facility in Bremerton offers a full tasting room to try out their brews or fill up a growler or two.

Beer Lover's Pick

Fat Scotch Ale
Style: Scotch Ale
ABV: 9.2%
Availability: Year-Round
Scotch ale is a unique malt-forward style that tends to be a bit on the bold side. Silver City has done such a phenomenal job over the years with its Fat Scotch Ale that it has racked up award after award at most of the major beer competitions. The brown brew has shimmering red shining through with a layer of white head that doesn't stay for long. Malts charge in with plenty of sweet caramel, chocolate, peat, smoke, and a touch of raisin in this true-to-style beer.

SLIPPERY PIG BREWERY

932 Slippery Pig Way, Poulsbo, WA 98370; (360) 394-1686; SlipperyPigBrewing.com
Founded: 2010 **Founders:** Dave and Shawna Lambert **Brewer:** Dave Lambert **Flagship Beer:** Rhubarb IPA **Year-Round Beers:** Rhubarb IPA, Dandelion Bitter, Stinging Nettle Pale, Hog's Breath Hefe **Seasonals/Special Releases:** Hampshire Stout, Kiwi Lager, Potbelly Plum, Sweet Belgium Pumpkin, Co-op Hop, Bitter Bunny CDA, Happy Sow Saison, Hog Thai'd, Piggly Wiggly Cucumber Ale, and many more **Tours:** None scheduled, just ask **Taproom:** Yes

The city of Poulsbo is quickly becoming one of the more interesting destinations for beer lovers in the state. One of the most unique breweries in the area is Slippery Pig Brewery, a small facility located on Red Rooster Farm. Founded by husband-and-wife team Dave and Shawna Lambert, the operation seems as if farm

Poulsbo Beer Run

Running and beer just go hand in hand. Each year the Poulsbo Beer Run (poulsbo beerrun.com) combines the two while giving you an option to drink beers from each of the three Poulsbo-based breweries. When you sign up you can choose which brewery you want to start at. First you drink a beer there, and head on to the next brewery, drink a beer, and so on. After you've completed the loop of three breweries, you run back to the start and drink a guest beer from your home brewery. Running to Slippery Pig Brewery, Sound Brewery, and Valholl Brewing is only about four miles, so you'll have plenty of time to drink.

living has collided with beer and created something very special. Going back three generations, the farm has been a part of Dave's family since his grandparents bought it and used it to raise cows, goats, and chickens. Today the farm is used to raise pigs and chickens and provides flowers, berries, greens, and of course beer. The couple have a passion for farming and for feeding their community in a sustainable way and have created the brewery as an extension of that.

Their farm-first philosophy has led to a variety of beers that don't really fit into any style, yet are delicious and fun to drink. Each of the ingredients is sourced as locally as possible, including all of their hops and most malts coming from within Washington. One distinguishing aspect of their beers is they are all brewed with seasonal ingredients, so you're always in for a treat depending on what they can get their hands on. **Hog Thai'd** is a brew that doesn't really fit any style, yet is a very intriguing recipe. Brewed with Crimson Cove smoked winter luxury pumpkin, toasted coconut, and curry leaves grown on the farm, it's almost strangely like drinking Thai food. They also brew a lot of beers with seasonal fruits, such as their **Kiwi Blonde,** brewed with 20 pounds of kiwis per batch. Make sure to stop by the farm and visit the kid- and dog-friendly taproom. You'll feel like a farmhand on break while sipping some interesting beers.

Beer Lover's Pick

Rhubarb IPA
Style: IPA
ABV: 9.9%
Availability: Seasonal

Wait, rhubarb in an IPA? Yes, it's true. The great masterminds at Slippery Pig crafted this huge IPA that uses 5 pounds of hops and 12 pounds of rhubarb in every barrel they produce. The result is a unique beer, which they mention has 209 IBUs (although there isn't much difference in taste after 100 IBUs). A hefty malt base along with the interesting rhubarb flavor holds the beer down from being overly bitter. They've also created a bourbon barrel–aged version that provided a strong bourbon aroma, yet was gentle in taste.

SOUND BREWERY

650 NW Bovela Ln., Ste. 3, Poulsbo, WA 98370; (360) 930-8696; SoundBrewery.com; @SoundBrewery

Founded: 2011 **Founders:** Mark Hood, Brad Ginn, John Cockburn, Alan Moum, and Steve Mattson **Brewer:** Brad Ginn **Flagship Beer:** None **Year-Round Beers:** Koperen Ketel Belgian Style Pale Ale, Bevrijder Belgian Style IPA, Dubbel Entendre Belgian Style Dubbel, Tripel Entendre Belgian Style Tripel, Monk's Indiscretion Belgian Speciality Ale, O'Regan's Revenge Irish Red Ale, Poundage Porter Brown Porter, Ursus Americanus American Stout, Reluctant IPA American Style IPA, Humulo Nimbus Double IPA **Seasonals/Special Releases:** Sound Sommerweizen Clea Unfiltered Wheat Ale, Latona IPA, Jublaum 10 Weizenbock, Ursus Spelaeus Belgian Imperial Stout, Entendez Noel Belgian Quadrupel, and many more **Tours:** No **Taproom:** Yes

Within just a few months of opening in 2011, Sound Brewery racked up six medals at the North American Brewers Association Beer Awards, one of the biggest competitions in the US. Over the next year they racked up multiple other awards at other competitions, bringing them both national and worldwide attention. Their brewing philosophy is fairly simple, but it works. They focus on using quality ingredients along with close attention to detail in the process of brewing while sticking with a simple grain bill and hop schedule. Each beer they brew is brewed to style, yet they add little touches to take them from average to award-winning recipes. While many of their beers are Belgian-style ales, they aren't bound by any particular style and brew a range of traditional German beers, English ales, and American styles.

With the brewery being based in the Northwest, it's no surprise **Humulo Nimbus Double IPA** is their top seller. Sweet malt is balanced by a citrus bitterness that finishes dry. Other favorites include their **Dubbel Entrendre Belgian Style Dubbel** that was based off a recipe brewer Brad Ginn created as a homebrewer; **Monk's Indiscretion,** based on a homebrew recipe from cofounder Mark Hood; and creamy **Poundage Porter,** which took home a 2012 World Beer Cup silver medal.

Around the state you can find their beers on draft as well as their beautifully created 22-ounce bottles. Each bottle is well designed, with the look of a nice bottle of wine, and includes a sticker over the cap. You can visit their tasting room in Poulsbo to taste up to 11 of their beers at any given time and fill up your growlers. They also offer a small selection of snacks.

Beer Lover's Pick

Monk's Indiscretion
Style: Belgian Strong Ale
ABV: 10%
Availability: Year-Round
The label on Monk's Indiscretion shows a monk offering a fine beer to a nun. Although he might not be showing indiscretion, he is offering her quite a treat if his cup is filled with this Belgian strong ale. Beautiful, sweet tropical fruit aromas come from both the hops and yeast, which also follows through to the flavor while giving off a delicious Belgian character. The 10% alcohol is scarily hidden and it's easy to get through the whole 22-ounce bottle without even realizing it.

TWIN PEAKS BREWING AND MALTING CO.

2506 W. 19th St., Port Angeles, WA 98363; (360) 452-2802
Founded: 1999 (pub started; brewery opened 2012) **Founders:** Ed and Wanda Smith
Brewer: Jeff Abbott **Flagship Beer:** None **Year-Round Beers:** Dry Hopped Elwha Silt,
Wanda Fuca Gold, Train Wrecked IPA, Ride the Hoh Red, Mt. Pleasant Porter, Ed's Big Ass
Red **Seasonals/Special Releases:** Hoh! Hoh! Hoh!, Spruce Tip **Tours:** No
Taproom: Yes

Twin Peaks Brewing and Malting Co. may have technically opened in 2012, but their beer has been delighting those in Port Angeles for some time. Ed and Wanda Smith have owned Peak's Brewpub since 1999, although at the time they weren't serving their own beers. By 2005 Ed acquired a two-barrel brewing system and started creating some very interesting beers that were sold in the pub alongside a range of guest beers. While crafting beers such as **Wanda Fuca Gold,** named after his wife, and the dry-hopped **Elwha Silt,** locals started to take note that the beers were pretty darn good. Brewing on such a small system does have its downfalls and pretty soon the couple started to look at expanding the business and producing more beer. After working on the idea for some time, they opened Twin Peaks Brewing and Malting Co. on a much larger 20-barrel system from Germany. The system itself is one of just a few like it in the US and had to undergo some changes with its electrical system to work with American voltage.

Beer Lover's Pick

Spruce Tip
Style: Imperial IPA
ABV: Unknown
Availability: Limited Release
For those who like to try new and interesting beers, Twin Peaks Spruce Tip may be one of the most unusual beers being brewed in the state. They end up brewing it as much as they can, yet it all depends on when and if they can get spruce tips from Alaska to put in the boil. Apparently spruce in Alaska tends to be sweeter than the more bitter trees that grow in Washington state. The result is a beer that is similar to drinking a forest, yet sweet enough that drinking a pint is very enjoyable.

You can visit the brewery's tasting room 7 days a week and try their line of beers or fill up your growlers. Try the sweet citrus-tasting **Train Wrecked IPA** or **Ed's Big Ass Red** with plenty of caramel and sweet malt. At the brewery as well as other locations around town, they also offer a selection of bottles you can purchase to take home. For those looking to get a meal with their beer, head on down to the Peak's Brewpub on Lincoln Street, just about 4 miles away. They're known for their beer and their chili, which shouldn't be ordered if you can't handle the heat.

VALHÖLL BREWING COMPANY

18970 3rd Ave. NE, Poulsbo, WA 98370; (360) 550-5825; ValhollBrewing.com; @ValhollBrew

Founded: 2010 **Founders:** Jeff Holcomb and Jordan Rodgers **Brewer:** Jeff Holcomb **Flagship Beer:** None **Year-Round Beers:** Porter, Valkyrie Red, Monster Double IPA, Belgian Wit, Brew Bitch IPA, Strong Scotch Ale, Golden Ale, Belgian Golden Strong, Spotty Dog ESB, and Stouty **Seasonals/Special Releases:** Stouty Stouterson, Pumpkin Stout, Blueberry/Raspberry Stout, Valhölapeno Red, Anise Nystagmus IPA, Sour Santa Winter Warmer, and many more **Tours:** No **Taproom:** Yes

Up in Poulsbo, Valhöll Brewing Company is one of the new and interesting breweries that have opened in town. In 2010 they turned on the kettles and started creating beer in a small garage space that immediately had people taking notice. Upon launching the brewery, they were using a Sabco Brew-Magic system that was capable of brewing only half a barrel of beer at a time. Since then the brewery has expanded into a larger space and upgraded to a 3.5-barrel system. The small batches allow brewer and owner Jeff Holcomb to use his out-of-the-box creativity to create some big and unusual beers.

In the tasting room they try to have 10 year-round beers with up to 4 others rotating, most of which have some kind of added ingredients. Their popular **Anise Nystagmus IPA** has been a hit, as it's nothing like you've ever had. Brewed with fennel bulb, tarragon, and licorice, and dry hopped with anise seeds, toasted fennel, and hops, it's like drinking black licorice but in IPA form. Also look for their big 8.8% **Valhölapeno Red,** an imperial red ale brewed with both fresh and roasted jalapeños that give it plenty of aroma, yet just enough heat in the flavor to keep you coming back to it. Year-round step up to the **Monster IPA,** a 10.4% ABV double IPA that will knock you down if you aren't careful. It can be a little too easy to drink.

Along with their own beers, they like to offer guest taps from area breweries in the taproom. Other than beer, Valhöll merchandise is the only type of product they offer on site. Their logo, with a tough-looking Viking, does make for some pretty good-looking apparel.

Stouty Stouterson
Style: Imperial Oatmeal Stout
ABV: 13%
Availability: Rotating
Valhöll Brewing Company used the word "stout" twice in naming Stouty Stouterson imperial oatmeal stout because it's so big you need to be reminded of it every time you order. It's similar to their Stouty Oatmeal Stout, but on beer steroids. They add sweet potatoes to both the mash and boil and dose it with cinnamon, brown sugar, and raisins. The end result is a smooth and chocolaty feast in liquid form that reminds you that it has 13% ABV, yet is a bit too easy to drink.

VASHON BREWING COMPANY (CLIFF'S BEER)
10124 SW Quartermaster Dr., Vashon, WA 98070; (206) 853-1719; CliffsBeer.com
Founded: 2012 **Founder:** Cliff Goodman **Brewer:** Cliff Goodman **Flagship Beer:** Alder Smoked Porter **Year-Round Beers:** Alder Smoked Porter, Inspiration India Pale Ale
Seasonals/Special Releases: Burton Blonde, Inspiration Stout **Tours:** No **Taproom:** No

The residents of Vashon Island got their own brewery in 2012 when Cliff Goodman started up the nanobrewery Vashon Brewing Company, or as locals know it, Cliff's Beer. At this small production-only brewery, Cliff is a one-man show producing a handful of beers out of his residence. Although Seattle is just a ferry ride away, he focuses on producing quality beer to serve his community on the island, so you probably won't find his beer elsewhere. However, if you can, consider yourself lucky. Around the island his beer is distributed in kegs and small growlers. Instead of bottles, he wanted to stick with only growler fills mainly because of the impact on the community and environment. In an effort to keep the carbon footprint as low as possible, most of the ingredients are sourced from around the state. They also recycle as much as they can, giving their spent grains to feed livestock on the island while also collecting cooling water from the brewery to use in their own garden.

Year-round they brew the flagship **Alder Smoked Porter,** a beer that has nice chocolate and smoky notes with very little of the bitterness common in porters. Because many people requested they brew an IPA, you can also find their Northwest-style **Inspiration India Pale Ale** at a handful of island restaurants. In the summer they release the light-bodied and floral **Burton Blonde** and in the summer a hefty

Alder Smoked Porter

Style: Porter

ABV: 4.8%

Availability: Year-Round

As one of the favorites on this island, the Alder Smoked Porter is a big, full-bodied dark porter with very little bitterness. It's made by cold smoking the barley with alder scraps that often come from the Vashon Forest Stewards. The result is a beer that has some subtle smokiness in both aroma and flavor, yet doesn't overpower the other chocolate and coffee notes. It's a complex brew that could easily be a hefty meal all by itself.

imperial stout named **Inspiration Stout.** They don't offer a tasting room, so your best bet is to contact Cliff to find out where his beer is currently being poured. In the summer you can look for the beer in growlers at the farmers' market.

Brewpubs

SLAUGHTER COUNTY BREWING COMPANY

1307 Bay St., Port Orchard, WA 98366; (360) 329-2340; SlaughterCountyBrewing.com;
@SCBC_Beer
Founded: 2012 **Founder:** Scott Kirvan **Brewer:** Scott Kirvan **Flagship Beer:** None
Year-Round Beers: None **Seasonals/Special Releases:** Ol' One Eye Pa, Wandering
Eye Sour IPA, Gorst Pilsner Style Ale, Regimental Scotch Ale, and more **Tours:** No
Taproom: Yes

Set to a nautical theme complete with jolly rogers, tricorn hats, and many other things pirate, this quirky watering hole is nestled in a strip mall near downtown Port Orchard. You may need a treasure map to find this place, as getting there is a little tricky. But when you do find it, you'll be greeted with an incredible view of the water of the Sinclair Inlet. The county in which Port Orchard resides is called Kitsap County, which was originally named Slaughter County, hence the name of the brewpub.

With fewer hops and a stronger malt flavor than many American versions, the **Ol' One Eye Pa** has some floral and citrus notes on the nose. Although there's not enough citrus to keep scurvy at bay, light bitterness and orange peel do make a presence on this pale ale. Pair this brew with the Musket Balls, which are meatballs accompanied by curry, Cuban, and sweet and sour sauces.

If you make it to SCBC before sunset, you can take part in their unique ritual. Every night at Slaughter County Brewing, the whole place takes a moment to stop, raise their glasses, and toast the sunset.

Beer Bars

POURHOUSE

2231 Washington St., Port Townsend, WA 98368; (360) 379-5586; PTPourhouse.com; @ptpourhouse
Draft Beers: 12 **Bottled/Canned Beers:** 200

While the town of Port Townsend isn't anywhere near being a craft-beer mecca, every town needs a place like the Pourhouse for beer lovers to flock to. Besides serving 12 rotating beers and offering around 200 bottles and cans, the taproom is situated in a perfect location, especially on warmer days. A beer garden in the back overlooks the water so you can relax while kicking back and enjoying a tasty beverage. Plenty of picnic tables offer outdoor seating, or you could get up and play a game on their concrete Ping-Pong table or on the petanque court. A wooden stage is situated right next to the building, offering live music frequently in the evenings. Inside, the spacious area offers small little nooks and crannies to sit and mingle with the generally friendly people there. You can also sit at the bar and watch a game on the TV. The beautiful plywood bar is almost an attraction by itself.

The 12 rotating taps are selected from many Northwest breweries along with others from around the country, such as Dogfish Head, Victory, and Shmaltz. One of their tap lines generally offers a local cider, while the 200 bottled and canned beers are also available. While there is a beer for everyone, they also offer an extensive wine list. Besides a few bar snacks, they don't offer food at the bar. However, ask for the take-out book that contains menus from just about every Port Townsend restaurant that will deliver to their location. Also, feel free to bring your four-legged friend to enjoy the Pourhouse with you.

South Puget Sound

For so long, the south Puget Sound has been in the shadows of Seattle's beer spotlight. For years Fish Brewing in Olympia and Harmon Brewing in Tacoma were the pillars of the craft-beer scene. However, the area now has a blossoming beer culture that is bringing in a new wave of breweries, pubs, and good craft beer. Tacoma, Puyallup, and Olympia have become known as exciting beer destinations. Even places such as Kent, where Airways Brewing is making a name for itself, are catching the eyes and mouths of those seeking the perfect pint.

Along with production breweries and brewpubs, the south sound is seeing an influx of nanobreweries, such as Duo Brewing, M.T. Head Brewing, and Soos Creek Brewing, entering the market. With continued growth, it will definitely be a part of the state that will just keep getting better each and every year.

South Puget Sound

BREWERIES

1	Airways Brewing Company
2	Airways Brewing Beer & Bistro
16	Duo Brewing
17	Elk Head Brewing
22	Fish Brewing Company
10	Harmon Brewery & Eatery
18	M.T. Head Brewing Company
12	Northwest Brewing Company
14	Puyallup River Brewing Company
4	7 Seas Brewing
3	Soos Creek Brewing Company
13	The Station U-Brew
9	Tacoma Brewing Company
11	Wingman Brewers

BREWPUBS

7	Engine House No. 9
19	Grove Street Brewhouse
15	Powerhouse Restaurant and Brewery

BARS

21	Eastside Club Tavern
8	Harmon Brewery & Eatery
5	Parkway Tavern
6	Pint Defiance
20	The Red Hot
	Skep & Skein

Breweries

AIRWAYS BREWING COMPANY

6644 S. 196th St., #T-100, Kent, WA 98032; (253) 200-1707; AirwaysBrewing.com;
@AirwaysBrewing
Founded: 2010 **Founder:** Alex Dittmar **Brewer:** Alex Dittmar **Flagship Beer:** Sky
Hag IPA **Year-Round Beers:** Sky Hag IPA, Jet City ESB, Starliner Stout, First Class IPA
Seasonals/Special Releases: Pre-Flight Pils, Midnight Departure CDA, Final Departure,
Uber Hag IPA, Tickel Your Zwickel, Maylani's Tropical Stout, T-Tail Blonde, Triple Chocolate
Stout, and many more **Tours:** Yes, by appointment **Taproom:** Yes

The business park that houses Airways Brewing Company might be the last place you would expect to find any type of brewery. However, for the small brewery, the odd location tucked between office complex buildings seems to work well. Founded in 2010 by homebrewer and former pilot Alex Dittmar, Airways Brewing crafts brews in an underserved area of the state and bases its business around an aviation theme.

When they first opened, they were brewing on a small system that produced just one keg per batch. As demand picked up they quickly felt the need to expand, and upgraded their tasting room, added a bistro just a few miles away in downtown Kent that serves food along with their beer, and beefed up their brewing system to 20 times the size of the original system. The expansion has allowed them to offer their lineup of regular and seasonal brews around Kent, as well as to start bottling and distributing to a handful of bottle shops around the state.

Their most popular offering is the flagship **Sky Hag IPA,** a huge IPA that is as bitter as the old flight attendant who hates her job. A must-try is their **Jet City ESB,** another year-round offering that's a beautiful balance of nuts, caramel, and bitter hops. At the bistro they occasionally will have Randall nights. During these special nights they pour their beer through a Randall, a contraption that allows you to fill it up with any type of ingredients you want, such as hops, coconut, orange peels, or other fruits. For example, they once poured their **Midnight Departure Cascadian Dark Ale** through coconut, coffee beans, and macadamia nuts to create an incredible-tasting beer you could find only at the source.

Sky Hag IPA

Style: Imperial IPA

ABV: 7.8%

Availability: Year-Round

Paying tribute to flight attendants who hate their jobs yet refuse to quit, Sky Hag IPA is just as bitter. The label shows a bitter-looking lady smoking a cigarette and obviously not all that excited about her job. Brewed with Northwest-grown malted barley and Columbus hops, this is one imperial IPA that is booming with citrus and piney hop flavor that has a big enough caramel backbone to help even things out. The finish is all bitterness that lingers on the tongue. Save this old hag for your last beer of the night, as it will wreck your palate if you're not careful.

DUO BREWING

719 4th St. SE, Puyallup, WA 98372; (507) 412-0071; DuoBrewing.com; @DuoBrewing
Founded: 2011 **Founders:** Dan and Heather O'Leary **Brewer:** Dan O'Leary **Flagship Beer:** Twin Ports Porter **Year-Round Beers:** Twin Ports Porter, Twin Ports Coffee Porter, Dúbailte Belgian Abbey **Seasonals/Special Releases:** Singular Fresh Hop Seasonal, Earth & Wind American Wheat Beer, Judas Kiss Belgian Golden Ale, Poles Apart Milk Stout, Chockablock Scotch Ale **Tours:** No **Taproom:** No

When Dan and Heather O'Leary were living in Portland, Oregon, they both discovered craft beer; it's tough not to when you live in the Northwest. However, they soon moved to Minnesota to be closer to family, but they soon realized the

Beer Lover's Pick

Poles Apart Milk Stout
Style: Milk Stout
ABV: 7.2%
Availability: Year-Round
It can be hard to find a brewery with a milk stout that fits the style perfectly. Duo Brewing does a fantastic job brewing Poles Apart Milk Stout just about exactly how a good milk stout should taste. With lactose added to the brew kettle, the result is a sweet yet creamy full-bodied stout with plenty of milk chocolate and coffee in the aroma and flavor that will make any sweets lover happy. It's good enough on its own to replace your birthday cake.

state had very few craft breweries to choose from. While Dan had never brewed before, he started dreaming of opening his own brewery in the state and went to work on setting up his business plan. The problem was that he was dreaming a little too big and couldn't find the money to make the plan a reality. He shut down the idea of the brewery and they moved to Puyallup because of his job. Even after they moved, the dream was still in the back of both of their minds and the duo decided to jump into it again. This time, however, they scaled it back and decided to open a nanobrewery to keep costs down while they slowly grew the business. Because the two of them were in it together, they decided on the name Duo Brewing.

While many brewers in the Northwest focus on hops, Duo's beers tend to let their malts give most of the character in the beers. They shine in brewing more malt-forward-style beers, such as porters, stouts, and scotch ales. One of their most popular beers is the **Twin Ports Porter.** A creamy beer with plenty of roasted malts, cocoa, and coffee, and just a touch of smoke from the use of Rauch Malt, Twin Ports is as complex as it is drinkable. For a refreshing summertime beer, their **Earth & Wind American Wheat Beer** is full of wheat, banana, and a touch of clove all packaged in a light body. Duo is a nanobrewery, so their beer can be hard to come by. Look for them on draft throughout the area using the beer finder on their website.

ELK HEAD BREWING

28120 SR 410 E, Buckley, WA 98321; (360) 829-2739
Founded: 2003 **Founder:** Rich Dirk **Brewer:** Rich Dirk **Flagship Beer:** Liberty Cap
IPA **Year-Round Beer:** Liberty Cap IPA **Seasonals/Special Releases:** Black Stag
Stout, Blast Zone, Glacier Pale, Kilted Elk, Hellfire, Figure 8, Big Rack Brown, Paradise,
Royal Black, Hellkoko, White Out, Lone Bull, Citronic, Elk Dandee, Back Track Barleywine,
Buckley Lager, ESP, Peacherino, Skookum Cherry, Glacier Pale, Sting-Ya, and many more
Tours: No **Taproom:** Yes

In between Boney Lake and Enumclaw on SR 410 lies the small town of Buckley. Toward the west side of town sits a business park that is an unlikely spot to find a craft brewery the caliber of Elk Head Brewing. With limited distribution and rarely spotted at many beer festivals, this brewery's beer goes unnoticed at times throughout the state. While small towns are often thought of as having a culture that clings to the almost clear yellow beers produced by macrobreweries, Buckley is different. Elk Head crafts an easy-drinking lager, but they are known more for the big and unusual beers using a range of ingredients.

From their 9.2% ABV **Elk Dandee,** brewed with dandelions, ginseng, and ginger, to **Sting Ya,** a seasonal containing stinging nettles, to **Figure 8,** a beer brewed with figs and cardamom pods, they are always coming up with new ingredients or ways

Blast Zone
Style: Chile Beer
ABV: 5.5%
Availability: Rotating

Chile beers tend to come in all different styles. From the knock-your-face-off heat to the more subtle touch of chile presence, they really do run the board. If you've tried one before and not liked it, make sure to seek out Blast Zone. Using 5 kinds of chiles that have been smoked with stout-soaked oak chips, the incredibly balanced beer is a joy to drink. With your first sip you'll wonder where the chile is. Give it a few seconds and then—bam! The smoky chile goodness comes out like few breweries can make it do.

to make unique beers. They also brew multiple beers that are more traditional, such as the **Liberty Cap IPA** and **Black Stag Stout,** a big stout with plenty of chocolate, nut, and vanilla flavors. If you visit the brewery, you can bring a growler to fill up with one of 14 of their beers they offer on draft in their taproom. If it's a growler from a brewery they don't already have, they'll trade one of theirs with yours and hang it on the ceiling. Other than Buckley, they also have a small tasting room in Ocean Shores on the Washington coast.

FISH BREWING COMPANY
515 Jefferson St. SE, Olympia, WA 98501; (360) 943-6480; FishBrewing.com
Founded: 1993 **Founders:** Crayne and Mary Horton **Brewer:** Paul Pearson **Flagship Beers:** Fish Tail Organic Amber Ale, Fish Tail Organic Pale Ale, Fish Tail Organic Wild Salmon Pale Ale **Year-Round Beers:** Fish Tail Organic Amber Ale, Fish Tail Organic India Pale Ale, Fish Tail Organic Wild Salmon Pale Ale, Fish Tail Soundkeeper Organic Pale Ale, Fish Tail Mudshark Porter, Fish Tail Trout Stout, Leavenworth Eightmile Alt, Leavenworth Whistling Pig Hefeweizen, Leavenworth Boulder Bend Dunkelweizen, Leavenworth Friesian Pilsener, Leavenworth Light **Seasonals/Special Releases:** Fish Tail Organic Blonde Ale, Fish Tail Organic Winterfish Ale, Leavenworth Oktoberfest Ale, Leavenworth Bakke Hill Black Lager, Reel Ales Swordfish, Reel Ales Monkfish, Reel Ales Starfish, Reel Ales 10^2 **Tours:** No **Taproom:** Yes

Fish Brewing Company got its start in 1993 with a 15-barrel brewhouse in downtown Olympia. At the time, their line of English-style beers was distributed lightly around the Puget Sound. It didn't take long for their demand to outgrow their production and they moved the brewery into a much larger facility across Jefferson Street. At the same time, they kept the brewpub at the original location so people could still come and drink their beers on site. Just a few years later, Fish Brewing started creating most of its core lineup of beer as certified organic and headed in a greener direction. Today most of the Fish Tail line is organic, including seasonals such as the **Organic Blonde** and **Organic Winterfish.**

In 2001 Fish Brewing merged with Leavenworth Bier, one of the Northwest's original German-style craft brewers, based in the Bavarian village of Leavenworth. They ended up moving the Leavenworth Bier line to the Olympia brewery and continue to distribute that line under the Leavenworth Bier name in 12-ounce bottles. Just a few years after that, they acquired Spire Mountain Ciders, the nation's oldest operating commercial craft cider maker, and moved operations to Olympia. Now they distribute 4 product lines including Fish Tail, Leavenworth Biers, Spire Mountain Ciders, and Reel Ales, a line of big and creative seasonal ales released in 22-ounce bottles.

Such a large lineup and a much larger brewing system means you can find their beers all over Washington, Alaska, Oregon, Idaho, and a handful of other states. In Olympia you can also try their lineup at the Fish Tale Brewpub as well as their newest location up in Everett. The original location should be on your list of must-visit brewpubs in the state. Their huge food menu has plenty of options for every taste, including selections such as an oyster burger, portobello burger, or the tasty fish tacos.

Beer Lover's Pick

Swordfish Double Cascadian Dark Ale

Style: Cascadian Dark Ale

ABV: 7.5%

Availability: April–June

Available both in 22-ounce bottles and on draft, Reel Ales' Swordfish Cascadian Dark Ale is a perfect dark beer for IPA fans. Brewed with plenty of citrusy Northwest hops, Swordfish drinks a lot like an imperial IPA, yet is balanced out with roasted malts, chocolate, and caramel. What really sets this CDA apart from the rest is how well the flavors play together so nicely and all the ingredients get to share the spotlight. Like other hoppy beers, this one is best when you drink it fresh and don't let it wait too long in the bottle.

HARMON BREWING CO.

1938 Pacific Ave. S., Tacoma, WA 98402; (253) 383-2739; HarmonBrewingCo.com; @HarmonBrewingCo

Founded: 1997 **Founders:** Fred Roberson and Pat Nagle **Brewer:** Jeff Carlson **Flagship Beer:** Point Defiance IPA **Year-Round Beers:** Mt. Takhoma Blonde, Pinnacle Peak Pale Ale, Brown's Point ESB, Puget Sound Porter, Point Defiance IPA **Seasonals/Special Releases:** Porter Porter, Black IPA, Rajah's Royal IPA, One Hop Wonder IPA, Imperial Red Ale, Steep & Deep Winter Ale, Dash Point Dark Wheat, Rusty Nail Pale Ale, Hop Art Ale, and many more **Tours:** No **Taproom:** Yes

In 1997 Harmon Brewing Co. opened its doors in Tacoma's historic warehouse district, also home to some of the city's historical breweries, such as the Heidelberg Brewery. The company is named after the Harmon manufacturing building it's located in, built in 1908 for F. S. Harmon, once the largest furniture manufacturer

Point Defiance IPA
Style: IPA
ABV: 6.1%
Availability: Year-Round

Named after Point Defiance Park in Tacoma, one of the largest urban parks in the US, Point Defiance IPA is easily Harmon Brewing's most popular beer. Although it was the first beer brewed on the original brewing equipment in 1997, it has changed slightly over the years. Since 2006 the recipe has stayed the same and provides IPA fans with a delicious brew. Hazy orange in color with grapefruit and crisp pine aromas that show up in the flavor, it starts with a gentle citrus bitterness before transitioning into a slightly sweet malt and finishing back to hoppy bitterness. A perfect beer to pair with their pizza.

west of the Mississippi. This building provides plenty of character throughout the brewery and restaurant. Along with the original location, Harmon Brewing also has a production facility with a taproom as well as a sister restaurant named The Hub, each offering a range of Harmon beers.

At the Harmon Brewery & Eatery, you'll generally find 8 beers on draft. Five of those are their year-round beers along with a rotation of seasonal and specialty-brewed beers. For dark-beer fans, their year-round **Puget Sound Porter** has plenty of chocolate and coffee notes to make you happy, while being pretty easy to drink. It also won a gold medal at the 1999 Great American Beer Festival. In 2012 the brewery brewed a special beer named **Hop Art Ale,** an IPA inspired by pop artist

Andy Warhol. In 1982 Warhol proposed draping the Tacoma Dome with a large pop-art flower. Although the proposal never went through, the Tacoma Art Museum was able to get some of the art. In collaboration with Harmon, the beer was brewed as what became the fourth seasonal beer the museum and brewery have conspired on.

If you're looking to experience Harmon brews, make sure to stop by their original brewery and eatery and enjoy their pub-style food. The taproom at the newer production facility also offers a range of food as well as a full calendar of live music. Make sure to bring a growler at either location to take some home. Outside of the Tacoma area you can also find their beer bottled around the Puget Sound area.

M.T. HEAD BREWING COMPANY

27307 159th Ave. E., Graham, WA 98338; (253) 208-8999; MTHeadBrewingCo.com
Founded: 2009 **Founders:** Tim and Renee Rockey **Brewer:** Tim Rockey **Flagship Beer:** Dark Marc **Year-Round Beers:** Golden Ale, No Brainer Ale, Twisted Head IPA, Bonehead Brown Ale, Dark Marc **Seasonals/Special Releases:** Punter's Special Ale, Bravo for Apollo, Two Head Imperial IPA, Smooth Head Cream Ale, Zeus's Revenge **Tours:** No **Taproom:** Yes

M.T. Head Brewing is a small two-barrel brewery based out of Graham, Washington, roughly 20 miles southeast of Tacoma. Founded by homebrewer Tim Rockey and his wife, Renee, the small brewery focuses mainly on a handful of

Dark Marc
Style: Cascadian Dark Ale
ABV: 8.19%
Availability: Year-Round
Named after Marc Martin, a Portland-area beer blogger and homebrewer, Dark Marc is M.T. Head's rendition of a Northwest-style Cascadian dark ale. About as true to the style as you can get, it's as dark as the name suggests with plenty of hops in the aroma. Four hop varieties add to the subtle caramel and dark malt flavors, giving the beer a lingering bitterness that is sure to please hop lovers. Dark Marc has very little of the roasted flavors many CDAs have, which you could say adds to the drinkability.

American-style beers that are sold mainly at the brewery. You'll find the taproom and brewery in a garage at a small farmstead in Graham with a beautiful view of Mount Rainier on clear days. Outside the brewery you can occasionally find M.T. Head beers on draft at some of the better craft beer bars around the south Sound.

Year-round they offer 5 beers along with a handful of seasonal and special-release beers. For those wanting something light, try their **Golden Ale,** a very light-bodied beer with plenty of hop flavor. Also check out the **Bonehead Brown Ale,** an American brown beer named for their brewhouse dog, Shuman, who is featured on the label. Seasonally you can try **Punter's Special Ale,** an Irish red ale that's malt-forward, yet boasts enough hops to keep it grounded.

If you plan on visiting the taproom, make sure to check their Facebook page for times and any unexpected closures if they are away at a festival. You'll want to bring your growlers and get them filled up while you're there.

NORTHWEST BREWING COMPANY

1091 Valentine Ave. SE, Pacific, WA 98047; (253) 987-5680; NWBrewingCompany.com; @NWBrewCo
Founded: 2007 **Founders:** Greg Steed and Dan Anthony **Brewer:** Greg Fleehart
Flagship Beer: Hoppy Bitch IPA **Year-Round Beers:** Hoppy Bitch IPA, Ginger Pale Ale, Mango Weizen, Joker Pale Ale, Jet Stream Lager, Three Skulls Ales Pale Ale **Seasonals/ Special Releases:** Sumatra Coffee Stout, Three Skulls Ales Poison, Three Skulls Ales Blood Orange Wit, Crazy Bitch Double IPA **Tours:** No **Taproom:** Yes

The tale of the Northwest Brewing Company is one of change. To clear things up, it's a completely separate entity from the Northwest Brewing Company that once brewed in Tacoma in the 1930s. The current rendition of the company starts back in Seattle in 2007, when Laughing Buddha Brewing started brewing its line of beers with an array of Asian ingredients, such as mango, pandan leaves, ginger, and palm sugar. While they were gaining traction in the Seattle beer scene, a trademark dispute occurred when an Australian brewery with a beer in a Buddha-shaped bottle objected to their name. By 2009 the Seattle brewery decided to just change their name and became Trade Route Brewing, while still keeping their original lineup of beers. At the same time they ended up moving operations out of the ultracompetitive Seattle market and ended up in Pacific, Washington. To keep things interesting, in 2012 under new ownership, Trade Route did two major things. First they acquired the Three Skulls Ales from the fledgling Baron Brewing of Seattle and took over their beers and distribution. The second change was once again changing their name to Northwest Brewing Company.

Today their beers can be found all over the state on draft and in 22-ounce bottles. Some of the original Laughing Buddha beers are still being crafted, such as the **Ginger Pale Ale** and **Mango Weizen,** along with the full line of **Three Skulls Ales.** They're also making a name for themselves with their Northwest-style IPA, named **Hoppy Bitch,** and its big sister, **Crazy Bitch Double IPA.**

The taproom has a small food menu including pizza, sandwiches, and barbecue to pair with your beers if you visit. Inside you can view the brewery while sipping on their beers. Stop in and stay awhile or get a growler fill to go.

Beer Lover's Pick

Mango Weizen
Style: Fruit Beer/Pale Wheat Ale
ABV: 5%
Availability: Year-Round
Northwest Brewing Company's Mango Weizen is one of those refreshing beers that are meant to quench people's thirst more than to have beer geeks dive into their intricacies. Brewed with both wheat and barley, along with a touch of hops and mangoes, it's a very drinkable beer. The hazy orange brew has a wheat flavor with a slight malty edge, citrus, and of course just a splash of mango juice. Give this to your non–beer drinking friends and see what they think.

PUYALLUP RIVER BREWING COMPANY

120 S. Meridian, Puyallup, WA 98371; (253) 268-0955; PuyallupRiverBrewing.com; @PuyallupBrew

Founded: 2011 **Founder:** Eric Akeson **Brewer:** Eric Akeson **Flagship Beer:** None **Year-Round Beers:** Electron IPA, Fryingpan Cascadian Red Ale, Lahard Imperial IPA, Paradise Blonde Saison, Point Success Porter, South Hill Pale Ale, Valley Farmhouse India Pale Ale **Seasonals/Special Releases:** Jack O'Lahar Pumpkin Ale, Aketoberfest Harvest Ale, Strawberry Farmhouse Saison, Gourdy Wow!, Pêche Farmhouse Saison, Sumner StrawBarbed Saison, One Hit Warrior IPA, and many more **Tours:** No **Taproom:** Yes

Puyallup River Brewing Company might be a small brewery, but it's doing some big things. Founded in 2011, they first started brewing in 2012. The brewery is definitely what you would consider a nanobrewery, as the brewing system is capable of producing only one barrel at a time. However, through hard work, their bottles

Beer Lover's Pick

Valley Farmhouse India Pale Ale
Style: India Pale Ale
ABV: 6.2%
Availability: Year-Round
In Washington pretty much everyone brews an IPA. Puyallup River Brewing Company created this one to stand out from the crowd. They brew it similarly to a Northwest-style IPA but ferment it with Belgian yeast, giving it a hoppy yet funky and spicy flavor. To take it up a notch, they add grains of paradise, green peppercorns, and lemongrass to the end of the boil, resulting in a very flavorful IPA that ends dry enough to keep you drinking it over and over.

have popped up all around the south Puget Sound in the area's best bottle shops. With a limited amount of beer being produced with each batch, it's tough to find any of their beers on draft, and when you do, it generally goes pretty fast.

After a year of operating the brewery in the small building, Eric Akeson decided to take the next step and opened up the Puyallup River Alehouse in what was once a Pioneer Bakery. The opening of the alehouse acts like a taproom for the lineup of Puyallup River beers and allows them to offer experimental and unusual beers that might not sell as well if they were bottled. The alehouse offers 24 taps of craft beer, most of them from other breweries. While they don't offer food, they do offer a killer selection of arcade games; Akeson collects vintage arcade games and was also inducted into the International Video Game Hall of Fame.

Many of their year-round beers are named after locations in and around Puyallup, such as **South Hill Pale Ale,** a brew that pairs nicely with a good summer barbecue. They also tend to brew a variety of saisons and other Belgian-inspired ales. Look for their **Strawberry Farmhouse Saison** if it's brewed again. They added 150 pounds of fresh strawberries after fermentation of a two-barrel batch of their **Paradise Blonde Saison,** creating a strong strawberry aroma and flavor with a saison spiciness.

7 SEAS BREWING

3006 Judson St., Ste. 110, Gig Harbor, WA 98335; (253) 514-8129; 7SeasBrewing.com; @7SeasBeer

Founded: 2008 **Founders:** Travis Guterson and Mike Runion **Brewer:** Travis Guterson
Flagship Beer: None **Year-Round Beers:** British Pale Ale, Cutt's NW Amber Ale, Rude Parrot IPA, Cascadian Dark Ale, Port Royal Export Stout, Ballz Deep Double IPA
Seasonals/Special Releases: Le Havre Belgian Winter Ale, Harvest Ale, Reign Man ESB, Saison Du Sept Mers, Wheelchair Barleywine, Hop Prophet **Tours:** Yes; call brewery for times **Taproom:** Yes

Starting a new business isn't the easiest task to take on; the countless amounts of paperwork and hoops you need to jump through to get off the ground can be brutal. 7 Seas Brewing hit a huge snag right before opening. Six weeks away from production a fire destroyed their operation, including pretty much everything that wasn't stainless steel. With the determination to succeed, founders Travis Guterson and Mike Runion pushed on and found a new location to begin brewing their beers. Since then the duo has expanded out of that space and moved the brewery to a much larger location in downtown Gig Harbor.

As the use of cans has been picking up in the craft-beer world, 7 Seas Brewing decided that was the route they would go to distribute their beers. In 2010 they became the first craft brewery in the state to can their beer, which they offer in

16-ounce tallboys around the state. Year-round they produce a handful of full-flavored beers that are greatly appreciated by even the most discerning beer geeks along with a rotating selection of seasonals available on draft in the taproom and around the Puget Sound. Keep an eye out for their **Ballz Deep Double IPA.** With a clever name that definitely stands out on the shelves, it's an incredibly malty and sweet double IPA. While the bitterness of the piney hops shines through, it is one of the more malt-forward beers in the state for the style.

You can visit the taproom 7 days a week to experience their beer, buy some cans and growlers, and simply have a good time. They don't offer food, but downtown Gig Harbor has plenty of places where you can stop to get food to go and bring it in.

Beer Lover's Pick

British Pale Ale
Style: English Pale Ale
ABV: 5.4%
Availability: Year-Round
In a quest to brew the proper pint, 7 Seas Brewing ventured out of the typical Northwest-inspired beer lineup and brewed this British pale ale. Although it might not have you weeping with delight at every sip, this approachable beer is meant for everyday consumption and is perfect in just about every situation. Earthy hops and slightly bitter citrus flavors give way to caramel and toasted bread malts and a finish with a dry lemon accent. Try pairing it with just about any type of British-style pub food for an excellent meal, or drink it after mowing the lawn.

SOOS CREEK BREWING COMPANY

16729 SE 251st Place, Covington, WA 98042; (253) 237-2739; SoosCreekBrewingCo.com; @SoosBrew

Founded: 2011 **Founders:** TJ Bloomingdale and Jason Brinkley **Brewers:** TJ Bloomingdale and Jason Brinkley **Flagship Beer:** None **Year-Round Beers:** Rua Beoir Irish Red, Beer Pressure IPA, Sine Lucis CDA **Seasonals/Special Releases:** Free Baller, "No Bollocks" IPA, Pavlik's **Tours:** No **Taproom:** No

When your brewhouse is 10 feet by 12 feet, you could definitely say you're a small brewery. For Soos Creek Brewing Company in Covington, they are the classic nanobrewery story. Both owners TJ Bloomingdale and Jason Brinkley got their start as homebrewers and dreamed about turning their hobby into a business. In 2011 the dream became a reality when they got licenses and fired up the brewing kettles. Although they have upgraded their brewing system to a "larger" one-barrel system, it still has the feeling of a slightly larger homebrew setup. Because of their smaller size, they don't have a taproom; however, you can still find their beers on draft around the south Puget Sound area.

Their beers come in a variety of styles ranging from their easy-drinking **Rua Beoir Irish Red** to their roasty-yet-hoppy **Sine Lucis Cascadian Dark Ale. Beer Pressure IPA** is an English-style IPA with a delicate balance of malt and hops.

Beer Lover's Pick

Pavlik's Pilsner
Style: Bohemian Pilsner
ABV: 5.1%
Availability: Year-Round

Although macrobreweries give Bohemian Pilsners a bad rap, they're actually very flavorful and refreshing when crafted just right. Soos Creek's Pavlik's Pilsner is one of those true-to-style beers that would make it very easy to drink an entire growler-ful all by yourself while watching a game or at the campsite. A spicy bitterness is present in the aroma from the use of Saaz hops, and it gives way to a smooth, crisp malty flavor with just a touch of spice that lingers.

THE STATION U-BREW

211 W. Stewart Ave., Puyallup, WA 98371; (253) 466-3721
Founded: 2010 **Founder:** Steve Samples **Brewer:** Steve Samples **Flagship Beer:** None
Year-Round Beers: None **Seasonals/Special Releases:** Railcar Pale Ale, I Like It on
Top IPA, Red Rye, Carry On Porter, Just in Time, Porter w/ Nutella, Honey Lemon Blonde,
Amber, Hobo Rhubarb Pale Ale, Raspberry IPA, Brown Sugar Brown Ale, Spice Ale, Black
IPA, Hit by the Train, Wet Sheep, and many more **Tours:** No **Taproom:** Yes

The Station U-Brew isn't your typical brewery. In fact, it's more the place you go if you want to brew your own beers while drinking some interesting beers in the process. Started by owner Steve Samples in 2010, the 1,500-square-foot store is set up in a way that people can make appointments to come brew on one of their Sabco Brew-Magic systems. You don't need to be an expert in brewing, as they help you along with the process. They make it so easy that you don't even have to clean up the kettles when your brew day is over. For around $150 you can brew about 10 gallons of beer that you will come back and bottle when fermentation is complete. For those who have brewed before, you'll know it's just not right to brew beer without a beer in your hand. That's where their own brewery comes into play. In fact, they use the same brew systems you use for a rotation of 6 beers on draft.

Each time you go in they will have a wide range of beers, ranging from IPAs to porters made with Nutella or Snickers bars. The taproom is open to anyone, not just

Beer Lover's Pick

Carry On Porter
Style: Porter
ABV: 6.1%
Availability: Rotating
Some things in life are really good, and then you add chocolate and they are amazing. For the Carry On Porter, they didn't just add any chocolate into the beer. They added the king of all candy bars, Snickers. The dark-as-night beer has some slight floral hoppiness to it, yet the caramel, nuts, and chocolate from both the candy bar and the specialty grains used make it just about the perfect dessert drink. If it's on draft, make sure to fill up a growler, or better yet, brew 10 gallons of it to take home and enjoy with all your friends.

those who are brewing. If you try one of the beers they have on draft and fall in love with it, you can sign up to brew that same beer in the shop. Inside they don't offer food other than pretzels, so you might want to come full, especially if you're coming to spend a few hours brewing your beer.

TACOMA BREWING COMPANY

625 St. Helens Ave., Tacoma, WA 98402; (253) 242-3370; TacomaBrewing.com
Founded: 2012 **Founder:** Morgan Alexander **Brewer:** Morgan Alexander **Flagship Beer:** None **Year-Round Beers:** None **Seasonals/Special Releases:** NW Pale Ale, Packwood Pale, Centennial IPA, Infinity Double IPA, Golden Ginger Ale, Coffee Porter, Pomegranate Porter, Pale Amber Irish Ale, Dark English Ale, Imperial Coffee Stout, Bourbon Oaked Imperial Stout, Bloody Mary IPA, Tacoma Lite, Honey Wheat Ale, Pale Amber, Penalty Kick IPA, Hop Fix Session IPA, End of the World Chocolate Chili Stout, and many more
Tours: No **Taproom:** Yes

Amocat Cafe (Tacoma spelled backward) owner Morgan Alexander has a passion for food. From crafting unique coffee drinks to the beers he brews at Tacoma Brewing Company, based in the back of the cafe, everything he creates is an extension of his foodie side. After years of homebrewing he decided to add the brewery as part of the cafe he runs. While those in Tacoma can visit and get a cup of coffee in the morning, they can visit the cafe, which doubles as the brewery's tasting room, and try his interesting beers. His brewing system is tiny, yet it allows him to

Pomegranate Porter
Style: Porter
ABV: 6.7%
Availability: Limited Release
Showcasing the creativity of brewer Morgan Alexander, Tacoma Brewing Company's Pomegranate Porter is just as it sounds. It's a thick and dark porter with pomegranates added in. It's a very dark beer with plenty of sweet fruit on the nose. Surprisingly the pomegranate flavor is strong enough to stand up to the coffee bitterness from the use of specialty grains in this delicious beer. If there is such a thing as a summertime evening beer, this would be it.

experiment with unique beers brewed with ingredients such as pomegranates, chiles, coffee, and even wasabi.

While the brewery is looking at growing to a larger system and new space, their current small size makes it so you'll most likely need to head to the Amocat Cafe to drink their brews. Their beers are made in a way so that even non–beer drinkers might be able to connect with at least one beer on tap. Beers such as their **Bloody Mary IPA** and **Pomegranate Porter** offer an experience you can't find anywhere else.

Visit on tap nights on Friday evenings inside the Amocat Cafe and sample some of their beer. Kids are welcome to come with you and they even serve child-friendly beverages. They also offer live music to kick back and relax to while drinking their beer.

WINGMAN BREWERS

509½ Puyallup Ave., Tacoma, WA 98421; (253) 651-4832; WingmanBrewers.com; @WingmanBrewers
Founded: 2011 **Founders:** Ken Thoburn, Derrick Moyer, Jason Sabol, and Daniel Heath
Brewer: Ken Thoburn **Flagship Beer:** None **Year-Round Beers:** P-51 Porter, Ace IPA, Stratofortress, Miss B Haven Tripel **Seasonals/Special Releases:** Pocket Aces Double IPA, Wingman ESB, Basil Lime Ale, Maori Warrior IPA, Black Widow and White Betty, and many more **Tours:** No **Taproom:** Yes

Wingman Brewers started out when three college housemates began homebrewing. After noticing that their beer brought people together, they brought on their fourth friend and turned the hobby into a business. When launching in April 2011 they decided on an aviation theme for the brewery's name and based on inspiration from head brewer Ken Thoburn's grandfather, who was in World World II. Everything from their logo and beer names to their tap handles that look like miniature bombs has a World War II theme to it.

Their beers tend to have a Northwest influence, but they don't stick to any specific style guidelines. Year-round they serve **P-51 Porter,** a smooth and malty porter with notes of chocolate and coffee, as well as **Ace IPA,** brewed with Belgian malts to give it unique characteristics. Both of those offerings are available in 16-ounce cans and can be found throughout the Tacoma area. Year-round they also brew **Miss B Haven Tripel,** where they have created a traditional-style Tripel and added Northwest hops to give it a little more flavor. Look for it along with many of their other beers on draft around the area.

You can also visit their tasting room 3 days a week, where they pour a variety of beers in 17-ounce glasses, including a handful of guest taps. Their sampler flight and growler prices are some of the best deals in the state. It's always nice to find a brewery that will fill a growler for less than $10. Since the guys are so invested in the local community, they also donate part of the profits from each keg to various charities.

Stratofortress
Style: Belgian Strong Dark Ale
ABV: 11.4%
Availability: Year-Round
As breweries continue to innovate and experiment with their beers, they end up creating some amazing concoctions, such as Wingman's Stratofortress. The Belgian strong dark ale is aged on cedar planks that have been soaked in dark rum, both of which are very apparent in the aroma along with a very characteristic Belgian yeast. Ripe fruit and hints of fig come out in the flavor and are balanced with a somewhat thick maltiness and Belgian spices. Watch out—the 11.4% ABV will sneak up on you all too quickly.

Brewpubs

ENGINE HOUSE NO. 9

611 N. Pine St., Tacoma, WA 98406; (253) 272-3435; EHouse9.com; @ehouse9
Founded: 1972 **Founders:** Win Anderson and Bob Lane **Brewer:** Shane Johns **Flagship Beers:** Tacoma Brew, India Pale, Rowdy Dick Amber, Belgian White **Year-Round Beers:** Tacoma Brew, India Pale, Rowdy Dick Amber, Belgian White **Seasonals/Special Releases:** Fire Engine Red, Imperial Stout, Irish Stout, Roasted Porter, Funky Farmer Ralph, Cabernet Barrel BDS, Dudas Priest, Petite Sour, Love Child Kreik, Hefeweizen, Scottish Ale, Old Dickens Barleywine, and many more **Tours:** No **Taproom:** Yes

Built in 1907 in Tacoma's north end, Engine House No. 9 served the people of the city until 1965, when it was abandoned and fell into disrepair. Restored and converted into a tavern in 1972, Engine House No. 9 is now on the National Register of Historic Places. With over 10 taps of E9 beers, plus more than 10 guest taps and even some out-of-country brews by the bottle, patrons are far from wanting in regard to selection. This family-friendly neighborhood brewpub also features karaoke as well as pub quizzes to go along with the beer and food.

Touted as being a favorite for nearly 40 years, the Famous E9 Northwest Taco is veggie, beef, or chicken in a giant tortilla baked with onions, cheddar-jack cheese, lettuce, tomatoes, and E9 sauce topped with salsa and sour cream. A famous taco deserves a special beer indeed. Pair it with a **Cabernet Barrel Aged Belgian Dark Strong** to round out the meal. With plenty of Cabernet and a hint of earthiness on the nose, the aroma follows through in the taste as the Cabernet boldly makes its presence known. The dry mouthfeel lingers into a well-balanced finish.

If you feel the need for another brew and maybe dessert, opt for the **Roasted Porter Float.** The beer is made with Martin Henry coffee and has the typical chocolate, coffee, and roasty notes indicative of the style. With a medium body and a caramel sweetness, this beer has a lingering roasty flavor.

GROVE STREET BREWHOUSE

233 S. 1st St., Shelton, WA 98584; (360) 462-2739; GroveStreetBrew.com
Founded: 2009 **Founders:** Jeff and Tessie Thompson **Brewer:** Jeff Thompson **Flagship Beer:** Ol' Pinchfister **Year-Round Beers:** Kölsch, Hefeweizen, GSB ESB, Ol' Pinchfister, Mahogany Knob Porter, Ivanna Stout **Seasonals/Special Releases:** Festivus Maximus, Slam Dunkle **Tours:** Yes **Taproom:** Yes

This Pontiac dealership–turned–brewery plays host to over 7 house-made beers, ciders, local wines, and house-made sodas, as well as an extensive variety of specialty teas. This family-friendly public house uses a seven-barrel pub system to create the ever-changing list of beers. With as many as 10 ales on tap at any given time, GSB is always brewing something new and is committed to providing patrons with new and exciting beers to enjoy.

The menu is quite varied, with many conventional, as well as unconventional, pizzas to choose from. Sandwiches, soups, salads, and appetizers are all part of the menu as well. If a light yet exciting lunch is what you're after, try the Twisted Tuna Croissant, composed of tuna salad, artichoke-jalapeño dip, shredded cabbage, and sliced pepperoncini. Softening the light sting from this croissan'wich is easy with a pint of Grove Street Brewing's **Kölsch.** With biscuit and light fruit notes, this well-balanced summer seasonal beer has light carbonation and finishes clean.

If a darker beer is more of your idea for a lunch brew, try the **Mahogany Knob Porter.** With a strong, sweet malty and chocolate aroma, the nose of this brew is typical for the style. With a lot going on in regard to flavor, the sugars, grain, and chocolate flavors mix together to create a well-balanced, very drinkable beer.

POWERHOUSE RESTAURANT AND BREWERY

454 E. Main, Puyallup, WA 98372; (253) 845-2799; PowerhouseBrewpub.com
Founded: 1995 **Founder:** Dusty Trail **Brewer:** Tim Patty **Flagship Beer:** India Pale Ale
Year-Round Beers: Belgian White, Powerhouse Pale Ale, Hefeweizen, Scottish Ale, India Pale Ale, Four Alarm Stout, Amperage Amber **Seasonals/Special Releases:** Brass Monk, Double Down IPA, Spring Saison, Summer Wheat, and more **Tours:** No **Taproom:** Yes

Originally constructed for the Puget Sound Electric Railway in 1907, the Puyallup substation–turned–brewpub originally supplied the current for the southern leg of the Interurban Electric Trolley that ran from Seattle to Olympia. Abandoned in 1969, the building was left to rainy Northwest weather until 1994, when it was purchased and extensively renovated into a restaurant and brewery. The rumbling of the trains that occasionally run by adds to the ambience of this historical reclamation. But if trains aren't your thing, then maybe just stick around for the beer. With 7 year-round beers as well as seasonal offerings, Powerhouse brews up enough small-batch beer to keep patrons amped up.

With light hop bite and Belgian yeast, the 9% ABV **Brass Monk** may be the high-voltage brew you're looking for. With banana and light fruit on the nose, this medium-bodied brew culminates with tastes of biscuity malt, yeast, and plenty of sweetness on the palate. Pair this with the smoked salmon pasta, which is smoked salmon, mushrooms, and green onions sautéed in a light garlic white wine cream sauce tossed in penne pasta. Topped with Parmesan cheese and parsley, this dish is sure to electrify the senses.

Beer Bars

EASTSIDE CLUB TAVERN

410 4th Ave. E., Olympia, WA 98501; (360) 357-9985; TheEastSideClub.com; @TheEastsideClub

Draft Beers: 42 **Bottled/Canned Beers:** About 20

As one of the oldest beer bars in the Northwest, the Eastside Club Tavern has been a local hangout for beer lovers since 1942. Over time the tavern has seen quite a lot, such as when it was partially destroyed in 1959 when a train crashed through the front of the building. Later, in 2001, the Nisqually earthquake caused some slight damage, creating a need for a new brick facade. Although the building looks a bit aged and the ambience isn't anything fancy, it still can be considered a beer lover's paradise. Inside feels a bit like your typical dive bar with old beer signs on the wall, multiple pool tables, a Ping-Pong table, foosball, TVs, video games, pinball, and a CD jukebox.

The beer selection is what sets the Eastside Club Tavern apart. With 42 rotating beers on tap, you can pretty much come back once a week and never get close to drinking everything on the menu; everything from IPAs and pale ales to Russian imperial stouts and everything in between grace the menu, from Northwest breweries and beyond. You'll find beers on draft you can't find anywhere else in Olympia, as well as a few on cask and nitro. They'll also fill growlers, so if you're not feeling in a mood to be out or are having a get-together, stop in and get a couple filled up with some of the best craft beer the state has to offer. On top of beer, they offer a window to order food from Alforno Ferruzza next door. Grab a slice of pizza to pair with any of your beers.

PARKWAY TAVERN

313 N. I St., Tacoma, WA 98402; (253) 383-8748; ParkwayTavern.com; @ParkwayTavern

Draft Beers: 37 **Bottled/Canned Beers:** About 25

It doesn't get any better than the Parkway Tavern if you're a beer lover in Tacoma. The neighborhood pub has been a staple in the city for decades. What once was an old house has been converted into a bar that fits into the neighborhood so well that you think you're headed over to your friend's house. There are plenty of seating options, including a front porch for nicer days, the bar area, booths, and a back area for kicking back and playing pool, shuffleboard, darts, or video games. On the walls are old photos of Tacoma history, including a picture from 1983 when a disgruntled customer rammed his truck into the tavern six or seven times. The relaxed yet clean atmosphere helps make it an unpretentious destination to drink and talk about craft beer with fellow beer lovers.

A rotation of 37 taps along with a good-size can and bottle selection will give you a little trouble in trying to figure out what to order. From rare beers from the West Coast to good Northwest standards and a few pedestrian beers to keep the PBR-loving crowd happy, there's something for everyone. If you're making a trip out of it, try coming on a Monday night when they bring out the Randall and pour some interesting beers through it. Along with that you'll usually find a beer pouring on nitro and a handful of cask-poured brews. You will also find a decent selection of pub fare ranging from burgers to sandwiches, although the drinks tend to outshine food.

PINT DEFIANCE
2049 Mildred St. W., Tacoma, WA 98466; (253) 302-4240; PintDefiance.com; @ PintDefiance
Draft Beers: 10 **Bottled/Canned Beers:** 1,000+

As one of the new kids on the block in Tacoma, Pint Defiance is part bottle shop and part taproom. Named as a play on words of Tacoma's Point Defiance Park, this haven of beer is located just off 19th and Mildred Street near Tacoma Community College. It's located in a strip mall with a Thai food place next door, which is perfect

Washington Beer Open House

Once a year, the Washington Beer Commission organizes an event that allows breweries statewide to open up their doors to the public. Across the state you can tour multiple breweries, chat with brewers, try new and special beers ranging from barrel-aged small batches to brand-spanking-new seasonal releases launched on the day you arrive. Each brewery does the event a little differently, so make sure to check with the breweries you're interested in and see what they have going on. For more information, check out the event's official website at washingtonbeer.com/open-house.

for ordering to go since the bar doesn't offer food. They do, however, carry lots of beer, ranging from Northwest favorites to rarities from the East Coast and beyond. Toward the back is the taproom, which pours 10 beers on draft. You can fill up a growler or enjoy beer while there. Their selection is a fantastic blend of beers ranging in styles, while you'll often find a keg or two coming from some of Washington's smaller breweries, not often found elsewhere. If you're in the mood for something specific that's not on draft, you can peruse the selection of over 1,000 bottles and cans of beer, cider, and mead to crack open in the taproom or take home with you.

Throughout the year they offer plenty of events including an almost-weekly meet-the-brewers night, where a brewery comes to take over the taps and talk about their beer. Also on Sunday they often do tastings around a specific theme. For example, around Valentine's Day they put together a flight consisting of beers to complement the holiday, such as a strawberry lambic and a chocolate cherry stout.

THE RED HOT
2914 6th Ave., Tacoma, WA 98406; (253) 779-0229; RedHotTacoma.com; @TheRedHot
Draft Beers: 15 **Bottled/Canned Beers:** About 20

In the short time The Red Hot has been serving Tacoma, it has quickly become a classic bar in the city. Walking in, you can look around and chances are the majority of the patrons are smiling. Located between a dog wash and a photography/wedding shop on 6th Avenue, the small bar may be in an odd spot, but it works perfectly. Upon entering you'll notice a big bar taking up the length of the room, with a few tables and booths. Look up and you'll see a ton of tap handles dangling from the ceiling as a tribute to beers past. There's a TV for sports or an occasional movie, but if you're a beer lover, the centerpiece is the big chalkboard showing the amazing selection of beers on draft. With 15 rotating taps of both local beers and those from afar as well as ciders, it isn't difficult to find something for every taste. You can also find a selection of Belgian beers in bottles and even cans of Rainier if your inner hipster wants to come out.

Their menu is focused on specialty wieners that have even been voted best hot dog in western Washington. If you decide on a beer first, you'll have to ask yourself what hot dog to pair it with. The 6th Ave. Strut is packed with cream cheese, fresh chopped onions, and tomatoes, while the Hilltop Strangler is loaded with bacon, Thousand Island dressing, fresh chopped onions, mustard, nacho cheese, and tomatoes. Don't worry if you don't eat meat; they also serve both vegetarian and vegan dogs.

SKEP & SKEIN

2106 Harrison Ave. NW, Ste. B14, Olympia, WA 98502; (360) 292-4400; SkepAndSkein.com
Draft Beers: 16 **Bottled/Canned Beers:** Over 5

Park next to a Dollar Tree and Grocery Outlet, walk into Skep & Skein, and you'll quickly forget you're in a strip mall. The name Skep & Skein is a mix of a few of the owners' passions. Skep is a dome-shaped beehive. Owner Dave Ross loves creating meads, which are made with honey. Skein is a quantity of yarn, which is a passion of his wife, Kriste, who co-owns the tavern. Inside you'll find a clean and open atmosphere with plenty of board games and no televisions.

What separates Skep & Skein from other taverns besides their great beer selection is that they are a licensed meadery. While you can order a number of craft brews, you can also order a selection of their own meads created in multiple flavors, such as lavender, raspberry, marionberry, blackberry, ginseng ginger, and other berry flavors. Along with their own mead selection, they offer a range of bottled meads and ciders that should please non–beer drinkers. Beer fans out there, however, are the main audience, with 15 of the taps dedicated to a range of both West Coast beers and beers from around the world. If you're in a rush, they offer the option to fill up a growler; however, the laid-back atmosphere will cause you to want to stick around and have a pint or two. If you want to sample multiple beers, they pour smaller glasses, so you can try quite a few of the brews on the menu. Although they don't serve food themselves, you can place an order for Apollo's, Vic's Pizzeria, and Wally Sandwich Shop next door and bring it into the tavern.

Southwest Washington

BREWERIES

Dick's Brewing Company	2
Everybody's Brewing	18
Ghost Runners Brewery	5
Heathen Brewing	6
Loowit Brewing Company	10
Mt. Tabor Brewing Company	9
St. Helens Brewing Company	3
Walking Man Brewing	15
West Highland Brewing	12
Westport Brewing Company	1

BREWPUBS

Acadian Farms	16
Backwoods Brewing Company	17
Laurelwood Public House and Brewery	4
The Old Ivy Taproom at Salmon Creek Brewery	8
Railside Brewing	13

BARS

A Beer at a Time	14
Brickhouse Bar & Grill	7
Northwest Liquid Gold	11

Southwest Washington

The southwestern part of Washington has a growing beer culture that shows just how thirsty the residents have been for many years. Much of the growth is occurring in and around Clark County, an area that is a part of the suburbs of Portland yet has never really had an identity of its own in the beer world. For years Vancouver has been home to the Great Western Malting Company, the oldest and one of the largest malting companies in the western US. However, most of that malt has been sent all over the country with very little staying in the county. Fortunately, those in the area no longer have to drive across the bridge to Oregon to find fresh beer. Just like Bob Dylan wrote, "the times they are a-changin'."

Downtown Vancouver is now home to Mt. Tabor Brewing, Loowit Brewing, and the Old Ivy Taproom at the Salmon Creek Brewery. Outside of downtown, smaller breweries have started up and experienced quick growth, while many restaurants and bars have focused on carrying better draft options. Beyond Vancouver the love of craft beer has been sprawling out to many other cities. From the gorge to the coast, southwest Washington is one of the best places in the state for beer lovers.

Breweries

DICK'S BREWING COMPANY

3516 Galvin Rd., Centralia, WA 98531; (360) 736-1603; DicksBeer.com
Founded: 1994 **Founder:** Dick Young **Brewer:** Dave Pendleton **Flagship Beer:** Dick Danger Ale **Year-Round Beers:** Dick Danger Ale, Dick's IPA, Dick's Cream Stout, Lava Rock Porter, Dick's Pale Ale, Dick's Golden Ale, Working Man's Brown **Seasonals/Special Releases:** Dick's Irish Ale, Dick's Barley Wine Ale, Dick's Hefeweizen, Dick's Belgian Triple, Dick's Imperial Stout, Dick's Grand Cru, Dick's Silk Lady, Dick's Double Diamond Winter Ale, Dick's Best Bitter, Dick's Mountain Ale, and many more **Tours:** Yes, every Fri and 3rd Sat of the month **Taproom:** Yes

It's fitting that Dick's Brewing Company has the first name of the founder and craft-beer pioneer Dick Young in its name. Although Young passed away in 2009, the Centralia-based brewery is a reflection of who he was. In 1984 Dick got hooked on homebrewing, so much so that he started selling homebrew supplies out of his business, Northwest Sausage & Deli, a small restaurant specializing in smoking Old World–style meats. By 1994 his idea of owning his own brewery came to fruition and Dick's Brewing Company opened in the back of the deli where he focused on brewing just three beers. One of those beers, **Dick Danger Ale,** is still the brewery's best-selling beer even though they have expanded considerably and brew over 20 beers. The name for the beer comes from Young's nickname of "Dick Danger," as he was an avid adventurer. Shortly before his passing, the brewery moved to a much larger 18,000-square-foot brewing facility, giving them ample room to meet a larger demand. Today you can either visit their tasting room to sample their beer or head over to the family-run Northwest Sausage & Deli to find their current offerings or to fill a growler.

Outside of Centralia, Dick's Brewing Company beers can often be found in 12- and 22-ounce bottles throughout 6 states. If you're lucky, you might even find them on draft occasionally throughout Washington. While you pretty much can't go wrong ordering any of their beers, chocolate lovers will be happy with **Dick's Imperial Stout.** Packed with rich chocolate and caramel malts, it's almost like drinking a beautifully crafted dessert. Also keep an eye open for **Dick's Belgian Triple,** a sweet brew with a Belgian spice to it, booming with subtle complexities. If you're near Centralia on a Friday, make sure to stop by the brewery for a tour and end up sampling their beer in the tasting room.

Double Diamond Winter Ale
Style: Winter Warmer
ABV: 7.5% ABV
Availability: Seasonal
Available in the winter months, Dick's Double Diamond Winter Ale is an almost perfect beer to sip on when the weather is cold. The label features the brewery's late founder, Dick Young, doing one of the things he enjoyed most: skiing. From the use of a lot of different malts, this brew packs a lot of sweet caramel, raisin, and dark fruit flavors that are balanced with piney yet subdued bitter hops. There is plenty of sweetness in the creamy finish that helps hide the alcohol. Try it after hitting the slopes.

EVERYBODY'S BREWING

151 E. Jewett Blvd., White Salmon, WA 98672; (509) 637-2774; EverybodysBrewing.com
Founded: 2008 **Founders:** Doug Ellenburger and Christine McAleer **Brewer:** Doug
Ellenburger **Flagship Beer:** Country Boy IPA **Year-Round Beers:** Local Logger
Lager, Bro Brah Bitter, Hoedown Brown, Pucker Huddle Porter, Cash Stout, Daily Bread
Common Ale, Goodwill IPA, Country Boy IPA, Law of Nature Pale Ale **Seasonals/Special
Releases:** Summer Lovin', Big Brother Imperial IPA, Little Sister India Session Ale, Sugar
Daddy, West Coast Common, Head Stash Pale Ale **Tours:** No **Taproom:** Yes

The small town of White Salmon may be sitting in Hood River's shadow (not literally; it sits at an elevation just about 500 feet higher than Hood River), but it makes a perfect destination for beer lovers. On the main strip in the town resides

Everybody's Brewing, which is in a fairly nondescript building that is pretty easy to miss. Once inside you'll find a beautifully designed pub that is the perfect hangout spot for both locals and those passing through on their way home from hiking, kite boarding, or whatever adventure they faced that day. On clear days you can sit on their back deck and take in some breathtaking views of Oregon's Mount Hood to the south. It's a full-service pub that offers a nice selection of food that uses locally sourced produce and meat.

Starting out as just a brewpub, they ended up buying a 20-hectoliter (17-barrel) brewing system from a company in Japan. The size was much larger than they needed to keep up with demand in the pub, so they've been able to expand distribution throughout the state, where they offer their beers strictly on draft. With a focus on mainly session beers brewed in the Northwest style, they have been very successful. Year-round look for their citrus-packed **Country Boy IPA,** which has a hop aroma that will put a smile on any hophead's face. Also try the well-balanced **Law of Nature Pale Ale.** At only 4.8% ABV yet packed with plenty of flavor, it's a highly sessionable beer. While you can find their beer around both the Portland and Seattle markets, you can't beat drinking on their back patio on a clear summer day. They also have plenty of live music, so make sure to check their website for listings.

Cash Stout Oatmeal Stout
Style: Oatmeal Stout
ABV: 6%
Availability: Year-Round
Even though Everybody's Brewing tends to specialize in hoppier beers, their Cash Stout is a must-try for dark-beer fans out there. They add over 100 pounds of flaked oatmeal to create such a smooth and rich body. Chocolate malts dominate the aroma and flavor with hints of vanilla, roasted coffee, and earthy hops to round things out. For an oatmeal stout, it's a beer that is going to pair superbly with just about any food you throw at it.

GHOST RUNNERS BREWERY

2403 NW 125th St., Vancouver, WA 98660; (360) 573-4872; GhostRunnersBrewery.com
Founded: 2012 **Founders:** Jeff Seibel and Rob Ziebell **Brewers:** Jeff Seibel and Rob Ziebell **Flagship Beer:** Hellacious Repeats Double IPA **Year-Round Beers:** Qualifier IPA, Hellacious Repeats Double IPA, Strong Leg Stout **Seasonals/Special Releases:** Negative Split Stout, Recover Ale, 10K Belgian IPA, Recovery Scotch Ale, and more **Tours:** No **Taproom:** No

Beer and running go hand in hand. It's almost as if the two were made for each other. After a long run or race, there aren't many better options to rehydrate the body and replenish yourself with much-needed electrolytes than by drinking a well-created craft beer. While that might be debatable, it's a good enough reason to drink a few pints from Vancouver's newest brewers, Ghost Runners Brewery, the next time you run. The one-barrel nanobrewery was founded in the Felida area in 2012 by neighbors Jeff Seibel and Rob Ziebell. Both have a background in homebrewing and have joined forces, equally sharing brewing responsibilities. Located in a small building in the back yard, the small running-themed production brewery is starting out distributing their beer strictly on draft at area restaurants and bars. While they don't offer a tasting room, it's worth searching around Clark County to sample their beers.

Beer Lover's Pick

Hellacious Repeats Double IPA
Style: Double IPA
ABV: 9.4%
Availability: Year-Round
Runners training for marathons know that training using repeats can help to improve your race time, yet they are pretty much hell to complete. In continuing with their running theme, Ghost Runners decided on the name Hellacious Repeats for their double IPA. It's a big IPA with a huge malt backbone that is incredibly well balanced with a marathon of hops. You get all of the big hop flavors, yet the bitterness is kicked to the back burner, leaving one smooth brew. However, repeating drinking too many pints of it might cause you a little hell at 9.4% ABV.

Each beer keeps their theme of running. Year-round they offer **Qualifier IPA,** a well-balanced IPA with plenty of citrus and pine; **Hellacious Repeats Double IPA,** a hefty 9.4% beast that has a big grain bill to keep the hoppiness in check; and **Strong Leg Stout,** a Russian imperial stout with a touch of bitterness and chocolate that finishes like coffee. Throughout the year they are also brewing up special-release beers, such as the delicious **Negative Split Stout,** a Belgian chocolate-vanilla stout brewed with both cocoa and whole vanilla beans. If your run didn't go as well as you would have liked, find their **Recovery Ale,** an 11.9% scotch ale that will have you forgetting the run after just a pint or two. Their tagline of "Run.Drink.Repeat." is pretty perfect. The more you run, the more you can drink. Just don't tell your doctor.

HEATHEN BREWING

5612 NE 119th St., Vancouver, WA 98686; (360) 601-7454; HeathenBrewing.com; @Heathen_Brewing

Founded: 2012 **Founder:** Sunny Parsons **Brewer:** Rodney Stryker **Flagship Beer:** None **Year-Round Beers:** Chillaxe Pale Wheat Ale, Son of Malice, Transcend IPA, Wicked Wheat, Indulge Amber **Seasonals/Special Releases:** Roasted Rhapsody, RIP Real Intense Porter, Promiscuous Blonde, Malice **Tours:** No **Taproom:** No

As one of the new breweries entering the Vancouver beer scene, Heathen Brewing got its start in 2012 by first offering its beer at the Vancouver Brewfest. Started by Sunny Parsons, a homebrewer who had the dream to go pro, the small brewery operating out of a shed is starting to pop up all around the city. The name Heathen Brewing honors a grandfather who would call all of his grandkids heathens when they were acting crazy running around everywhere.

Using locally sourced ingredients, Heathen Brewing is crafting up an array of beers common with traditional American craft breweries. One interesting beer that is worth a drink is the **Chillaxe Pale Wheat Ale.** Brewed like a traditional pale ale, Chillaxe has a wheat-style backbone that gives it a hoppy yet subtle wheat flavor and makes for a brew that's a bit different yet very drinkable.

While you won't find a pub to drink their beer, you can check out their website for times when they open up the brew shed for growler fills. Although they are brewing extremely small batches, they are aiming to offer up to 12 beers at a time. You can also find their beers on draft at various Vancouver-area bars, restaurants, and beer events.

Transcend IPA
Style: IPA
ABV: 6.4%
Availability: Year-Round

Heathen Brewing claims this beer might "Transcend" IPAs as we know them. Taking a sip, you might find it hard to disagree. A slight caramel malt plays a supporting role, but lets the Simcoe, Warrior, and Citra hops take the spotlight. Plenty of citrus and piney notes are present in this light-bodied brew with solid bitterness that doesn't distract from the taste. The murky glowing orange color draws you in while the balanced and artistically smooth flavor causes you to stay and enjoy every sip.

LOOWIT BREWING COMPANY

507 Columbia St., Vancouver, WA 98660; (360) 566-2323; LoowitBrewing.com; @LoowitBrewing

Founded: 2012 **Founders:** Thomas Poffenroth and Devon Bray **Brewers:** Thomas Poffenroth and Devon Bray **Flagship Beer:** Lucid Golden Ale **Year-Round Beers:** Loowit Red Ale, Extrabeerestrial ESB, Couverino CBA, Rollins CDA, Lucid Golden Ale, Shadow Ninja IPA, Shimmergloom Stout **Seasonals/Special Releases:** Winter Stout, Vandalia Summer Ale, Shimmergloom Stout, Brewthulhu Coffee Stout, P-P-P-Pepper Pete's Power Ale, The Walking Red **Tours:** No **Taproom:** Yes

Downtown Vancouver has never exactly been a center of excitement past 6 p.m. Fortunately, the area is growing with new businesses that are catering to those looking for a little nightlife, many of which center on beer. As downtown started its rebuilding project, homebrewers Thomas Poffenroth and Devon Bray decided it was the perfect time to open a brewery they had been working on for years. When deciding on a name, they ended up choosing Loowitt after Thomas recalled a hike on the Loowit Trail #216 around the base of Mount St. Helens. The name is actually a Native American name given to the mountain, which you'll find in their logo.

Their brewery and tasting room has been a breath of fresh air to Vancouver, giving residents a local brewery they can get behind. In downtown Vancouver you can visit their tasting room a few nights per week and try up to 6 of their own beers on draft, as well as fill up a growler to go. Inside the tasting room you can get a peek of the brewery itself or head over and play the free *Street Fighter II* arcade game.

Beer Lover's Pick

Shadow Ninja IPA
Style: IPA
ABV: 6.8%
Availability: Year-Round
Like a ninja hiding in the shadows, Shadow Ninja is very skilled at what it does.
The glowing orange beer has plenty of floral hop aromas to get your mouth water-
ing. Its balance between malts and an array of floral, citrus, and piney hops adds
to the intrigue of this well-rounded IPA. A slight bitterness hangs in the shadows
but reveals itself as you get further into your pint, which might be sooner than you
think, as the almost creamy texture makes it an easy drink.

Outside of the brewery they have been distributing their beers around Clark County
at various restaurants and bars.

With a solid core of beers, they offer an array of mostly American-style ales.
Their **Lucid Golden Ale** has become one of their most popular beers, with plenty
of taste compared to many golden ales available. Look for their **Couverino CBA,** a
brown ale brewed darker than normal. Named after Vancouver, it has a slight roasted
nutty flavor with plenty of hops to keep things in line.

MT. TABOR BREWING COMPANY
113 W. 9th St., Vancouver, WA 98660; (360) 696-5521; MtTaborBrewing.com;
@MtTaborBrewing
Founded: 2010 **Founder:** Eric Surface **Brewer:** Eric Surface **Flagship Beer:** P5 Pale
Ale **Year-Round Beers:** P5 Pale Ale, Hudson's Bay CDA, Red Lion Red, Little Bull Stout,
Bridge Lifter IPA **Seasonals/Special Releases:** The Calf Stout, Rocket Blonde, Butch's
Angry Beaver, Bike Lane IPA, Pale Torque Ale, Sibeerian Bull, Orange Glo IPA, Asylum Ave.
IPA, Block 9 Porter, Angry Bull Stout, and many more **Tours:** No **Taproom:** Yes

Mount Tabor is a volcanic cinder cone in Portland that is home to a neighborhood that bears its name along with a big city park on top. So how does a
brewery located in Vancouver, Washington, end up with a name from the other side
of the river? Eric Surface and Brian Maher originally founded Mt. Tabor Brewing
Company in the Mount Tabor neighborhood in 2009. In 2011 Eric set his eyes on
Vancouver and noticed that the once-barren downtown was starting to show some

Beer Lover's Pick

Hudson's Bay CDA
Style: Cascadian Dark Ale
ABV: 6.2%
Availability: Year-Round

In Vancouver, Hudson's Bay is an area high school, a neighborhood, and a hopped-up Cascadian dark ale. The beer is as dark as a stout yet has a light enough body that makes you feel like you're drinking an IPA. Rich roasted malts with a touch of chocolate give way to a big and dry hoppy finish. This is a CDA that hop lovers will really enjoy, as it gives you a little punch not often found in middle-of-the-road beers of this style.

signs of life. In October 2011 he relaunched the brewery in downtown Vancouver with a much bigger brewing system.

Since the move, Mt. Tabor has been producing its Northwest-style beers and distributing them around the area in kegs. They also run their taproom on Thursday and Friday nights so you can come in and try their beer and have a good time. You can also get a growler fill to go and choose out of their 6 beers they usually have on draft.

They offer a handful of year-round and seasonally brewed beers. Their **P5 Pale Ale** is a crisp and citrusy pale ale that doesn't have your typical American pale ale flavor that scares away non-hopheads. If you enjoy good Northwest-style beers, chances are you'll find something you'll enjoy.

ST. HELENS BREWING COMPANY
117 Grand Fir, Toledo, WA 98591; (360) 864-4029; StHelensBrewingCo.com
Founded: 2011 **Founders:** Chris and Callie Fraser **Brewer:** Chris Fraser **Flagship Beers:** Fire Dog Red and Apocalypse Ale **Year-Round Beers:** Callie's Comet, Ashkiker Trappist, American Classic Pilsner, Apocalypse Ale, Fire Dog Red **Seasonals/Special Releases:** Pumpkin Butt, Winter Warmth **Tours:** No **Taproom:** Yes

The small town of Toledo is home to fewer than 1,000 residents. It's known more as a town you pass through to go visit Mount St, Helens. Because of its proximity to the famous volcano, brewer Chris Fraser decided to name his brewery St. Helens Brewing Company. The small brewery was launched in 2011 with distribution in just a handful of locations around the area. Most of their beer was available

Callie's Comet
Style: Dark Ale
ABV: 5.2%
Availability: Year-Round
Named after brewer Chris Fraser's wife, Callie, this is one dark ale that would be difficult to classify as any particular style. Think of it as a non–dark beer drinker's dark beer. Despite being fairly black in color, it has an incredibly light mouthfeel that could make this into a very good session beer. Callie's Comet has subtle roasted coffee and chocolate notes without the bitterness of a porter, and gets better the farther you get into your pint. If you're looking for big, bold flavors, look elsewhere. However, if you want an easy-drinking darker beer, give Callie's a try.

around Toledo but could be found in 22-ounce bottles as far south as Camas. After just a short while it was time for the next step, so Fraser and his wife bought the one bar in town, named Harry's Place, and turned it into the family-friendly St. Helens Tap Room and Grill. You can now find their lineup of St. Helens Brewing Company beers on the taps along with a range of beers from other breweries. Along with beer at the taproom, which is located at 112 Ramsey Way, you can also find a decent dinner menu with everything from burgers to prime rib. The place definitely has the small-town local-joint feel, with live rock and blues music a regular occurrence.

Year-round you can find a small but interesting beer selection. Their **Callie's Comet** is a dark ale that is light enough to drink all night. They also offer another easy-drinking and true-to-style **American Classic Pilsner.** One of their more interesting beers is the **Apocalypse Ale,** brewed with anise to give it a strong black-licorice taste. Along with their main beers they also offer a few seasonal small-batch beers throughout the year.

WALKING MAN BREWING

240 1st St., Stevenson, WA 98648; (509) 427-5520; @WalkingmanBeer
Founded: 2000 **Founder:** Bob Craig **Brewer:** Cory McGuinness **Flagship Beer:** Walking Man IPA **Year-Round Beers:** Walking Man IPA, Homo Erectus, Knuckle Dragger, Crosswalk Wheat, Ramblin' Raspberry, Walking Stick Stout **Seasonals/Special Releases:** Santa's Little Black Homo, Big Black Homo, Sas-Squash Pumpkin Ale, Jaywalker, Black Cherry Stout, Barefoot Brown, Iron Man, Nomadic ISA, Pale Strider, Foot Fetish, Right of Way, Flip Flop Pilsner, Porter Porter, Biped Red, Stumblefoot, Kriek, High Road, and many more
Tours: No **Taproom:** Yes

What started as a hobby to make good, cheap beer turned into Bob Craig creating one of the most well-known brewpubs in the country. In 2000 he found a big house just a block off Highway 14 and turned the basement into a brewpub. He also created an outdoor area for people to enjoy on those few days of the year when it isn't raining. It didn't take long for word to spread and people came flocking to the small-town pub. With a specialization in big, flavorful beers, from hopped-up IPAs to thick, robust stouts, there isn't a beer they make that's bad. Along with multiple

Beer Lover's Pick

Jaywalker
Style: Russian Imperial Stout
ABV: 12.7%
Availability: Special Release
If you happen to come across Walking Man's Jaywalker Russian imperial stout, forget whatever else you were planning on ordering and order it. You won't be disappointed. Although it's rarely brewed, it does tend to show up at special occasions around the area. Dark roasted coffee flavors balance out the big typical stout flavors with a touch of oak that all comes together to hide the huge alcohol content. They've even released a bourbon barrel-aged version that could very well push it to be considered one of the best stouts in the world.

awards for their beer at international competitions, they were also named the 15th best brewpub in the world by RateBeer.com in 2010.

Beer drinkers in southwest Washington have been lucky that Walking Man has been able to brew enough to distribute their beers in kegs on a regular basis. Most people know them and appreciate them for their hoppy beers, such as their almost creamy **Walking Man IPA** and their big and balanced **Homo Erectus** imperial IPA that has a scarily unnoticeable 9% ABV. Their darker ales, such as the **Walking Stick Stout** and **Black Cherry Stout,** are all crafted so artistically in balance that you almost feel privileged to drink them. If you're visiting Stevenson, make sure to go to the pub. However, check their Facebook page for times or give them a call before you leave. Since it's a small town, they don't stay open all that late. And if you enjoy fish, try the smoked salmon pizza.

WEST HIGHLAND BREWING

18012 NE 22nd Way, Vancouver, WA 98684; (360) 883-5357; WestHighlandBrewing.com; @WestHighlandAle

Founded: 2010 **Founders:** Don Stewart and Sam Simms **Brewers:** Don Stewart and Sam Simms **Flagship Beer:** None **Year-Round Beers:** Michel's Brown Porter, Harris Hawk IPA, Morning Mist Ale **Seasonals/Special Releases:** Mango Ale **Tours:** No **Taproom:** No

Don Stewart and Sam Simms had a combined 25 years of homebrewing experience before they decided to take their hobby and turn it into a business. Between their passion for brewing and their love of West Highland terriers, they ended up naming their business West Highland Brewing Company. Based in a garage in Vancouver, the pair produces their line of beers one barrel at a time and distributes it in kegs to a handful of restaurants around the area. While many breweries in the area choose to create ultra-bitter hop bombs for beers, their philosophy is to lower the IBUs (international bittering units) and create beers with low bitterness, low alcohol content, and low carbonation. The result is a range of beers that aren't meant to wreck your palate, but provide an enjoyable time of drinking.

Their beers do tend to be tough to find at times, though restaurants around the area, such as the Blind Onion, Juliano's Pizza, and the Cascade Bar & Grill, have all been known to carry a few on draft. Instead of brewing a lot of styles, they tend to offer just a few and do each of them pretty well. Their **Michel's Brown Porter** is a low 4.5% ABV brown ale with hints of coffee and nuts that is excellent to drink on its own or alongside a chocolate-based dessert. **Harris Hawk IPA** is only 4.3% ABV, but plenty of Northwest-style hops give it a tasty floral flavor. While they don't offer a taproom, their Facebook page is your best bet to find out where their beer is pouring.

Mango Ale
Style: Pale Ale
ABV: 6.4%
Availability: Seasonal

At the inaugural Vancouver Brewfest in 2012, most attendees had their first experience with West Highland Brewing and their Mango Ale. Of all the beers being poured, this particular beer ended up winning the people's choice award. Brewed with mangos and spices, this pale ale is all about the fruity sweetness, yet it has enough bitterness to rein it in. Try pairing it with either Hawaiian teriyaki-based dishes or Asian barbecue for the ultimate summertime treat.

WESTPORT BREWING COMPANY

118 W. Pacific Ave., Westport, WA 98595; (307) 421-4411; WestportBrewing.com; @WestyBrewing
Founded: 2011 **Founder:** Mark Wagner **Brewer:** Mark Wagner **Flagship Beer:** None **Year-Round Beers:** Wetsuit Wheat, Bleach Bottle Blonde, Cohasset Cream Ale, Kaleidoscope Kölsch, Horizontal Premium Bohemian Pilsner, Sailor's Delight Amber Ale, Bucking Orca Bock, Bottle Beach Brown Ale, Plank Island Porter, Shoalwater Stout, Navigator India Pale Ale, Riptide India Red Ale, Neptune's Imperial India Pale Ale, Dungeness Dark India Black Ale **Seasonals/Special Releases:** Cranberry Stout, Cranberry Kölsch, Cranberry Blonde Ale, Cranberry Kriek, Cranberry Porter **Tours:** No **Taproom:** Yes

For years the Washington coast has been lagging behind the rest of the state when it comes to beer culture. It's an area that caters to tourists and offers plenty of adventure, but all along the coast there hadn't been a craft brewery in operation since 1944. Then in 2011, brewer Mark Wagner set up his brewery in the coastal town of Westport. With a long background in brewing and advanced degrees in both cell physiology and biology, Wagner turns brewing into a beautiful blend of science and art. The brewery itself is a three-barrel system similar to many others out there, but they use plastic fermenters instead of the commonly used stainless steel. According to Mark it isn't about cost savings, but he believes that polyethylene fermenters help to produce better beer. Upon tasting their beers, you would have a hard time arguing any other way.

With a lineup of close to 20 beers along with a series of seasonally brewed styles, they give you plenty of options to sample. In their India ale series, they offer 4 hop-packed brews, including their popular **Navigator India Pale Ale,** the balanced **Riptide India Red Ale,** the big and hefty **Neptune's Imperial India Pale Ale,** and the dark and roasty **Dungeness Dark India Black Ale.** Seasonally they release a series of beers using locally grown cranberries including a stout, Kölsch, porter, blonde ale, and Kriek, a tart beer released in the fall. You can find Westport beers on draft at multiple locations on the west side of the state from Seattle all the way down to Vancouver. In Westport make sure to visit their taproom to get a sample, pint, or growler fill of a great number of beers.

Beer Lover's Pick

Cohasset Cream Ale
Style: Cream Ale
ABV: 4.9%
Availability: Year-Round
If you're looking for a beer to help cross over your macrobeer-loving friends into craft-beer fans, Cohasset Cream Ale just might be what you reach for. It's also a go-to beer after working hard doing yard work. Heck, you can enjoy it while doing yard work. This cream ale uses lager yeast that's fermented at ale temperatures to create the creaminess. Light and crisp, it has gentle flavors of grainy cereal, corn nuts, and just a touch of earthy hops to keep you engaged.

Brewpubs

ACADIAN FARMS

342 Carson Creek Rd., Carson, WA 98610; (509) 427-4297; AcadianOrganics.com
Founded: 2012 **Founder:** Benton Bernard **Brewer:** Benton Bernard **Flagship Beer:**
None **Year-Round Beers:** Porter, IPA, 4 Grain Pale Ale **Seasonals/Special Releases:**
Strawberry Wheat, Chocolate Espresso Stout, Butternut Squash Barleywine, Saison,
Berliner Viesse, English Mild, as well as various IPAs **Tours:** Yes **Taproom:** Yes

A small family farm located in the breathtaking Columbia River Gorge, Acadian
Farms grows a wide variety of organic fruits and vegetables. In the nanobrewery
located on the farm, they brew farmhouse ales when they are not tending to the
crops. Made with certified organic malts, barley, and regional hops, this farm brews
only small batches of handcrafted beer only 10 gallons at a time. With an outdoor
seating area that has beautiful views of the gorge, patrons can relax with a great
view and enjoy any one of the more than 5 beers on tap at Acadian Farms.

Try a refreshing **Strawberry Wheat** from Acadian while you're relaxing in the
outdoor seating area. This American pale wheat ale has plenty of strawberry and
light wheat malts. This is definitely a brew to enjoy on a nice day. Fresh-baked
bread, cheese, jams, pickles, and even farm-fresh eggs are available at this farm
as well. This is a very family-friendly environment—even the farm animals love
visitors.

BACKWOODS BREWING COMPANY

1162 Wind River Rd., Carson, WA 98610; (509) 427-3412; BackwoodsBrewingCompany
.com
Founded: 2012 **Founder:** Kevin Waters **Brewer:** Kevin Waters **Flagship Beer:** None
Year-Round Beers: Copperline Ale, Red Bluff Ale, Ridge Run Stout, Imperial Brown,
Clear Cut Pale, Blueberry Wheat, Log Yard IPA **Seasonals/Special Releases:** The
Bumbler, Shortfall IPA, End of Summer Ale, Red Sled IMP, Spring Ahead Red, Beacon Rock
ESB, Carson IPA, Backwoods Brown, and more **Tours:** No **Taproom:** Yes

Located in the heart of the Columbia River Gorge, this rustic 10-barrel brewpub
reflects the legacy of logging that is a big part of the area. The bar is made of
3- to 4-foot slabs of wood with the seating area using the same, and the bar stools
utilize heavy branches for their legs. To give an idea of the rustic-ness of this establishment, one can sit outside, sip a brew, and watch cattle grazing in the fields set
against a backdrop of the Oregon Cascade Mountains.

While enjoying the serenity of the Cascades and the cows, taste a pint of **The Bumbler,** a buzzing 10.3% ABV brew that weighs in at a whopping 104.5 IBUs. Each batch is made with 20 pounds of honey and uses all Cascade hops. Pair it with the IPA Braised Brisket Nachos, which include jack cheese, pico de gallo, jalapeños, black beans, roasted corn, sour cream, and olives.

Feeling a bit on the patriotic side? Opt for the Red, White, and Bleu pizza. With pepperoni, olives, and blue cheese, you may as well pair it with a pint of the **Backwoods Brown.** With mellow malt flavor and a clean finish, this is a good brew to get the delicious yet pungent bleu cheese to wave the white flag.

LAURELWOOD PUBLIC HOUSE AND BREWERY

1401 SE Rasmussen Blvd., Battle Ground, WA 98604; (360) 723-0937; LaurelwoodBrewpub.com; @Laurelwood1

Founded: 2001 (Battle Ground location opened in 2009) **Founders:** Mike De Kalb and Cathy Woo–De Kalb **Brewer:** Vasili Gletsos **Flagship Beer:** Workhorse IPA **Year-Round Beers:** Organic Free Range Red, Mother Lode Golden Ale, Workhorse IPA, Space Stout, Organic Tree Hugger Porter **Seasonals/Special Releases:** Organic Portland Roast Espresso Stout, Mexican Mocha Ale, Organic Pale Ale, Imperial Workhorse IPA, Moose & Squirrel, Battle Ground Bock, Organic Deranger Imperial Red Ale, Vinter Varmer, Stingy Jack Pumpkin Ale, Portlandia Pils, Green Mammoth, Ink Heart, Portland Pale Project Series, and many more **Tours:** No **Taproom:** Yes

While you could technically say Laurelwood is an Oregon brewery since it's based in Portland, the brewpub in Battle Ground has brought fresh much-needed craft beer to this area of Washington. The majority of the beer both served at the pub and distributed in bottles is brewed at their Sandy Boulevard location in Portland. However, when you walk into the Battle Ground public house, look to your left and you will notice a small two-barrel system crammed in the corner. You can find experimental and small-batch beers that have been brewed on the small system, although it often seems that it goes unused. Don't let that stop you from making a visit. Their flagship location is just 30 minutes away, so they always have plenty of good, fresh beer on draft. On top of that, Laurelwood's owner Mike De Kalb is from Battle Ground, so he has a good feel for what people in the area want. What makes the pub such a wonderful addition to the area is its family-friendly aspect. With a kids' play area and a tasty children's food menu, the little ones will be kept busy while the adults relax and drink good beer.

IPA fans going to Laurelwood need to order their **Workhorse IPA.** It's one of the best in the Northwest. Aside from the Workhorse, they also offer a handful of other year-round beers, including their creamy **Space Stout,** a roasty **Organic Tree Hugger Porter,** and their well-known and highly drinkable **Organic Free Range Red.** In Battle Ground you'll usually find 4 or 5 more seasonal and rotating beers to choose from as well. Look for the **Organic Deranger,** a hefty imperial red with plenty of caramel malt sweetness. Outside of their pubs you can also find Laurelwood's beers around Oregon and southwest Washington in bottles.

THE OLD IVY TAPROOM AT SALMON CREEK BREWERY
108 W. Evergreen Blvd., Vancouver, WA 98660; (360) 993-1827
Founded: 1994 **Founders:** Larry and Ana Pratt **Brewer:** Tomas Munoz **Flagship Beer:** None **Year-Round Beers:** Creekfest, Main Street Ale, Weizenbock **Seasonals/Special Releases:** Creekfest, Ma Liberty IPA, Weizenbock, Fresh Hop IPA **Tours:** No **Taproom:** Yes

The Old Ivy Taproom is a cozy brewpub located in downtown Vancouver. Once named the Salmon Creek Brewpub, it changed owners in 2012 and everything including the beer was changed when it was relaunched. With lots of real ivy climbing up the rustic redbrick exterior, the courtyard is nestled between the brewpub as well as the next-door business, which just happens to be a bottle shop. After dinner and a few pints at the Old Ivy Taproom, make the five-step trek to By the Bottle, located in the old Salmon Creek Brewpub's party room, to peruse the selection of beers from all over the world available for purchase.

With an antique-looking wood bar and a stamped ceiling, the atmosphere of the Old Ivy Taproom beckons patrons to come in and imbibe. With 4 or 5 in-house brews, as well as over 18 guest taps, there is plenty of brew to choose from. **Creekfest,** an amber ale that is a spin on an Oktoberfest beer, has a light floral aroma and a hint of malt on the nose. With light malts on the palate, this beer finishes bitter as the floral hops make their presence known. Pair it with a Fressen pretzel with beer cheese and stone-ground mustard. This is a pretty standard soft pretzel, but dipped in the beer cheese, it becomes quite a bit more. The cheese comes out quite hot and contains the house-made Weizenbock beer.

RAILSIDE BREWING

421 C St. 1B, Washougal, WA 98671; (360) 907-8582; RailSideBrewing.com
Founded: 2012 **Founders:** Mike Davis and Anna Davis-Postrozny **Brewer:** Mike Davis
Flagship Beer: None **Year-Round Beers:** Hopper Car IPA, Railside Pale, Northwest IPA
Seasonals/Special Releases: Cherry Stout, Winter Warmer, Oktoberfest, Pumpkin Ale
Tours: By appointment **Taproom:** Yes

Railside Brewing, run by a husband-and-wife team, is nestled in a little industrial area right next to the Amtrak Empire Builder rail lines in Washougal. You'll know you have arrived when you're inside this cozy, cabin-esque building. The stone fireplace and rustic mantel have a quaint, homey feel and welcome patrons to come in for a brew. With country music playing and a train rattling down the track, this place is aptly named.

So if you're in the area or just train hitching, pop in for a **Northwest IPA.** This Northwest-style IPA has a citrus nose with hints of earthiness. A medium mouthfeel with hints of pine balances this brew on the finish. Pair it with the house beer cheese, made with sharp cheddar cheese and one of the three in-house beers and served with crackers. Looking for an extra-hearty meal before they call "All aboard"? Try the **Cherry Stout,** which has intense coffee and chocolate notes with just a hint of cherries. Complete the meal with *bigos* (Hunter's Stew), a traditional Polish dish made with two kinds of cabbage and the finest cuts of beef and pork.

Beer Bars

A BEER AT A TIME

2926 E St., Washougal, WA 98671; (360) 835-5200; ABeerAtATime.com; @ABeerAtATime
Draft Beers: 46 **Bottled/Canned Beers:** 450

Washougal residents are finally able to enjoy decent beer without having to head into Portland or Vancouver. With the addition of Railside Brewing and Amnesia Brewing opening up in town, beer lovers are fortunate to have A Beer at a Time to experience an amazing selection of great craft brews. In fact, the small bar attached to a liquor store offers more beers on draft than any other establishment in the county. With a rotating 46 beers on draft, deciding what to drink is the toughest part of your visit. You won't find any macrobrews filling up the tap lines either. Each beer selected is unique, with plenty of seasonal and hard-to-find beers that can't be found pouring anywhere else in the area.

The outside looks more like an old liquor store than a beer bar flowing with malt and hoppy goodness. Inside, however, you can turn right and shop for liquor or head

left into the wood-filled bar and bottle shop. Big wooden tables that look as if they were sliced right out of a big log fill the room, while deer-antler chandeliers give you the feeling you're out in the country. A wall of coolers filled with around 450 bottled and canned beers line one wall, giving you the option to do a little shopping while enjoying your beers. The shop doesn't have a kitchen on site, but the owners bought what was previously Evergreen Pieway and turned it into Beacon Rock Pub and Grill just a few doors down from A Beer at a Time. Patrons of the bar can order right off the Beacon Rock menu and they'll bring it over and add it to your tab.

BRICKHOUSE BAR & GRILL
109 W. 15th St., Vancouver, WA 98660; (360) 695-3686; VancouverBrickhouse.com; @WABrickhouse
Draft Beers: 20 **Bottled/Canned Beers:** About 20

For years downtown Vancouver was a pretty sad place if you were a beer lover. There wasn't any place that had the same love for craft beer as the neighbors to the south in Portland. That all changed once Brickhouse Bar & Grill took over a building that has seen its share of dive bars over the years. Inside, the dimly lit building has lots of character, with old brick walls, multiple couch seating areas, wooden floors, neon signs, bikes hanging around and plenty of interesting art. Up

MashFest

Twice a year homebrewers around Clark County get together in downtown Vancouver for MashFest, a small festival celebrating homebrewed beer. You can sample over 15 beers from local homebrewers and chat with them about their brewing process. Brewers can win People's Choice and Brewer's Choice awards. Due to Washington law, you can't show up at the door expecting to buy tickets, so make sure you get tickets in advance to this limited event. For more information, visit the event website at mintteaimports.com/events/mashfest.

front is a small bar where you can choose to head right into the dining area, which also houses a stage for live music, or keep walking straight to the lounge in the back where the second bar is located with plenty of options for entertainment. Up front is a large shuffleboard, as well as pool tables, darts, and a jukebox. On nice days you can enjoy your drinks and food out in the covered patio. What sets Brickhouse apart from other bar-style restaurants is their focus on being family-friendly. In the dining area is a kids' play area along with a varied children's menu. Don't worry, if you don't want to be surrounded by kids, just head to the lounge, where it's strictly 21 and over and the little ones are nowhere to be seen.

The rotating tap list focuses heavily on West Coast beers, offering a wide range of styles to fit pretty much any mood. From brewery standards to seasonal and special releases, they often carry beers not found anywhere else in Vancouver. You'll find plenty of pub food available, including a menu of salads, sandwiches, burgers, and a handful of entrees. Make sure to check their Twitter account for upcoming events, as they often have live music on the weekends.

NORTHWEST LIQUID GOLD

11202 NE Fourth Plain Blvd., Vancouver, WA 98662; (360) 326-4281;
NorthwestLiquidGold.com; @NWLiquidGold
Draft Beers: 20 **Bottled/Canned Beers:** About 200

When Northwest Liquid Gold first started out, it offered Northwest-brewed beers strictly through their website, shipping beer all over the country. Over time owners Pete and Travis decided to open up a bottle shop to bring quality beer to a fairly neglected area of town for those seeking craft brews. Shortly afterward they turned the business into a bottle shop/tavern and were forced to stop online sales due to state regulations. Luckily for the thirsty residents of Clark County, they have gotten better as time has passed, and now offer 20 rotating taps of a wide range of beers that are available for growler fills, pints, and even 4-ounce pours.

Located in an older strip mall off Fourth Plain Boulevard, the shop doesn't look like much from the outside. With a few seats at the bar up front and a couple of small tables, it does tend to get packed during weekend evenings and game days. During the summer they open up the beer garden outside, providing plenty more seating and the chance to enjoy some quality beer in the fresh air. Along with a fantastic tap list and a bottle selection of a mix of local beers, rare and hard-to-find special releases, and seasonals, they also offer many events throughout the year. Quite often you'll find brewery tastings, where a brewery takes over a handful of their taps and sends out a representative to talk beer. You'll find frequent tap list updates and event details on their Facebook page. Although they don't serve food on the premises, there are plenty of restaurants nearby to grab some grub to bring in on your way to the bar.

BREWERIES

Brewery	No.
Alpine Brewing Company	1
Ancient Lakes Brewing Company	6
Bale Breaker Brewing Company	11
Columbia Valley Brewing	5
Horse Heaven Hills Brewery	13
Ice Harbor Brewing Company	21
Ice Harbor Brewery @ The Marina	20
Icicle Brewing Co	4
Iron Horse Brewery	9
Old Schoolhouse Brewery	2
Roslyn Brewing Company	8
Snipes Mountain Brewing	12
St. Brigid's Brewery	7
Yakima Craft Brewing Co.	10

BREWPUBS

Brewpub	No.
Atomic Ale Brewpub & Eatery	18
Kimo's Sports Bar	19
Methow Valley Brewing Company/ Twisp River Pub	3
Shrub Steppe Smokehouse Brewery	15
White Bluffs Brewing	16
Whitstran Brewing Company	14

BARS

Bar	No.
West Richland Beer & Wine	17

Central Washington

0   20   40 miles

0   0.4   0.4 mile

Inset

Central Washington

For years central Washington has been a pivotal part of the brewing industry in the state and beyond. This section of the state, specifically the Yakima Valley, is home to about 75 percent of the total US hop acreage. Yakima is also home to the nation's very first brewpub, Yakima Craft Brewing, which was opened in 1982. You would think an area that is so engulfed in beer culture would also produce some of the state's best beer. While good beer has been brewed in central Washington, it hasn't been until recent years that it has started picking up and getting beer lovers excited.

In Ellensburg, Iron Horse Brewery has exploded on the scene, while up in Oroville, Alpine Brewing Company is producing some of the best German-style beers around. In Sunnyside, Snipes Mountain Brewing is brewing styles that would excite beer geeks in Seattle. All over the area you can find brewpubs in even the smallest of towns. It might not be an area of the state you'd think of first if you're looking at doing pub crawls, but hop in the car (responsibly) and get your central Washington beer-cation started.

Breweries

ALPINE BREWING COMPANY

821 14th Ave., Oroville, WA 98844; (509) 476-9662; Alpine-Brewing.com
Founded: 2000 **Founder:** Bart Traubeck **Brewer:** Bart Traubeck **Flagship Beer:**
Bohemian Pilsner **Year-Round Beers:** Märzen, Bohemian Pilsner, HefeWeizen,
DunkelWeizen **Seasonals/Special Releases:** Oktoberfest, WeizenBock, Bavarian Light,
WinterBock **Tours:** Call if interested **Taproom:** Yes

Right in the center of the state near the Canadian border lies the small town of Oroville, right on the southern tip of Osoyoos Lake. The town of less than 2,000 residents is surrounded by the eastern outskirts of the Cascade Mountains. Founded in the late 1850s as a mining settlement, it's now known mainly for tourism. It's also an interesting place to find one of the state's best lager-producing breweries, Alpine Brewing Company. In the 1990s it was originally founded as Buchanan Brewing. Current owner Bart Traubeck was involved with the brewery at the time but wasn't an owner. After securing a 35-barrel copper brewhouse from a brewery that closed in Bavaria, the company was able to produce beer for just a year before the economy got the best of it. Bart was able to purchase the brewery, sitting empty for almost three years, from the bank and reopened it as the Alpine Brewing Company.

The choice to brew authentic German-style beers was an easy one for the brewery. Bart grew up in Germany, where he went to school at the Technical University of Munich to study the art of brewing. His past experience has helped him create a lineup of authentic German beers rivaled by few in the state. Year-round they offer a malty-tasting **Märzen;** a **HefeWeizen** with plenty of banana and clove notes; and the popular **Bohemian Pilsner,** one of the easiest-drinking and best lagers in the state. While they don't offer a whole lot of seasonals, they do offer a couple. They also celebrate Oktoberfest with one of their most popular beers, their own smooth, full-bodied **Oktoberfest.**

Their distribution reaches across central and eastern Washington and parts of the Puget Sound area, where they make their brews available both on draft and in 22-ounce bottles. If you're in Oroville, you can visit the brewery, which is housed in a downtown building that was a car dealership in the early 1900s. Their beer garden is fantastic on clear days, especially when they have live music playing.

Beer Lover's Pick

Märzen
Style: Märzen
ABV: 5.2%
Availability: Year-Round
Just like its simple name, Alpine's Märzen is a beer that's simply brewed true to style. Conditioned for eight weeks before being served, this lager is incredibly clean, very smooth, and packed with a well-balanced flavor and malty aroma. A touch of hops is backed by a fruity yet caramel taste in this full-bodied brew that is tasty enough for just about any palate to appreciate. As with any traditionally brewed Märzen, pair it with German cuisine, such as sausages, wiener schnitzel, or anything with sauerkraut.

ANCIENT LAKES BREWING COMPANY
21547 Road 11.2 NW, Quincy, WA 98848; (888) 270-2760; AncientLakesBrewing.com
Founded: 2010 **Founder:** John Cedergreen **Brewer:** Mike Silk **Flagship Beer:** None
Year-Round Beers: Quincy Gold, Fossilhead Hefeweizen, Silk Pale, I-90 IPA, Antler Dance Amber, Small Town Brown, Potholes Porter, Steamboat Stout **Seasonals/Special Releases:** Cherry Bomb, Tribulation **Tours:** No **Taproom:** No

The number of wineries opening in the town of Quincy and the surrounding areas has been increasing exponentially over the past few years. While on a trip to the Napa Valley, Quincy resident John Cedergreen found out that many of the winemakers are also fans of good beer. He realized that there were only a few breweries around Washington wine country and set out to fix that. The only problem was that he didn't know how to brew beer. Fortunately, he joined with local homebrewer Mike Silk and created the Ancient Lakes Brewing Company in a garage outside of town. The name comes from a small chain of lakes in the area known as the Ancient Lakes and fits perfectly with who they were trying to become.

The small brewery isn't open to the public, yet they distribute their beers around the Quincy area one keg at a time. The ^{2}/$_3$-barrel system they brew on allows them to keg just four ^{1}/$_6$-barrel kegs with each batch, classifying them as one of the smallest nanobreweries in the state. Their size isn't holding them back from creating some delicious and well-crafted beers. With 7 year-round beers, their lineup consists of fairly standard American-style beers, ranging from a blonde ale all the way to a creamy, roasty, and chocolaty stout that they both keg and bottle from time to time.

Small Town Brown
Style: American Brown Ale
ABV: 6.4%
Availability: Year-Round
One of the great aspects of beer is that where a beer is made doesn't impact the flavor. In fact, some really good beers are produced in small towns across the US, such as Ancient Lakes' Small Town Brown. A true-to-style American brown ale, Small Town is dominated by sweet malts that have a hoppy presence in the background. The versatile brown ale would pair perfectly with a number of foods, such as a thick steak on the grill, a roast beef sandwich, or a side of baked fall vegetables.

They also release a handful of seasonal beers including their **Tribulation** barleywine, a big 10% ABV beer that gets released in bottles and disappears fairly quickly. Since they're still fairly small, make sure to check their website to find out where you can sample some of their beers.

BALE BREAKER BREWING COMPANY
1801 Birchfield Rd., Yakima, WA 98901; (509) 424-4000; BaleBreaker.com; @BaleBreaker
Founded: 2012 **Founders:** Mike and Cheryl Smith, Patrick Smith, Meghann and Kevin Quinn, and Kevin Smith **Brewer:** Kevin Smith **Flagship Beers:** Topcutter IPA, Field 41 Pale Ale **Year-Round Beers:** Topcutter IPA, Field 41 Pale Ale **Seasonals/Special Releases:** None yet **Tours:** No **Taproom:** Yes

Since the late 1800s, Washington's Yakima Valley has been one of the premier hop-growing regions in the world. In fact, over 75 percent of the country's commercial hop production happens in the state. While many hop farms in the area are third and fourth generation, the area has always lagged in the number of breweries compared to the rest of the state. Because no breweries in the area were as close to the harvest as they could be, a family who was no newcomer to hops started Bale Breaker Brewing Company. In fact, the 10,000-square-foot brewery, constructed in 2012, is located in field 41 of the Smith family's hop field that was started by their great-grandparents in 1932, just a year before Prohibition ended. Within minutes of harvest, the hops technically could be in the brew kettle giving the beer its bitterness, flavor, and wonderful aromas.

Moxee Hop Festival

The Moxee Hop Festival kicks off the first weekend of August each year at Moxee City Park, right in the center of hop-growing country. The event offers plenty of food and craft vendors, games for kids, live music, a parade, karaoke, fireworks, a 5k run, a pancake breakfast, and of course plenty of beer. While you probably won't find rare beers pouring, the event is worth the trek out to celebrate the coming hop harvest. For more information, check out the event website at moxeehopfestival.org.

The name Bale Breaker comes from a specialized piece of equipment used by hop processing companies. When the hops are harvested, they're packed in 200-pound burlap-wrapped bales. The bale breaker is then used at the processing center to break apart the compressed bales before they are sent off to a pelletizing machine.

Field 41 Pale Ale
Style: Pale Ale
ABV: 4.5%
Availability: Year-Round
Named after the hop field the brewery is located in, Field 41 Pale Ale is packed with incredible hop aroma. However, once you take a sip you'll realize that even though there is a slight bitterness, the crisp citrus flavor and light malts make this an incredibly easy-drinking pale ale. It's very sessionable and would make an excellent accompaniment to a weekend camping trip, as the cans cause it to be an easy traveling companion.

Since launching in 2013, Bale Breaker Brewing Company has produced two beers available in cans. Their **Field 41 Pale Ale** has been dry hopped aggressively, giving it a powerful hop aroma, yet it's light and easy body makes it easy to drink. **Topcutter IPA** also is packed with plenty of Yakima Valley hops giving it a fruity, citrus, and floral flavor as well as aroma. The name comes from equipment used on the farm to remove hop vines from their trellis. Make sure to visit the taproom if you want to sample a pint or two, fill a growler, or buy a six-pack to take home.

COLUMBIA VALLEY BREWING

538 Riverside Dr., Wenatchee, WA 98801; (409) 888-9993; ColumbiaValleyBrewing.com
Founded: 2011 **Founders:** Dick Oakley, Rich Rossmeisl, Roman Rossmeisl **Brewer:** Oscar Castillo **Flagship Beer:** None **Year-Round Beers:** CVB Porter, Twisted Brown Ale, Bavarian Weizen, Lookout Lager, La Rubia the Blonde, Triple "C" Pale Ale **Seasonals/ Special Releases:** Wenatcheeweizen, The Suffocator, Oscar's Oktoberfest, Oscars Pale Ale, Suffocator Imperial Amber, Powerhouse IPA, Wild as Ale Pale, Liberator Amber, Pasayten Porter, Dirty Santa, and many more **Tours:** No **Taproom:** Yes

Columbia Valley Brewing became the first brewery to open its doors in Wenatchee in 2011. Located right near the Columbia River, the brewery offers plenty of comfy indoor seating at both tables and couches as well as 3 glass roll-up doors that open up to a 1,600-square-foot beer garden. Featuring both indoor and outdoor stages, the brewery can be a blast, especially in the summer months. While they don't offer food in the brewery, they do something few places don't: They offer free use of a propane grill so you can bring your own meat and cook it outside. On warm days it feels like an outdoor party with food cooking on the grill and live music.

On draft at the brewery you'll find a decent mix of their own house-brewed beers and guest taps from breweries all over the US. In the spring and summer, their **Wenatcheeweizen** does its job of quenching thirst. This Hefeweizen is full of wheat and lemon flavors and is very approachable. In the fall look for **Oscar's Oktoberfest,** a beer named after brewmaster Oscar Castillo.

For those in Wenatchee or surrounding areas, keep an eye out for their event schedule, as they offer plenty of fun ways to be entertained: everything from hot dog–eating contests and chili cook-offs to a range of live music and games on the 16-foot big screen. Plus they allow you to bring your dog.

Beer Lover's Pick

Suffocator Imperial Amber
Style: Imperial Red Ale
ABV: 8.6%
Availability: Rotating
Like a cross between an imperial red ale and a strong ale, Suffocator is a delicate monster of a brew. It's dark and mysterious looking with a small glow causing you to stop and stare at the beauty of its unfiltered body. Rich caramel, nuts, and dark fruit offer several layers of complexity to wade through before the earthy hops kick in for just a second and the malty sweetness takes over once again and finishes strong.

HORSE HEAVEN HILLS BREWERY

1118 Meade Ave., Prosser, WA 99350; (509) 781-6400; HorseHeavenHillsBrewery.com
Founded: 2009 **Founders:** Gary and Carol Vegar, Dave and Brenda Keller **Brewer:** Gary Vegar **Flagship Beers:** Dark Cherry Stout, Honey Girl, Buck Off IPA **Year-Round Beers:** Honey Girl, Horse Heaven Wheat, Stallion Stout, Dark Cherry Stout, Buck Off IPA, Ruby Spur, Live Long Lager, Delta Pale Ale **Seasonals/Special Releases:** Apricot Honey Girl, Saison, Smokin Anvil, Festivus IPA, Calyptonite Fresh Hop, Mustang Red, Heaven's Hefeweizen, Nut Brown, and many more **Tours:** No **Taproom:** Yes

Smack in the middle of wine country, Prosser is home to thriving wine culture and tourism. Horse Heaven Hills Brewery founder Gary Vegar and his wife, Carol, along with business partners Dave and Brenda Keller, have set out to make the town an attraction for beer lovers as well. From their beer names to the theme in their taproom, you'll find references to horses just about everywhere.

Back when they were setting up, they bought a seven-barrel copper brewery from a company in Auburn, Alabama, to put into their building, which once served as the area's Laundromat. Today you can visit their taproom to try their beers while checking out their brewing equipment. The building isn't anything spectacular, but it's a very comfortable spot to sit and drink beer, watch a game, or sing songs with friends on the piano. They've also been known to host live music and special events ranging from wakes to weddings and other celebrations.

They offer a wide range of what they call transitional beers; for those looking to make the crossover to craft beer, they have a wide range of styles that should draw

Central Washington

Breweries [193]

Dark Cherry Stout
Style: Stout
ABV: 4.9%
Availability: Year-Round

To make their Dark Cherry Stout, Horse Heaven Hills Brewery takes its standard Stallion Stout and amps it up with Yakima Valley cherries. The aroma will make you think you're smelling a cherry cola with a touch of roasted goodness. A touch of chocolate and coffee supports the cherry flavor, creating one delicious dessert beer. At the brewery they serve it on nitro, which is about the only way this creamy beer should be served other than with a scoop of vanilla ice cream in it.

you in. **Honey Girl** is one of their most popular offerings. At the end of the boil, they add 25 pounds of Snowberry honey to give it a smooth sweetness that balances out the slight bitterness. Since Prosser is so close to an abundance of wheat- and hop-growers, many of their beers use local ingredients; however, they also like to bring in specialty hops and malts from around the world to create styles outside the typical Northwest lineup.

ICE HARBOR BREWING COMPANY

206 N. Benton St., Kennewick, WA 99336; (509) 582-5340; IceHarbor.com
Founded: 1997 **Founders:** Mike Hall and Bill Jaquish **Brewer:** Russ Corey **Flagship Beer:** India Pale Ale **Year-Round Beers:** Columbia Kölsch Brand Ale, Runaway Red Ale, Harvest Pale Ale, Sternwheeler Stout, India Pale Ale, Tangerine ExBEERience, Hefeweizen
Seasonals/Special Releases: Dry Irish Stout, ESB, Fresh Hop IPA, Lighthouse Lager, India Winter Ale, Irish Red Ale, Nut Brown Ale, Pilsner, Uncle Herbert's Scottish Ale, Wallula Red, Barley Wine Style Ale, and many more **Tours:** No **Taproom:** Yes

Since 1997 residents of the tri-city area have been fortunate enough to drink consistent and quality beer produced by Ice Harbor Brewing Company. Started by two homebrewing friends who were former workers at the Hanford Site, the brewpub now offers two locations in Kennewick along with a small bottling line that allows them to distribute around eastern Washington. The brewery itself, along with the main brewpub, is located in what was once a grain mill right next to some

Sternwheeler Stout
Style: Stout
ABV: 5.5%
Availability: Year-Round

While stouts aren't often known as session beers, Ice Harbor's Sternwheel Stout could easily be classified as one. With a picture of a sternwheeler puffing smoke on the bottle, this brew has been a staple in Ice Harbor's yearly lineup. The dark-as-night stout has plenty of chocolate and roasted aromas with a touch of coffee in the background. While it looks thick, it actually has a fairly medium mouthfeel, allowing you to not get bogged down too much with the coffee, chocolate, roasted malts, and slight bitterness of the flavor. This is the stout for the non–stout drinker.

railroad tracks. Fittingly, much of their brewing equipment comes from old dairy equipment that has been given new life as fermenting tanks, although they have been slowly switching them out with conical fermenters.

Their core brand of beers is available year-round in 12-ounce and some 22-ounce bottles at both of their pubs. The 7 year-round beers include a Kölsch, red ale, stout, Hefeweizen, barleywine, pale ale, and their most popular: **India Pale Ale,** which was first brewed on September 11, 2001. Throughout the year you'll also find a range of seasonally brewed beers available mainly in their pubs. Over the years they've brewed over 100 different beers, with many being one-hit wonders while others continue to return year after year.

In Kennewick their two pubs offer the same beer, yet different experiences. At the brewery and pub you get the feeling you might be in a time warp. Inside looks old and well used, but it works. It has a definite local, comfortable vibe, allowing you to kick back and enjoy some solid brews and pub-style food in a relaxed atmosphere. Just a short drive away is their location at the Port of Kennewick marina. Built in 2007, it has a much more updated decor and a slightly different food menu. You'll find multiple menu items made using their beer, such as their Runaway Red Ale Meatloaf, or the Stout & Shroom Burger made with their delicious **Sternwheeler Stout.**

ICICLE BREWING COMPANY

935 Front St., Leavenworth, WA 98826; (509) 548-2739; IcicleBrewing.com; @IcicleBrewing

Founded: 2011 **Founders:** Oliver and Pam Brulotte **Brewer:** Dean Priebe **Flagship Beer:** Bootjack IPA **Year-Round Beers:** Khaos Kölsch, Lokal Lager, Dirtyface Amber, Bootjack IPA, Priebe Porter **Seasonals/Special Releases:** Apres Harvest, Raspberry Wheat, Freund Festbier, Big George, Fist Full of Quarters, Woody Goomsbock, Colchuck Hefeweizen, Ill Eagle Imperial IPA, Betty White Ale, Chumsticke Alt, Dark Persuasion, and many more **Tours:** Noon Sat and Sun by phone or e-mail reservation **Taproom:** Yes

For years the Bavarian town of Leavenworth was without a brewery after the Leavenworth Brewery merged with Fish Brewing Company and moved their operation to Olympia. Each year thousands of people visit the tourist town, yet while there, they had to settle on beer that was trucked in from other areas. Then in 2012 husband-and-wife team Oliver and Pam Brulotte decided to change that and opened up the Icicle Brewing Company after successfully starting München Haus, a Bavarian grill and beer garden just down the road. Being in a German-themed town, the brewery doesn't necessarily stick to that mold. It's true they produce some excellent German-style beers, such as their **Colchuck Hefeweizen** and **Khaos Kölsch,** but they also make sure to have a few American-style favorites, such as their **Bootjack IPA** and **Priebe Porter,** on draft so all palates will have something to enjoy.

Outside the tasting room, you can find their beers on draft and in bottles throughout central Washington and a few select locations as far east as Spokane and as far west as Federal Way. The best place by far to enjoy their beer is either at their München Haus restaurant in Leavenworth or the brewery's actual tasting room. The all-ages tasting room features a small handful of food items on the menu and a full selection of both their regular and seasonal beers.

Bootjack IPA
Style: IPA
ABV: 6.5%
Availability: Year-Round

Just about every brewery in the Northwest offers an IPA, yet all aren't created equal. While some wander over to the English IPA style, Icicle Brewing sticks to the traditional Northwest-style IPA with its hop-forward yet balanced Bootjack. Citrus and floral notes fill the aroma and are present throughout in the taste; however, a blend of caramel malt sweetness keeps the bitterness from getting too excessive. The emphasis on hop flavor and aroma without too much bitterness would make this a perfect IPA to pair with Indian curries, especially those with a little heat to them.

IRON HORSE BREWERY

1000 Prospect St., Ste. 4, Ellensburg, WA 98926; (509) 933-3134; IronHorseBrewery.com; @IronHorseBeer

Founded: 2004 **Founder:** Jim Quilter **Brewer:** Tyson Read **Flagship Beer:** Quilter's Irish Death **Year-Round Beers:** Quilter's Irish Death, 509 Style, High Five Hefe, Iron Horse IPA, Light Rail Ale, Malt Bomb **Seasonals/Special Releases:** Cozy Sweater, Black IPA, Double Rainbow, Mocha Death, Hop Hub Pale Ale, Loco Imperial Red, Cinco de Drinco, Insane with the Grain, and many more **Tours:** Call to schedule **Taproom:** Yes

In 2004 Jim Quilter founded Iron Horse Brewery in the city of Ellensburg. At the time the brewery looked very different than it does today, which can be attributed to a 2007 sale of the brewery to son-and-father team Greg and Gary Parker. While the brewery wasn't doing so well during its first few years of existence, Greg whipped things into shape once he took the reins and helped create one of the most beloved breweries in the state. Although a lot was changed in the transition, Quilter's legacy has lived on in the brewery, as he created the flagship **Quilter's Irish Death,** a huge malt bomb they like to call beer candy.

Along with their flagship Irish Death, Iron Horse also brews a range of both year-round and seasonal ales that don't adhere to traditional styles. If you enjoy a good beer after a day of mowing the lawn, hiking, or doing any kind of physical activity, give their smooth and hoppy **509 Style** a try. Named after the Eastside

Central Washington

Quilter's Irish Death
Style: Unclassified
ABV: 7.8%
Availability: Year-Round

When you see a skull and cross-bones on the label and a name such as Quilter's Irish Death, you know you are in for something big. The name Quilter is the last name of the brewery's founder, who created the recipe. It's so unique it's a tough beer to classify. While some call it a strong scotch ale, others call it something else. Whatever the style, it's a malty beer for sure. With very little hop presence in the flavor, it's all about the caramel and sweet bready malts. In fact, they use a massive amount of malt in each batch. It's the perfect beer for those non-hopheads out there.

area code, it's similar to their IPA in that it has plenty of hop flavor without the bitterness, yet it's a lot lighter, so you won't fill up on it so fast. **Mocha Death** is the perfect seasonal to drink with a late-night dessert; they take Irish Death and add locally roasted espresso beans and pure cocoa to create a sweet and creamy malt bomb booming with coffee.

Their tasting room is open 6 days a week for you to enjoy a few pints, fill up a growler, or buy some bottles to go. They also offer The Micropub on Main Street, which is exactly what it sounds like. You can visit The Micropub, housed in a tiny building, to enjoy at least 8 beers on draft, including a guest tap and a small selection of wines.

OLD SCHOOLHOUSE BREWERY

155 Riverside Ave., Winthrop, WA 98862; (509) 996-3183; OldSchoolHouseBrewery.com; @OldSchoolBrew

Founded: 2008 **Founders:** Casey and Laura Ruud **Brewer:** Blaze Ruud **Flagship Beer:** Ruud Awakening IPA **Year-Round Beers:** Ruud Awakening IPA, Imperial IPA, Imperial Stout, Uncle Big's Brown, Rendezvous Porter, Epiphany Pale, Hooligan Stout, New School ESB **Seasonals/Special Releases:** Fresh Hop IPA, Backcountry Coffee Stout, Barley Wine Style Ale, Double D Blonde, Blazing Amber, Winterbreak, School of Rock, Nightmare CDA, and many more **Tours:** No **Taproom:** Yes

In the tiny Old West–themed town of Winthrop you'll find rugged wooden buildings that remind you of many western movies. You'll get the urge to hop on your horse and ride down Riverside Avenue and make a stop at Three-Fingered Jack's

Beer Lover's Pick

Imperial Stout
Style: Imperial Stout
ABV: 9.9%
Availability: Special Release
With the waxed bottle and an elegant monochrome label with the Old Schoolhouse logo on it, you know you're in for a treat. Old Schoolhouse Brewery's Imperial Stout is a beer that needs to be drunk slowly to enjoy its complexities. Dark as night, the beer has an aroma filled with chocolate, roasted coffee, and vanilla. The creamy body coats your mouth, making sipping on this sweet beer delightful. With dark fruit, coffee, chocolate, roasted malts, and a touch of hops in the flavor, try closing your eyes and appreciate what you're drinking.

Saloon. While you might fit in, you'll probably want to head a little farther down the road until you see a worn red building, which is home to the Old Schoolhouse Brewery. The brewery itself was once home to Winthrop Brewing Company before Casey and Laura Ruud bought it, renamed it, and put their son Blaze to work as the head brewer in 2008. Since then they have grown the business in the small town to include distribution of their beer in 22-ounce bottles as well as taking home multiple awards on both the national and international levels.

If you get a chance to visit Winthrop, you should, especially in the summer. Old Schoolhouse Brewery's back beer garden is easily one of the best places to drink beer on the West Coast. The patio is located right along the banks of the Chewuch River and the beauty that surrounds it. They offer a full menu of pub fare that changes with the seasons.

Although the location is fantastic and the food tasty, their beer alone is worth making the trip. Luckily, if you're in other parts of the state, you can still find a selection of their beers in bottle shops around Washington and parts of Idaho and Oregon. IPA fans will appreciate both their Northwest-style **Ruud Awakening IPA** and its big brother, the **Imperial IPA.** Both have won awards at the Denver International Beer Competition.

ROSLYN BREWING COMPANY

208 Pennsylvania Ave., Roslyn, WA 98941; (509) 649-2232; RoslynBrewery.com; @Roslyn_Brewery

Founded: 1990 **Founders:** Dino Enrico, Roger and Lea Beardsley **Brewer:** Kent Larimer **Flagship Beer:** Roslyn Dark Lager **Year-Round Beers:** Roslyn Dark Lager, Brookside Pale Lager, #9 Root Beer **Seasonals/Special Releases:** Fa La La Lager, Roslyn Belgian Ale **Tours:** No **Taproom:** Yes

In the late 1800s large deposits of coal were found in the Roslyn area, prompting Northern Pacific Coal Company, a subsidiary of the Northern Pacific Railroad, to establish the town. For years the town was built around coal mining, which meant it didn't take long for a smart entrepreneur to open a brewery in the area. For close to 25 years the Roslyn Brewing and Malting Company brewed German-style beers that were delivered to local saloons by wagon. For just a nickel, the miners who were thirsty after a hard day of work would get a whole bucket of beer. Unfortunately, due to Prohibition the brewery was shut down in 1913.

Although coal mining in the area ceased in the 1960s, the tiny town survived. To carry on the tradition of days past, the Roslyn Brewing Company was formed in 1990. Much like the original brewery, the focus was on German-style lagers using malted barley and hops grown in Washington. With over 20 years of brewing experience, they still focus on what they do best and brew just 2 year-round beers. The flagship **Roslyn Dark Lager** was their original brew, resembling a recipe created by the German brewmeisters of the original Roslyn Brewing and Malting Company. They also offer their **Brookside Pale Lager,** a light beer that's been mildly hopped and named after the Brookside neighborhood in Roslyn. During the end of the year you can also find their **Roslyn Fa La La Lager,** which is a red lager brewed for the holidays.

In Roslyn the brewery has the appearance of an old saloon on the outside. Step inside and the taproom offers their beers along with a house-made root beer. No food is available, but they have a nice beer garden out back, perfect for bringing a picnic or food from other nearby establishments. Look for their beer throughout Washington both on draft and in 22-ounce bottles.

Beer Lover's Pick

Roslyn Dark Lager
Style: Dark Lager
ABV: 4%
Availability: Year-Round
At 4% ABV, this dark lager is a session beer that might not be for everyone, although it is well brewed, for those who enjoy the style. Brewed with four types of malts and three hop varieties, this smooth lager is full of sweet and roasty malt flavor with just a touch of coffee bitterness and a soft yet noticeable hop presence. For such a light session beer, you'll find a lot of complexities that would pair well with many smoked meats.

SNIPES MOUNTAIN BREWING

905 Yakima Valley Hwy., Sunnyside, WA 98944; (509) 837-2739; SnipesMountain.com; @SnipesBeer

Founded: 1997 **Founders:** Maryann and Gene Bliesner **Brewer:** Chad Roberts **Flagship Beer:** IPA **Year-Round Beers:** Coyote Moon, Extra Blonde Ale, IPA, Porter, Sunnyside Pale Ale **Seasonals/Special Releases:** Harvest Ale, Roza Reserve, Hefeweizen, Vaquero, Little Chief, Quinceañera: Prieta, New Sheriff, Quinceañera: Concepción, Red Sky ESB, No-Bake Stout, Golden Ale, Dos Borrachos, Dark Matters, Pumpkin Death, Coyote Azul, and many more **Tours:** No **Taproom:** Yes

In the mid 1800s a man by the name of Ben Snipes drove his cattle and settled in the Yakima Valley. He found the perfect spot to manage his cattle range, believed to have numbered over 35,000. A headquarters of sorts was built, consisting of a modest log cabin that fellow ranchers could recognize for miles. The area was known as Snipes Mountain. Unlike Snipes's small cabin, Snipes Mountain Brewing is housed in a fairly large building made of logs in the central Washington town of Sunnyside. The big brewpub is a spacious mountain lodge–style building offering a wide range of food and beers that will pique any beer geek's interest. Inside the pub you can look through the glass windows and watch as the beer is made right in front of you.

From blonde ales, pale ales, and IPAs, to more interesting styles, such as sour beers, saisons, and barleywines, they offer a wide range to choose from, especially in the pub. Outside the pub they offer limited 12- and 22-ounce bottles as well as

Vaquero
Style: Imperial IPA
ABV: 8.5% ABV
Availability: Special Release

A Spanish word for cattle herder, Vaquero is big and tough just like the name implies, yet has a soft side. Dark amber in color with a thin head, the beer has aromas of mandarins, orange peels, grapefruit and piney hops that are a delight to smell. Big, citrusy fruit flavors are incredibly balanced with pale grains and a finish that has very little lingering bitterness. In the past, they have served this on cask infused with Satus hops and ghost pepper jelly, resulting in a very interesting brew with a slight bite.

distribution across the state in kegs. Their **Coyote Moon** brown ale is just about the perfect beer to take camping or drink on a hot day. At 3.9% ABV and packed with plenty of toasted nut and chocolate flavors, it is quite refreshing. For those looking for something heftier, their **Roza Reserve** barleywine has plenty of complexity and a nice warming alcohol presence for sipping by the fire. Look for any of their sour beers, barrel-aged, or Belgian-style beers for some truly unique creations.

ST. BRIGID'S BREWERY

10333 Road 5.6 NE, Moses Lake, WA 98837; (509) 750-8357; StBrigidsBrewery.com
Founded: 2011 **Founders:** Tom and Whitney Wytko **Brewer:** Tom Wytko **Flagship Beer:** TKO Amber Ale **Year-Round Beers:** TKO Amber Ale, London Calling Brown Ale, Zone Three Pale Ale **Seasonals/Special Releases:** Snow Fall, The Great Pumpkin **Tours:** No **Taproom:** No

In 2011 Tom and Whitney Wytko figured it was time to take their 20-year hobby of homebrewing and turn it into a business. Moses Lake was the perfect destination of choice for their brewery since they were the only brewers in the city. The story behind the name St. Brigid's Brewery is very interesting for both beer geeks and for those interested in faith. Born around 457, St. Brigid of Ireland had an intriguing association with beer. One miracle attributed to her was when she once turned one barrel of beer into enough to supply 18 churches during the entire Easter season.

St. Brigid's Brewery offers 3 year-round beers. Their flagship **TKO Amber Ale** is packed with malt and citrus flavor and features tiny boxing gloves dangling on

London Calling Brown Ale
Style: English Brown Ale
ABV: 5.4%
Availability: Year-Round
With a name like London Calling Brown Ale, you can probably figure out that this is an English brown ale. One of the best parts of ordering this beer on draft is the tap handle, which features a red English phone booth on top. The smooth light-bodied ale is nutty with hints of molasses and chocolates shining through and ends with a fairly dry finish. The hop presence is barely there, making this a solid beer for the style.

top of its tap handle. Other than that, they brew **London Calling Brown Ale,** an English-style brown; and **Zone Three Pale Ale,** an easy-drinking pale ale packed with Cascade hops.

Since the brewery is built into the Wytkos' backyard, they don't currently offer a tasting room. However, make sure to check their website, as they have plans to open one in the near future. Until then you can look for their beer on draft around Moses Lake at multiple bars and restaurants, and pouring at various area beer festivals.

YAKIMA CRAFT BREWING CO.

2920 River Rd., #6, Yakima, WA 98902; (509) 654-7357; YakimaCraftBrewing.com; @YakimaCraftBrew

Founded: 2008 **Founder:** Jeff Winn **Brewer:** Chris Swedin **Flagship Beer:** None **Year-Round Beers:** Pale Ale, 1982, IPA, Vern, Twin Stag **Seasonals/Special Releases:** Bad Monk, Good Monk, Stout, Imperial Red, Heather, Lincoln Avenue Coffee Stout, Inland ESB, Fresh Hop Imperial Red, Summer Snow IPA, Winter Ale, and many more
Tours: Call to set up **Taproom:** Yes

Located in the heart of the nation's top hop-producing region, the Yakima Valley, Yakima Craft Brewing Co. has been carving out a name for itself using a historical piece of brewing equipment. The 3.5-barrel boil kettle they brew on was what

Beer Lover's Pick

Twin Stag Scottish Ale
Style: Scotch Ale
ABV: 6%
Availability: Year-Round
With a green label that has two stags in the background, Yakima Craft Brewing's Twin Stag Scottish Ale almost has a Christmas vibe to its look. Like many scotch ales, it tends toward the red side, complementing the green label. However, this is one dark brown beer with just a glimmer of copper highlights. They claim it's mysterious and complex, and that's the truth. Flavors of raisins, toffee, chocolate, roasted malt, earthy hops, and a touch of smoke lead to a full-flavored beer that is equally as drinkable as it is mysterious.

the legendary Bert Grant used when opening up the nation's first post-Prohibition brewpub in Yakima back in 1982. For those who haven't heard of Bert, he was one of the leading figures in the craft-brewing industry. At the time, no one else had created the brewpub model for a business, which was a pretty big deal. Today Yakima Craft Brewing Co. brewmaster Chris Swedin is crafting up plenty of tasty ales on the old copper kettle.

Year-round the brewery produces 5 beers along with a selection of seasonal and special releases available in both bottles and on draft. Locals love **1982,** a clean amber ale named after the year Bert Grant opened the first brewpub. Another favorite is their Northwest-style **IPA,** a well-balanced beer that received an A+ by the magazine *Beer Advocate*. Toward the end of the year keep an eye out for their seasonal **Bad Monk,** a Belgian-style dark ale with a beautiful nutmeg, clove, and spicy Belgian yeast aroma. Since their system is pretty small, your best bets for finding Yakima Craft Brewing beers are around Yakima and central Washington. The taproom in Yakima is the best spot to try all of their beers, and they'll occasionally have beers they don't release anywhere. It's a small room, so go with the mind-set that you're there to drink beer or fill up a growler. If they're slow, you might be able to ask them to show you the brewhouse featuring their old kettle.

Brewpubs

ATOMIC ALE BREWPUB & EATERY

1015 Lee Blvd., Richland, WA 99352; (509) 946-5465; AtomicAleBrewPub.com
Founded: 1997 **Founder:** Aaron Burks **Brewer:** John Kerley **Flagship Beer:** Atomic Amber **Year-Round Beers:** Half-Life Hefeweizen, Plutonium Porter, Atomic Amber **Seasonals/Special Releases:** Chinook IPA, Oppenheimer Oatmeal Stout, Seaborgium 106 Scottish Ale, Burs Blonde, International Proton Pale Ale, B-17 Brown Ale, Backscatter Blackberry Wheat, Snake Spice Ale, Jim's Radioactive Ale, Dysprosium Dunkel Weisen, Rad Dog Russian Imperial Stout, Happy Hippy Honey Red Ale, KRA Strawberry Blonde, Proton Pale Ale, Einstein's Enriched Barleywine, Einstein's Depleted Blonde Ale, Szilard's Cup of Coffee **Tours:** Yes

Just south of the site of the world's first operating plutonium reactor, Atomic Ale, a nuclear-themed three-barrel brewpub, lights up the tri-city area with its handcrafted ales. Founded in 1997, the Atomic Ale Brewpub was the first brewpub in Washington's Tri-Cities. With nuclear-themed brews and food, imbibing diners can enjoy all the word play without all the fallout. For instance, **Atomic Amber,** with slight maltiness on the nose, is a light-bodied brew with hints of fruit. Pair it with an Atomic giant soft pretzel, a hand-made pretzel shaped like an atom, served with spicy nuclear butter and blue cheese dressing.

Labeled as "world famous," the Atomic Ale'd Red Potato Soup is made with thin-sliced red potatoes, Canadian bacon, chopped onion, and a hint of thyme. This soup is also made with the house-brewed **Half-Life Hefeweizen,** so picking a beer to pair it with isn't difficult. Made with 60 percent wheat, the Half-Life Hefeweizen is a cloudy and crisp beer with hints of banana and pear.

Known for its wood-fired pizzas, Atomic Ale Brewpub has an interesting selection of pies to choose from as well. With more nuclear-themed cleverness, such as **Positron Pineapple, Atomic Red, Manhattan Project,** and the **Reactor Core,** you're assured of finding a pizza to match your specific tastes.

KIMO'S SPORTS BAR

2696 N. Columbia Center Blvd., Richland, WA 99352; (509) 783-5747; KimosSportsBar.com
Founded: 1997 **Founders:** Steve and Renea Metzger **Brewer:** Doug Ryder **Flagship Beer:** Helluva Hefe **Year-Round Beers:** Helluva Hefe, Honey Red Ale, Helluva Honey, Smoked Porter, Oatmeal Stout, Screaming Eagle IPA **Seasonals/Special Releases:** The Americans Amber, The Winter Wee **Tours:** Impromptu

Located in Richland, Kimo's Sports Bar (formerly Rattlesnake Mountain Brewing Company) is located right by the Columbia River. With a great view of the river, patrons get plenty of ambience as they dine and imbibe on the brews. With 6 year-round offerings as well as seasonals, there are a fair amount of options to choose from if you pop in to watch the game at this sports bar.

Washington Tops in Hops

To make beer you need four main ingredients: water, grains, yeast, and hops. In brewing, the flower of the hop plant (which is a member of the hemp family) is used to give beer bitterness, flavor, and aroma. The types of hops used, at what point the brewers add them to the boil, and the amount used all determine the outcome of the beer. Even stouts use hops to add dimension and balance out the flavor.

Washington is fortunate to be home to one of the premier regions in the world for growing hops, one of the most important ingredients in producing beer. Not only does it allow breweries in the state to get the freshest ingredients, but it also is big business and brings a lot of revenue into the state.

The Yakima Valley in central Washington is home to many multigenerational hop farms that account for over 77 percent of the total US hop crop. It's so big that nearly two-thirds of the hops grown in Washington are exported to other countries.

So why do hops grow so well in the Yakima Valley? A mix of plentiful irrigation created by the Yakima River watershed and desertlike conditions create a very productive and fertile growing area. The conditions are so stable in the area that crops tend to be fairly consistent year after year. Next time you're drinking a Northwest-style IPA or pale ale, make sure to stop and appreciate its hoppiness and take a drink for all the wonderful Washington hop farmers who made it possible.

If you stop in at this honky-tonk-looking joint, try a pint of the **Smoked Porter.** With an aroma of smoke and caramel, this reddish brown beer has a nice peppery flavor that has been smoked in-house using hickory. The light smoky malts finish this beer off well. Pair this pint with the earthiness of the portobello mushroom stuffers, which is large mushroom caps, lots of diced tomatoes and cheese. If lighter beer is more your thing, then try the **Rattlesnake Mountain Helluva Hefe.** This American-style wheat ale has notes of apple and banana on the nose. Crisp and dry, this beer is medium-bodied and has a sweet finish. Drink this for dessert with an order of the homemade Dutch apple cobbler.

METHOW VALLEY BREWING COMPANY / TWISP RIVER PUB

201 N. Methow Valley Hwy., Twisp, WA 98856; (509) 997-6822; MethowBrewing.com; @TwispRiverPub
Founded: 1998 **Founder:** Aaron Studer **Brewer:** Aaron Studer **Flagship Beers:** Cream Ale, ESB, Vienna Lager, Porter **Year-Round Beers:** Cream Ale, ESB, Vienna Lager, Porter **Seasonals/Special Releases:** Bock, India Pale Ale, Spiced Winter Ale, Cherry Hefeweizen, Summer Ale, Organic Pale Ale, Coffee Stout, Oatmeal Stout, Oktoberfest Double Stout, and more **Tours:** No

Methow Valley Brewing Company/Twisp River Pub has been serving patrons since 1998. For having such a small brewing system (3.5 barrels, about 100 gallons), the brewery has an impressive 10 taps of house-made brews for guests to choose from as well as a few guest taps. Methow Valley has a traditional beer engine that pulls the cask-conditioned offering into your glass. Although having different names, with Methow Valley Brewing providing the brew and the Twisp River Pub delivering the food, both reside in the same building.

If you find yourself in this dusty mountain town, stop by for a **Methow Valley Cream Ale.** With a fair amount of carbonation and a grainy aroma, this light golden brew is creamy with just a touch of bitter hops. The dry finish and smooth mouthfeel make this a great session beer that lends itself to food pairing rather well. Pair it with the sweet potato fries, which are thin-cut, crispy sweet potatoes topped with local goat cheese crumbles and drizzled with a balsamic glaze.

If you're looking for a heftier brew, grab a pint of the **Methow Valley Oatmeal Stout.** With heavy chocolate malt on the nose, this brew is more of a dark, dark brown as opposed to the more traditional black associated with stouts. Smooth with notes of vanilla and coffee, this brew culminates with the oatmeal and the sugars making their presence known. Chocolate and oranges go together quite well, so pair this pint with the Grand Marnier chocolate mousse, which is a combination of chocolate, coffee, and whipped cream, with a touch of orange liqueur.

SHRUB STEPPE SMOKEHOUSE BREWERY

2000 Logston Blvd., Ste. 122, Richland, WA 99354; (509) 375-9092;
shrubsteppebrewing.com

Founded: 2012 **Founders:** Steve Maiuri, Kevin Miller, and Kyle Roberson **Brewer:** Kyle Roberson **Flagship Beer:** Black Tail Jack **Year-Round Beers:** Bad Kitty, Hopgoddess, Mo Otter, Ringold, Vadozz, Wildfyre **Seasonals/Special Releases:** Black Tail Jack **Tours:** Yes

Barbecue and brewing. These are the interests that bring the three owners of Shrub Steppe together. A mechanical engineer, a millwright, and an electrical engineer, this trio decided to take their hobbies to the next step in Richland. The unique name of this brewpub comes from the most abundant plant species in their particular ecosystem in Richland (shrub) and a Russian word that means vast treeless plain (steppe). Historically dominating the landscape of eastern Washington, shrub steppe is a type of natural grassland with a continuous overstory layer of shrubs.

Offering more than 7 house beers, the brewery has slated 2 taps for guest homebrews to be included in the lineup as well. While the owners consider Pilsner-style lagers to be their specialty, don't expect one-note beers. Look for West Coast–style IPAs as well as other craft beers brewed with smoked malts, which will act as a signature flavor. Try one of their signature brews with a beef brisket sandwich and a side of mac and cheese for a well-rounded barbecue experience.

WHITE BLUFFS BREWING

2000 Logston Blvd., Ste. 126, Richland, WA 99354; (509) 554-7059;
WhiteBluffsBrewing.com; @WhiteBluffsBeer

Founded: 2010 **Founders:** Mike and Chardell Sutherland **Brewer:** Mike Sutherland **Flagship Beers:** Bluffdiver IPA, Miss Chievous' Biere De Garde **Year-Round Beers:** Bluffdiver IPA, Miss Chievous' Biere De Garde **Seasonals/Special Releases:** Ale Ferme Noire, Biere De Ambre, Beire De Mars, Biere De Noel, St. Doc's Saison, #1 IPA, Dirty Double IPA, Exploding Galaxy IPA, Mindbender IPA, Midnight Summit IPA, Oatmeal IPA, RyePA, Snickering Owl IPA, Thundersnake IPA, American Wheat, Dunkelweiss, Rye Not, Oatmeal Porter, Oatmeal Stout, Northside Brown, ROCKtoberfest, Blonde Bomber, Smurfdiver, Kölsch, Red Alt, Blufftop Pale Ale, Summer Gose, and many more **Tours:** No

Stating that it is the "people's brewery," White Bluffs Brewing makes it a point to listen to the people. Having a credo that states, "We brew beer with character for people with taste," this brewpub has a likeable attitude with an impressive list of beers to back it up. With over 25 years of experience, this Tri-Cities-based operation has more than 7 house-made beers on tap as well as at least 4 on deck waiting to take the stage. Offering a wide selection as well as having a pleasant view, White Bluffs Brewing is located in Richland. With active brewing as a backdrop, imbibers/diners get some great brewing ambience.

First, grab a pint of **Bluffdiver IPA.** This brew, which comes with a "No hops rookies" warning, has big grapefruit and pine notes thanks to the Simcoe, Cascade, and Citra hops it's brewed with. Boasting a light malt body to accompany the citrus and pine, this beer is well-rounded as well as aggressive. Pair this elegant warrior of a brew with the Mr. Popular, a panini composed of grilled flatbread, chicken, sharp cheddar cheese, pepperoncini, mayo, and barbecue sauce.

Done with IPAs? How about a nice **Summer Gose**? Made with wheat, Pilsner, and acidulated malt, this beverage combines sweet and sour in one brew. With orange, pineapple, and tangerine on the nose, the sea salt and coriander complete the style. Pair it with the Cubano: grilled flatbread, pulled pork, sharp cheddar, dill pickles, house mustard, and mayo.

WHITSTRAN BREWING COMPANY
1427 Wine Country Rd., Prosser, WA 99350; (509) 786-4922; WhitstranBrewing.com; @Whitstran

Founded: 1996 **Founders:** Larry and Sue Barbus **Brewer:** Larry Barbus **Flagship Beer:** None **Year-Round Beers:** Steamy Cream California Common Ale, Pavlov's Pilsner, Horse Heaven Hefe, Highlander Scottish-Style Ale, 11th Hour Pale Ale, Over-the-Edge Dry-Hopped Pale Ale, Palouse Porter, D20 Heavy Water Stout **Seasonals/Special Releases:** Friar Lawrence Belgium-Style Ale, Friar's Blessing Raspberry Lambic, Friar's Decadence Chocolate Chocolate Imperial Stout, Friar's Sahib Imperial IPA, Friar's Penance Barley Wine Ale **Tours:** No **Taproom:** Yes

Whitstran Brewing is located on Wine Country Road, surrounded by vineyards and wineries. This brewpub resides in a strip mall seemingly entirely dedicated to wine and all its accoutrements. A stranger in a hostile land, or an oasis in a desert of vines and grapes, Whitstran Brewing offers an alternative for those seeking suds. Not that there is anything wrong with wine, but this book is about beer!

The **11th Hour Pale Ale** has a sweet malty aroma with a light hop presence. With light bitterness and mellow fruit notes, this brew has a nice malt-to-hop balance. Make sure not to fill up on the complementary seasoned pretzels, because the pub offers a decent selection of appetizers, pizzas, sandwiches, burgers, and entrees.

If something more "decadent" is what you seek, try **Friar's Decadence Chocolate Chocolate Imperial Stout,** which is made by adding a touch of baker's cocoa to the boil. With cocoa and coffee on the nose, this brew has a chocolaty texture with a dry, malty finish. The light booziness in the flavor lets the imbiber know it is an imperial stout.

Beer Bars

WEST RICHLAND BEER & WINE
4033 W. Van Giesen St., West Richland, WA 99353; (509) 967-9726;
WestRichlandBeerAndWine.com; @WRBeerShop
Draft Beers: 20 **Bottled/Canned Beers:** Over 450

Those in the tri-city area really have to search for decent craft beer. Your best bet is to head over to West Richland and visit a bottle shop off West Van Giesen Street in a little strip mall called West Richland Beer & Wine. Open since 2009, the shop has seen quite a few changes over the years, making it what it is today. Though they specialize in both beer and wine, you'll notice that the beer selection is a big focus of their business. When they first started out, they were strictly a bottle shop that also filled growlers, but have since expanded to over 20 unique taps and have started offering pints and beer flights to sip on while you shop or relax. The tap list rotates frequently with many beers from Washington, Oregon, California, Colorado, and Alaska, as well as a handful of Belgian and other international beers. Inside are plenty of beverage coolers filled with hundreds of bottles and cans that can be bought to take home or drink at the shop.

Eastern Washington

Okanogan National Forest

Colville National Forest

Little Pend Oreille National Wilflife Refuge

WASHINGTON IDAHO

Curlew Lake State Park

1 Republic

2 Kettle Falls

3 Colville

Columbia River

Spokane R.

Inset

Maple St.

Monroe St.

Mission Ave.

8

9

10 Sprague Ave.

7

Grand Blvd.

High Dr.

29th Ave.

11

0   1   2 miles

4

Spokane

5

Airway Heights

See Inset

6

Spokane Valley

12 Odessa

Snake River

Pullman 13

Clarkston 14

15 Waitsburg

N

Walla Walla

16–17

0   15   30 miles

WASHINGTON
OREGON

BREWERIES

Budge Brothers Brewery	10
Iron Goat Brewing	9
Laht Neppur Brewing Co.	15
Laht Neppur Ale House	16
Lost Falls Brewery	3
No-Li Brewhouse	8
Northern Ales	2
Orlison Brewing Company	5
Paradise Creek Brewery	13
Republic Brewing Company	1
Riverport Brewing	14
Rocky Coulee Brewing Company	12
Twelve String Brewing Co	6

BREWPUBS

Mill Creek Brewpub	17
Steam Plant Grill	7

BARS

Manito Tap House	11
Pints Alehouse	4

Eastern Washington

The beer culture in eastern Washington is very interesting, yet extremely exciting. Recent growth around Spokane has been transforming the largest city on the east side of the state into a true beer lover's destination. Between brewers and beer bars popping up all over the town and its suburbs, great beer is constantly being poured.

Outside of the Spokane area you'll find plenty of breweries located in some of the smallest towns in the state, showing that it doesn't take very many people to support a local brewery. Breweries such as the Republic Brewing Company in Republic, Rocky Coulee Brewing Company in Odessa, Northern Ales in Kettle Falls, Laht Neppur Brewing Co. in Waitsburg, and Lost Falls Brewery in Colville have all been supported by the small communities they serve.

Breweries

BUDGE BROTHERS BREWERY

2018 E. Riverside Ave., Ste. 1, Spokane, WA 99202; (509) 426-3340; BudgeBrothers.com
Founded: 2010 **Founders:** Bruce and Brad Budge **Brewers:** Bruce and Brad Budge
Flagship Beers: Spokamber Ale, Orangutan Pale Ale, Hop Train IPA, Extra Stout
Year-Round Beers: Spokamber Ale, Orangutan Pale Ale, Hop Train IPA, Extra Stout
Seasonals/Special Releases: 13th Reindeer Eggnog Stout, Cream Ale **Tours:** No
Taproom: Yes

When brothers Bruce and Brad Budge got the idea to start their brewery, there wasn't much in the way of stopping them other than their age—Bruce was only 18. They didn't let that interfere with their plans and just a short four years later Budge Brothers Brewery opened in Spokane's international district. The duo has expanded into their location on East Riverside Avenue, focusing on a core lineup of beers. Outside their taproom, which is open only a few days a week, they have light distribution of kegged beers at restaurants and bars around Spokane.

Year-round they brew up a line of 4 beers. **Spokamber Ale** is their light and malty amber with Spokane's area code of 509 on the label. They also offer their **Orangutan Pale Ale,** packed with so many hops you could almost classify it as an IPA. Their **Hop Train IPA** is a powerhouse, packing in 8% ABV and plenty of bitter hops. **Extra Stout** is their one year-round dark beer with plenty of chocolate and coffee in the aroma. Aside from their core lineup, they release a few seasonal beers throughout the year, including their **13th Reindeer Eggnog Stout,** a rich and creamy ale that should please fans of chocolate and eggnog.

A couple days a week the taproom is open and you can go sample their beers, fill up a growler, or buy one of their party pigs. Make sure to check their Facebook page, as they like to do specials where you can fill a growler for only $5. It's a basic taproom, so no food is available.

Orangutan Pale Ale

Style: Pale Ale

ABV: 5%

Availability: Year-Round

The orangutan on the label of Budge Brothers' Orangutan Pale Ale stares you down, but don't let him scare you—he's really nice. Outside the Northwest people might classify this as an IPA, but in Spokane it's a pale ale. Plenty of Summit and Cascade hops are added to the beer, giving it both a citrus and a floral aroma and flavor. Caramel malts round out the flavor, helping to create an extremely sessionable pale ale. It's a versatile enough beer to pair with many foods, such as Cajun dishes, seafood, or chicken wings.

IRON GOAT BREWING

2204 E. Mallon Ave., Ste. B, Spokane, WA 99202; (509) 474-0722; IronGoatBrewing.com; @IronGoatBrewing

Founded: 2012 **Founders:** Paul Edminster, Sheila Evans, and Greg and Heather Brandt **Brewers:** Greg Brandt and Paul Edminster **Flagship Beer:** None **Year-Round Beers:** Head Butt IPA, The Impaler IPA, Garbage Pale Ale, Goatmeal Stout, Bleating Red Ale **Seasonals/Special Releases:** Goatnik, Damn Hot Blonde, Trashy Blonde, Cap'n Kidd Scotch Ale, Fresh Hop Pale Ale, and many more **Tours:** No **Taproom:** Yes

In Spokane's Riverfront Park resides a well-known sculpture known as the "Garbage Goat." The metal sculpture allows people to put bits of trash in its mouth and off it goes, similar to the appetite of a real goat. Taking that as inspiration, two Spokane-based couples got together and created a brewery themed around the sculpture and named it Iron Goat Brewing. By the middle of 2012 the brewery was open and the small taproom was serving up fresh beer to those in Spokane.

They brew 5 year-round beers and a handful of seasonals. Year-round they offer their **Head Butt IPA,** a unique beer packed with citrus and tropical fruit that comes from the use of New Zealand Motueka hops. Their **Garbage Pale Ale** is a perfect sessionable brew that has just the right balance of malt and nice and clean Australian

Beer Lover's Pick

The Impaler
Style: Double IPA
ABV: 8.5%
Availability: Year-Round

Even though Washington state is such a perfect place for growing hops, there are still many other regions around the world growing unique hop varieties that aren't often found in Northwest beers. The Impaler is brewed with Australian-grown Galaxy hops, giving it a passion fruit–like flavor that is equally as delicious to smell as it is to taste. Balanced with biscuity malts, The Impaler just gets better with every sip. A complex flavor profile makes it a big double IPA that those who don't just want to be blasted by hops will enjoy.

Sylva hops that give a slightly herbal yet somewhat spicy finish. Make sure to look out for **Goatnik,** their 9.9% ABV Russian imperial stout. Big roasted malt flavors dominate the beer with a body that is a lot lighter than you'd expect from a beer of the size.

You can find Iron Goat beer mainly on draft around the Spokane area. The small taproom provides a good spot to try their lineup of beers, listen to live music, or play some Thursday-night trivia. Their taster tray allows you to sample all the beers pouring, often including a beer you can't find anywhere else. Bring your growler and fill it up with their brews.

LAHT NEPPUR BREWING CO.

444 Preston Ave., Waitsburg, WA 99361; (509) 529-2337; LahtNeppur.com; @LahtNeppur
Founded: 2006 **Founder:** Court Ruppenthal **Brewer:** Court Ruppenthal **Flagship Beer:** India Pale Ale **Year-Round Beers:** Peach Hefeweizen, Mike's Golden Ale, Neddy's Brown Nut, Oatmeal Porter, India Pale Ale, Piper Canyon Scotch Ale, Stout **Seasonals/Special Releases:** Winter Warmer, Wild Hop Ale, Strawberry Cream Ale, Belgian Wit, Laughing Boy Stout, Backseat Blonde **Tours:** No **Taproom:** Yes

Approximately 20 miles northeast of Walla Walla in the small 1,200-person town of Waitsburg, Laht Neppur Brewing is crafting a selection of both beer and wine. This generally brings up a couple questions. First, what the heck does Laht

Peach Hefeweizen

Style: Hefeweizen

ABV: 5.3%

Availability: Year-Round

It's always fun to find a beer to give to people who say they don't like beer and watch their faces light up upon that first sip. Laht Neppur's Peach Hefeweizen is one of those beers that non–beer drinkers can easily love. It's a traditional hazy Hefeweizen that's brewed with both peaches and peach puree to create a sweet and very refreshing beer. Its light body makes it perfect to pair with a scorching summer day.

Neppur mean and what language is it? The name actually isn't in any language. It does, however, come from brewery founder and head brewer Court Ruppenthal's name. Just spell Ruppenthal backward and add a space and you get Laht Neppur. Another question is why did they decide on the small town of Waitsburg instead of the more populated Walla Walla to open the brewery? You have to visit the small town to fully grasp its charm, which is what drew Ruppenthal to open up shop there. The relaxed pace of life makes it the perfect scene to kick back and enjoy a beer or two with both the locals and those passing through.

They offer a wide selection of beers ranging from light summer beers brewed with fruits such as strawberries, peaches, and apricots to heavier beers, such as their **Barley Wine, Winter Warmer,** and the award-winning **Piper Canyon Scotch Ale,** aged for complexity.

Aside from the brewery in Waitsburg, the Ale House in Walla Walla serves their brews along with a similar small food menu of pizza and pub fare. During baseball season you can also visit their outfield pub at Borleske Stadium during any Walla Walla Sweets home games. Outside of the area, their beers are also showing up throughout the state in limited bottles as well as on draft.

LOST FALLS BREWERY

347 W. 2nd Ave., Ste. D, Colville, WA 99114; (509) 684-0638; LostFallsBrewery.com
Founded: 2003 **Founder:** Chip Trudell **Brewer:** Chip Trudell **Flagship Beer:** IPA **Year-Round Beers:** Porter, IPA, Pale Ale, Rye **Seasonals/Special Releases:** Nut Brown, Wheat Ale, Imperial Stout, Barley Wine **Tours:** No **Taproom:** Yes

Colville is most known in the Washington beer world as the small town that was home to Hale's Ales. Then in 1992 while they were growing, Hale's ended up moving out of the town, leaving the area without a brewery to call its own. Fortunately, Lost Falls Brewery eventually opened, giving locals a place to go drink beer a few nights a week. Unfortunately for the rest of the state, they don't get to experience the beers that owner and head brewer Chip Trudell is producing on his three-barrel system.

Located in a warehouse that is somewhat hard to find, it doesn't feel like anything special. Inside the taproom you'll find a few seats and tables intermixed with the brewing equipment. A roll-up door is in the front that can be lifted on warmer

Beer Lover's Pick

Porter
Style: Porter
ABV: 5.5%
Availability: Year-Round
Lost Falls' Porter is a beer that can double as a session ale or be served for dessert. Either way, it's delicious. Dark black in color, it has minimal carbonation and a thin mouthfeel that help it go down easy. A dark roasted aroma wafts out of the glass and follows you to your first sip. Big malts hit you with an almost ashy flavor that is quickly subdued by a malt sweetness with very little bitterness. The roasty finish will have you wanting to order another pint once it's gone.

summer days, providing space for imbibers to sprawl out and often fire up a grill—just make sure to bring your own meat. The tasting room itself doesn't provide any food, but that doesn't stop people from bringing in their own. One word of caution: You might want to call before you visit, as their operating hours and days tend to fluctuate. However, you can be sure to have a good time on Friday nights, when locals flock to the brewery ready to have a good time with the music cranked. Trudell brews just a handful of beers, but all are well done. Most popular is the Northwest-style **IPA** that's hopped up. Also make sure to try the **Rye,** a beer similar to the IPA yet with subtle spicy notes from the rye.

NO-LI BREWHOUSE

1003 E. Trent Ave., #170, Spokane, WA 99202; (509) 242-2739; NoLiBrewhouse.com; @NoLiBrewhouse

Founded: 1993 **Founder:** Mark Irvin **Brewer:** Mark Irvin **Flagship Beers:** Crystal Bitter and Born & Raised **Year-Round Beers:** Born & Raised, Silent Treatment, Crystal Bitter, Jet Star Imperial IPA, and Wrecking Ball Imperial Stout **Seasonals/Special Releases:** Chocolate Dunkel, Blueberry Crème, Winter Warmer, Stellar Stout, Solar Winds, Horned Aviator, Summer Wheat, Amber, and many more **Tours:** No, but call if interested **Taproom:** Yes

Born & Raised IPA

Style: IPA

ABV: 7%

Availability: Year-Round

A tribute to those who were born and raised in Spokane, No-Li Brewhouse's Born & Raised IPA is by far their most popular beer. Brewed with Washington-grown Cascade, Columbus, and Chinook hops, the shining copper-colored ale booms with citrus, floral, and biscuity aromas. The hops are present in the beginning before transitioning over to a somewhat sweet malt and earthiness before a lingering bitterness follows. This is a total IPA lover's IPA that packs in a bold 7% ABV.

Back in 1993, a local production brewery opened in Airway Heights that self-distributed to local bars and restaurants. The company was named Northern Lights Brewing Company and operated for eight years before packing up and moving into their current Spokane location. A new, bigger facility meant they could serve their beer in a pub setting and offer food, helping them become a known icon in the city for people to imbibe in a selection of delicious craft beers. Owners Mark Irvin and John Bryant recently decided to rebrand Northern Lights Brewing Company to No-Li Brewhouse. While the name may have changed, the quality of their beers has remained the same.

Today the brewery focuses on distributing a handful of beers, such as their **Silent Treatment Pale,** which got its name from their dispute with another brewery; **Crystal Bitter Ale; Jet Star Imperial IPA;** and their flagship **Born & Raised IPA.** Each is available in 22-ounce bottles around Spokane and a few other select spots around the country, such as Denver and New York City. You can't go wrong with most of their seasonals. Make sure to try their **Winter Warmer,** a warming beer whose ingredients are all sourced within 300 miles of the brewery.

In Spokane the pub is by far the best place in the city to try their beers, especially since they offer a handful you won't find anywhere else. Along with a selection of pub food ranging from burgers to jambalaya and pasta, you can enjoy a selection of their beers at incredible prices. The sample trays allow you to try anywhere between 4 and 10 beers, depending on how thirsty you are.

NORTHERN ALES

325 W. 3rd Ave., Kettle Falls, WA 99141; (509) 738-7382; NorthernAles.com
Founded: 2007 **Founders:** Steve and Andrea Hedrick **Brewer:** Steve Hedrick **Flagship Beer:** None **Year-Round Beers:** Smoked NorthPorter, Flume Creek IPA, Okanagan Highlander, Honey Basil, Smelter's Ash, The Grouch Lager **Seasonals/Special Releases:** THE Oatmeal Stout, Flagstaff Amber Scotch ale, Pete's Czech Pilsner, Rice Pale Ale, and many more **Tours:** No **Taproom:** Yes

Northern Ales opened its doors in 2007 in the most unlikely spot in the state. Even if you've lived in Washington your whole life, you may not even know that there is a town called Northport. Located in the northeastern part of the state near the Canadian border along the Columbia River, Northport is home to roughly 300 residents. With the next closest US town Kettle Falls 40 miles away, it wasn't exactly the ideal place for a brewpub. It didn't, however, prevent them from creating some interesting and tasty brews. After a few years in the small town, it was time to move and they settled in the "much larger" town of Kettle Falls, where the population is around 1,600.

The brewpub is still the best place to find both their beers and a good time. They brew on a small system, yet produce a great number of beers that are constantly rotating. Available both on draft and in a handful of 12- and 22-ounce bottles, most of their beer sticks around Kettle Falls. It has been known to pop up in bottle shops around the Puget Sound from time to time as well. You'll find bottles of their **Smoked NorthPorter,** named after their original location. Dark black in color, it's a smooth porter with plenty of coffee and sweetness with a touch of smokiness in

Beer Lover's Pick

Honey Basil Ale
Style: Herbed/Spiced Beer
ABV: 13%
Availability: Year-Round

Just like the name implies, Honey Basil Ale is made with a ton of honey and hints of basil. The recipe was a favorite of the brewer before Northern Ales opened and it has stuck with them ever since. It pours an almost honey-like amber color with a strong basil aroma balanced with a touch of sweetness. If you don't like basil, you probably won't like this beer because it's strong in the flavor. However, it's incredibly refreshing and the sweetness of the honey turns it into a very interesting beer.

the finish. Also look for their imperial stout named **Smelter's Ash** or the **Okanagan Highlander** scotch ale.

If you happen to make it to Kettle Falls, make sure to look at their schedule, as they offer plenty of live music and a small menu of food options. You can fill a growler or pretty much any size container as long as its quantity is marked. Also note that they're only open Wed through Sun.

ORLISON BREWING COMPANY

12921 W. 17th Ave., Airway Heights, WA 99001; (509) 244-2536; OrlisonBrewing.com; @OrlisonBrewing
Founded: 2009 **Founder:** Bernie Duenwald **Brewer:** Bernie Duenwald **Flagship Beers:** Clem's Gold, Lizzy's Lager, Brünette, Orlison's IPL **Year-Round Beers:** Clem's Gold, Lizzy's Lager, Brünette, Orlison's IPL **Seasonals/Special Releases:** Em's Easy, Havanüther
Tours: No **Taproom:** No

Founded as Golden Hills Brewing in 2009, the brewery underwent a branding change in 2013 and changed the name to Orlison Brewing Co. The name itself is a combination of Orlin and Jason, the names of the two investors that jumped on board to take the brewery to the next level. Orlison is doing things a bit differently than other craft brewers in the Northwest. Instead of taking aim at the craft-beer geeks by producing ultracreative and varied styles of beer, they have their sights set on converting macrobeer drinkers by producing a portfolio of easy-drinking lagers.

Instead of worrying about quantity, the production-only brewery creates just a few lagers that range in both color and flavor. On the lower end of the spectrum is **Em's Easy,** a light lager that is comparable to Bud Light in body, yet has a much better flavor. The next step up is their **Clem's Gold,** a pale lager with a little more flavor and body than Em's and that is highly sessionable. It's a beer you can drink and enjoy while watching an entire football game and still be able to function even if it goes into overtime. One of the newest beers to their lineup is the Orlison's IPL, formerly named **7 Seventy India Pale Lager** it has 7% ABV and has 70 IBUs. It's a beer that has all the hops of an IPA but with the cleaner finish you find in most lagers. Currently Orlison doesn't offer a taproom, but its beers are showing up on draft across the state from Spokane to Seattle as well as parts of Idaho.

Beer Lover's Pick

Lizzy's Lager
Style: Premium Lager
ABV: 5.5%
Availability: Year-Round
Owner Bernie Duenwald named Lizzy's Lager after his daughter because it was her favorite beer. Similar to an ESB but brewed as a lager, it pours a dark amber color and has plenty of caramel sweetness in the aroma. It starts off with a citrus flavor before giving way to its caramel malt body and finishes nice and clean. This is one enjoyable lager that is bursting with flavor yet won't bog you down.

PARADISE CREEK BREWERY

245 SE Paradise St., Pullman, WA 99163; (509) 338-9463; ParadiseCreekBrewery.com; @PCBrewery

Founded: 2010 **Founder:** Tom Handy **Brewer:** Tom Handy **Flagship Beers:** Over the Hop IPA and Pokerface Blonde **Year-Round Beers:** Postal Porter, J-Dub's Pale Ale, Over the Hop IPA, Pokerface Blonde Ale, Paradise Hoe Belgian Wit, Sacred Cow Milk Stout **Seasonals/Special Releases:** Espresso Stout, Bad Dawg Belgian Pale, Hop Hammer IPA, Hoe's Daddy Dunkelweizen, Pullman Water American Lager, Hopocalypse Imperial Black IPA, Oktopuss Märzen, Alpha Madness Fresh Hop, Hector's Revenge, Grizzly Brown, Cougar City Sour, Bavarian Bombshell, Stocking Stuffer, and many more **Tours:** No **Taproom:** Yes

In downtown Pullman sits a building known as the Old Post Office Building. The US Postal service used the building, built in 1930, for almost 50 years before it moved on to a new location. In 2002 the building was sold to Tom Handy, who opened a wine bar named the Old Post Office Wine Gallery. He also leases part of the building to a new winery named Merry Cellars. After Handy and winemaker Patrick Merry struck up a friendship, the two started homebrewing together and honed in on their brewing skills. While Merry Cellars' business grew, they eventually moved out and Handy decided to change directions and closed down the wine bar. In 2010 he set up Paradise Creek Brewery in the building, creating a very beautiful brewery.

While in the beginning they had a tough time keeping up with demand in the brewpub, they have since been able to brew enough to start distribution of their brews across eastern Washington and parts of northern Idaho in both kegs and bottles. They offer plenty of year-round seasonal beers to look for, such as their sweet and flavorful **Pokerface Blonde,** their smooth **Hoe's Daddy Dunkel** that has a distinct banana bread smell, or their hopped-up **Postal Porter.** In the winter try the **Sacred Cow Milk Stout,** a creamy and sweet beer brewed with Bucer's Tanzanian coffee.

The brewpub is one of those places you must visit if you find yourself in or around Pullman. A comfortable yet elegant decor fills the space. Multiple flat-screen TVs are at the bar, and during big games and other occasions they'll bust out the 12-foot HD projection screen. They also offer an excellent menu consisting of burgers, sandwiches, salads, and a few appetizers, with options for those with dietary needs.

Eastern Washington

Postal Porter
Style: Porter
ABV: 5.5%
Availability: Year-Round
Named after the brewery's location in the Old Post Office Building, Postal Porter's brilliant logo shows a gun wrapped around a mug of dark beer. As one of the beers they bottle, this is a traditional Northwest-style porter brewed with plenty of dark malts and two hop varieties. The result is a dark-as-night brew beaming with chocolate and roasty malts in the aroma. A somewhat smoky flavor peeks through the roasted malt and chocolate with noticeable yet not overpowering coffee bitterness.

REPUBLIC BREWING COMPANY
26 Clark Ave. N., Republic, WA 99166; (509) 775-2700; RepublicBrew.com
Founded: 2011 **Founders:** Billy and Emily Burt **Brewer:** Billy Burt **Flagship Beer:**
Republic Pale **Year-Round Beers:** Republic Pale, Big Mischief Porter, Brush Fit Brown
Seasonals/Special Releases: Belgian Tripel, Kettle River Drifter, Widowmaker IPA,
Rusty Bucket Amber, Krohnie's Bliss Kölsch, Irish Eyes Stout, Falligan's Red, Bavarian
Weizen, Dunkel **Tours:** No **Taproom:** Yes

The small town of Republic, Washington, isn't the first place you'd expect to find a brewery. Republic is the most populated town in Ferry County, but you could pretty much say it's in the middle of nowhere. In this town of roughly 1,000 residents you won't find any traffic lights, fast food chains, or traffic. However, you will find a small brewery offering the locals and those passing through a place to stop and drink fresh beer. Opened in 2011, Republic Brewing Company is actually the town's second brewery. The first was called by the same name and provided liquid gold to area gold miners in the 1890s. After years of operating, it finally closed down in 1913, but its history is still remembered. Inside the taproom at the current rendition of the Republic Brewing Company, you'll find a lot of history and paraphernalia hanging around on the walls.

Today the small brewery is located on Clark Avenue. The company is the creation of Billy and Emily Burt, both longtime locals of Republic. You'll find Billy heading up brewing operations while Emily heads up the tasting room, a real family business. The little taproom provides a perfect place to enjoy a pint or two of beer and mingle with people from all walks of life. Year-round they offer 3 beers, **Republic Pale, Brush Fit Brown,** and **Big Mischief Porter,** all of which are local favorites. Along with their regular lineup you can find 3 other beers on draft. Of those they generally offer a lighter beer on one tap, an amber or red on another tap, and the third is a variety ranging everywhere from a Kölsch to a Belgian Tripel.

Republic Pale
Style: Pale Ale
ABV: 5.8%
Availability: Year-Round
Brewed as a traditional American-style pale ale, Republic Pale is the brewery's top seller, and no wonder. Sure, small towns tend to enjoy pale ales over obscure styles, but this is one well-brewed pale. The crisp beer has a light body yet has plenty of flavor from the Cascade hops. It's the type of beer that is pretty much perfect to drink in any situation, no matter whether that is hanging out at the local brewery or sitting on the lake with a fishing pole in your hand.

RIVERPORT BREWING

150 9th St., Ste. B, Clarkston, WA 99403; (509) 758-8889; RiverportBrewing.com
Founded: 2008 **Founders:** Marv Eveland, Karen Eveland, Pete Broyles, and Nancy Broyles
Brewer: Pete Broyles **Flagship Beer:** River Rat Red **Year-Round Beers:** Bedrock Bock, Blonde Moment, Cedar Rock Pale Ale, Seven Devils IPA, Old Man River Oatmeal Stout, River Rat Red, Bullseye PA **Seasonals/Special Releases:** Alpha Reign, 5/5 Pepper Beer, Hellsgate Hefeweizen, Magruder's Porter, Grande Ronde Rye, B-Run Red, Oktoberfest Bier, Ol' Harold, Winter Spirit, and many more **Tours:** No **Taproom:** Yes

If you're from Clarkston or have spent time there, chances are you'll understand that it's not exactly the most thriving place for craft beer. As Riverport Brewing co-owner Pete Broyles put it, "This is Keystone country." Since both Clarkston and Lewiston residents deserved beer that had flavor, Pete and homebrewing friend Marv Eveland created a brewery designed to convert the masses. That by no means implies they make bland beer, but rather they seek to educate people and create beers that will draw the mass-produced-beer drinkers to realize it's better to drink beer that tastes good. The business partners built the brewery from scratch doing almost everything themselves, including putting together the brew system.

They have created a taproom that fits the area perfectly. It offers a relaxed atmosphere that allows you to bring your kids, or just come and watch a game on the big screen while enjoying their beer. Popcorn is the only food option, but a few different places will deliver if you get hungry. On warm days they'll open up their 3 garage doors facing the hills so you can kick back and take life easy.

Beer Lover's Pick

Old Man River Oatmeal Stout
Style: Oatmeal Stout
ABV: 5%
Availability: Year-Round
Riverport's Old Man River Oatmeal is what you would call a session stout. At 5% ABV and sporting a creamy yet not-too-heavy mouthfeel, it's a drink you can sip on all night and not feel bogged down. Cocoa and roasted malts billow out of the glass, creating an inviting aroma. A touch of coffee, roasted oats, chocolate, and nuts are all present in the flavor, yet none are that dominant. Pair this with a dessert consisting of rich dark chocolate or caramel or pretty much any game dishes or hearty stews.

Outside of the draft room their beer is available only on draft, mainly in the Lewiston metropolitan area. A range of year-round beers includes a fairly standard offering of Northwest beers. Their **Blonde Moment** is a favorite in the area and is perfect for those looking to explore craft beer for the first time. **Bullseye PA** is an IPA with a little more malt forwardness than many in the state, resulting in a very drinkable beer full of toasty malts.

ROCKY COULEE BREWING COMPANY

205 N. 1st St., Odessa, WA 99159; (509) 750-7921; RockyCouleeBrewingCo.com
Founded: 2002 **Founder:** Tom Schafer **Brewer:** Tom Schafer **Flagship Beer:** Fireweed Honey Blonde **Year-Round Beers:** Fireweed Honey Blonde, Golden Lite Summer Ale, Creamed Copper Ale, Brown Ale, Dunkle **Seasonals/Special Releases:** White Out Winter Ale **Tours:** No **Taproom:** Yes

In Washington plenty of small towns have a brewery to call their own. When craft brewers are dialed into the community they serve, they tend to make beer that people actually want to drink. This is exactly the case for Odessa-based Rocky Coulee Brewing Company, which has been crafting beer since 2002. The picturesque small town with fewer than 1,000 residents has been a big supporter of the brewery ever since.

The brewery itself is a production facility with just a small tasting room that is open only on Friday. Outside of the tasting rooms you can find their beer on draft around the tri-county area and as far as Spokane at times. They also bottle their **Fireweed Honey Blonde,** a favorite among locals. Since the town is situated in the

Beer Lover's Pick

Fireweed Honey Blonde
Style: Blonde Ale
ABV: 6.4%
Availability: Year-Round
As the only year-round beer Rocky Coulee bottles and their flagship ale, Fireweed Honey Blonde makes the perfect beer to drink on a hot summer day. Brewed with Fireweed honey, the light ale has a smooth and somewhat sweet flavor with plenty of malt and just a hint of floral in the finish without being bitter. This is a beer that appeals to the masses, yet has plenty of flavor and is extremely refreshing.

middle of farming country, their beers tend to be on the maltier side and less bitter to please the tastes of the region. Their flavorful creations aren't bland in any way; they just tend to stay away from creating bitter beers so they are more approachable to newer beer drinkers. If you like a good wheat beer, make sure to try their **Dunkle,** a traditionally brewed Dunkelweizen with a touch of smokiness.

TWELVE STRING BREWING COMPANY
11616 E. Montgomery Dr., Ste. 26, Spokane Valley, WA 99206; (509) 990-8622; 12StringBrewingCo.com
Founded: 2011 **Founder:** Terry Hackler **Brewer:** Terry Hackler **Flagship Beer:** None
Year-Round Beers: G String Blonde, Archtop Amber, Electric Slide IPA, Don't Fret Porter, Drop D Stout, Double Drop D Stout, Jam Session IPA **Seasonals/Special Releases:** 12 Strings of Winter Ale, Mango Mamba Summer Ale, C#7#5 IPA, Roundabout Confusion Harvest Ale, Spring Reverb, Wet Hop Pale Ale, Hip Hop Doo Wop, and many more
Tours: No **Taproom:** Yes

The 30 years Terry Hackler spent brewing beer at home gave him enough expertise and knowledge to take the plunge and open his brewery in Spokane Valley just east of Spokane. Just like the business name, Twelve String Brewing Company carries the guitar theme into their beer names as well as the taproom with guitars mounted on the walls.

The seven-barrel steam-heated brewing system was pieced together by Hackler, who built a lot of it from scratch. With the brewery in place, Twelve String Brewing Company opened their doors in 2011 with the focus on brewing Northwest-style ales. Most of their beer is sold around the Spokane area and their own taproom. Don't be surprised to find 3 or 4 IPAs on draft at any time; this is the Northwest, of course. **Electric Slide IPA** is their original single-hop IPA brewed with Calypso hops. Another IPA that has become one of their most popular beers is the **Jam Session IPA,** also brewed with Calypso hops. Along with their year-round offerings, you'll usually find a handful of seasonals on the tap list. Look for their winter warmer named **12 Strings of Winter.** It's a hoppy beer with a touch of spice and a lingering sweetness that isn't your typical dark winter brew.

The taproom is covered with beautiful woodwork, another hobby of owner Terry Hackler. A cozy atmosphere makes it a perfect place to sit and enjoy up to 10 beers on draft, some of which are guest brews. Along with a TV for Gonzaga and other important games, they also offer live music on many Fridays. Go ahead and bring your wine-loving friends, as the taproom has them covered as well. Make sure to also come with your growler in hand, especially if it's Tuesday, when they have discounted growler fills.

Beer Lover's Pick

Don't Fret Porter
Style: Porter
ABV: 5.5%
Availability: Year-Round

Falling in line with their guitar-themed brewery, Twelve String Brewing Company named this year-round drink Don't Fret Porter. It's a traditional Northwest-style porter brewed with plenty of hops, yet the aroma is all chocolate malt with a touch of peanut butter. The medium- to light-bodied porter has flavors of chocolate, roasted nuts, coffee, and just a touch of bitterness from the

hops. They suggest pairing it with a scoop of vanilla ice cream with raspberry topping. Yes, please!

Brewpubs

MILL CREEK BREWPUB

11 S. Palouse St., Walla Walla, WA 99362; (509) 522-2440; MillCreek-Brewpub.com
Founded: 1997 **Founder:** Gary Johnson **Brewer:** Troy Robinson **Flagship Beer:**
Penitentiary Porter **Year-Round Beers:** Walla Walla Wheat, Wildwood IPA **Seasonals/
Special Releases:** Penitentiary Porter, Brew 22 **Tours:** No

Located smack in the middle of wine country, Mill Creek Brewpub was the first brewpub in Walla Walla. This family-friendly establishment features a 1,500-square-foot outside patio with a river-rock fireplace. Mill Creek Brewpub brews 4 in-house beers and features guest taps as well. Stop in for a **Wildwood IPA,** which has a fruity hop aroma and a light trace of caramel. With light citrus and a hint of brown sugar on the palate, this brew is almost more of an English IPA than one from the West Coast. Pair this with a Zesty, Snappy, and Sassy Chicken Sandwich, which is char-broiled with grilled onions, swiss cheese, spicy mayo, lettuce, and tomato and served on a bun.

If an IPA isn't your thing, try a **Brew 22,** a Bavarian-inspired blonde ale that has light brown sugar and toast on the nose. This pale lager has some light buttery qualities and very light hop presence at the tail end of the brew. Pair this beer with the 5 Alarm Arson Burger, which is a spicy ⅓-pound burger with smoked bacon, jalapeños, grilled sweet onions, chipotle mayonnaise, tomato, lettuce, dill chips, and 3 cheeses.

STEAM PLANT GRILL

159 S. Lincoln St., Spokane, WA 99201; (509) 777-3900; SteamPlantSpokane.com
Founded: 1999 **Founder:** Ron Wells **Brewer:** Ben Quick **Flagship Beer:** Double Stack
Stout **Year-Round Beers:** Blonde Ale, Cutter's Pale Ale, Big Brick Brown, Highland
Scottish Ale, Huckleberry Harvest Ale, Whitman's Wheat Beer, Firebox IPA, Doublestack
Stout **Seasonals/Special Releases:** Jalapeno Ale, Stack's Frost, Strawberry Wheat,
Barleywine, Pumpkin Spice Ale, Chocolate Bock **Tours:** By appointment

The Steam Plant was originally constructed to provide steam heat as well as electrical power for downtown Spokane. The facility had outgrown its economical viability by 1986, but the 225-foot smokestacks were not done serving a purpose. With a 10-barrel system in the back of the restaurant, this is not just an architectural/historic preservation; this place means business. Stop on in for a pint of the

Highland Scottish Ale. With strong yeast, citrus, and floral notes, this brew also has a light caramel malt aroma as well. With light bitterness and a slightly nutty quality, the light hops kick in at the finish. Pair it with the smoked steelhead antipasto, which is a naturally raised Columbia River steelhead, smoked in-house and served with herbed cream cheese, a rotating selection of pickled and roasted vegetables, and rye crostinis.

The most popular brew from this place, though, is the **Double Stack Stout.** Accentuated with vanilla and bourbon flavors, with a nice warm, vanilla aroma, it is easy to see why this creamy, chocolaty beverage is the flagship beer of Steam Plant. Use this brew to mellow out the jalapeño white bean chili, which is tender chicken breast seasoned with Southwest spices, marinated in Steam Plant's Jalapeno Ale, boiled, and simmered with poblano peppers, onions, and white beans.

Beer Bars

MANITO TAP HOUSE

3011 S. Grand Blvd., Spokane, WA 99203; (509) 279-2671; ManitoTapHouse.com; @ManitoTapHouse
Draft Beers: 50 **Bottled/Canned Beers:** About 50

Manito Tap House is an eco-friendly gastropub that boasts 50 rotating beers on draft. With an emphasis on taking care of the environment, they became the first three-star certified green restaurant in Spokane. While the inside has a modern, upscale vibe to it, most of the materials used in constructing the space were reclaimed or recycled materials. The walls are lined with reclaimed wood from an old barn in Rearden, and benches have been created using old bleachers from area schools. You'll even find bathroom countertops made of recycled paper among a host of other environmentally friendly options. If you're there for the beer, take a look at the windowed barback so you can see straight through to the many kegs of beer hooked up to the draft system.

Speaking of beer, you'd better come thirsty. Their 50 taps rotate regularly from breweries all over the world. You'll find a mix of both local and international beers ranging from hard-to-find seasonals to standards such as Young's Double Chocolate Stout and Newcastle Brown Ale. Along with pints you can order a taster paddle of 6 beers for only $5 if you're in the mood to try multiple beers, or bring a growler to fill and take home with you. You'd also better come hungry, as all of their food is prepared fresh in-house, including the ketchup. The handmade burgers are among the best in the city, so try either the Grand Beef Burger loaded with bacon or the Tap House Burger filled with Cambozola cheese, lettuce, tomato, smoked onion, pancetta, and bacon marmalade with a touch of mayo.

PINTS ALEHOUSE

10111 N. Newport Hwy., Spokane, WA 99218; (509) 368-9671; pintsalehouse.com
Draft Beers: 18 **Bottled/Canned Beers:** Over 60

Finding quality craft beer in north Spokane has been a daunting task for years. Derek and Patricia Quist opened Pints Alehouse to serve the beer lovers to the north. Located off Newport Highway, the alehouse is all about the beer. They don't serve food in the bar, but they occasionally have other companies serving food out front. Across the street is a shopping complex with plenty of food options that you can pick up to take in with you.

Inside you'll find a beautifully decorated bar with warm colors, a brick bar-back, and 2 TVs on each side of the bar so you can watch most big games. They offer a decent selection of wines, so your non-beer-drinking friends can tag along. Eighteen rotating beers fill the tap lines with a blend of local, national, and international brews. Along with Washington breweries you'll find Lagunitas, Dogfish Head, Ayinger, Great Divide, Stone, and plenty of others that can be tough to find in Spokane. They also offer over 60 bottles and cans with a focus on barrel-aged beers, Trappists, imperial stouts, and ciders. If you're not sure what to order, the staff are well versed in beer and more than happy to help you choose the right beer.

Beer Festivals

If you love beer, very few things are more enjoyable than spending a day or weekend at a beer festival. Depending on the festival, you get to try beers rarely tasted or not available in your area. You also get to try new styles and beers from breweries just down the road to breweries on the other side of world, all while having a ton of fun. From big beers in the winter, to fruit and lighter beers in the summer months and everything in between, each event will give you a wide range of styles to try from multiple breweries.

This chapter is a small selection of some of the bigger festivals around the state that should be added to your calendar. By no means is this an all-inclusive list. With the number of beer festivals happening in Washington, it would take a whole book just to write about each one. Get a group of friends and hit some festivals this year. Just make sure you bring a designated driver.

January

STRANGE BREWFEST

The American Legion, 209 Monroe St., Port Townsend, WA 98368; StrangeBrewfestpt.com/index.htm

Strange Brewfest is a celebration of uniquely crafted beers from all over the Northwest. This festival plays host to around 30 craft breweries and cideries and delivers as many as 60 strange brews to try. This annual event takes place at the end of January and is meant to be a celebration of stand-out beers from around the area. Strange Brewfest allows attendees to see the creativity and genius of Washington's brewing community. But don't look for these odd concoctions at your local bottle shop. Most of the creative beers that are tasted at this festival can only be tasted there. The participating brewers are encouraged to be as creative as possible when mixing up their strange offerings, which doesn't always yield a "mainstream" brew. The theme of Strange Brewfest changes from year to year and is as quirky as some of the brews. There is plenty of entertainment to take in as you partake of the unique creations of the featured breweries. With multiple bands to listen to over the course of the event, don't get too distracted to check out the many other forms of entertainment at this celebration. Previous years' events have included everything from costume contests to chainsaw carving exhibitions. Tickets are $25 per person and include admission for all 3 days, a souvenir tasting glass, and 4 free tasting tokens.

February

BELGIANFEST

Bell Harbor International Conference Center, 2211 Alaskan Way, Pier 66, Seattle, WA 98121; WashingtonBeer.com/Belgianfest

Hosted by the Washington Beer Commission, Belgianfest takes place at Bell Harbor International Conference Center on Seattle's waterfront. This annual event showcases the beer culture of Belgium by offering over 60 Belgian-style beers crafted by Washington breweries. The featured beer styles for this festival include Tripels, Dubbels, saisons, Wits, Abbeys, and lambics. These beers, all brewed with Belgian yeast, can be tasted with a $35 admission to the event. This price comes with a commemorative tasting glass as well as ten 4-ounce tastes. Designated-driver admission is $5 and includes free water and soda. If you happen to be a member of WABL (Washington Beer Lover), then bring a current passport and you can enjoy two bonus tokens as well as a chance to taste an exclusive WABL beer. This event is 21 and over, so be sure to bring a valid ID.

June

GORGE BLUES AND BREWS FESTIVAL

Skamania County Fairgrounds, 710 Rock Creek Dr., Stevenson, WA 98648; GorgeBluesAndBrews.com

This annual festival takes place at the Skamania County Fairgrounds in Stevenson and has a lot going on. Walking Man Brewery, Stevenson's local brewery, pours the brews while talented local bands play the blues. With over 16 regional breweries and plenty of wineries present, you would do well to pace yourself. The featured beers are the best the Gorge and surrounding areas have to offer. Soaking up the suds will be an easy feat as there is a huge selection of food. With multiple blues bands playing the festival, your ears won't get bored from all the beer talk. This is truly a festival to make a weekend out of with the family. Camping is available, so you can continue your evening safely after the official festivities have wrapped up. Look for the registration form on the event website. With the unforgettable scenery around the area, attendees can experience Stevenson, as well as all the Columbia Gorge has to offer. Admission to this event is $15 per person and includes a commemorative beer glass or wineglass. This is a 21-and-over event, so make sure to bring valid ID.

Washington Beer Commission

Since 2006 the Washington Beer Commission has been promoting the state's brewing industry. The state legislature authorized the creation of the Beer Commission, making it the first of its kind in the US. Since its inception the commission has been given the task of raising awareness of the quality of beers produced in the state.

So why would a state get involved in promoting the local beer industry? Simple. Back in 2008 the brewing industry in Washington alone brought in over $1.2 billion. Not only does helping the industry grow bring in massive federal, state, and local taxes, but it also affects our local communities. Most breweries are small family-owned businesses that provide many jobs in the state.

To help promote the local beer industry, the Washington Beer Commission is actively involved in a number of ways. Each year it puts on six large beer festivals ranging from the massive Washington Brewers Festival to the Spokane Oktoberfest and Bremerton Summer Brewfest. They also organize other events, such as the Washington Beer Open House, where breweries across the state open up their doors for tours and other events.

If you're interested in getting involved, you can join their WABL program (Washington Beer Lovers). A yearly membership fee gets you into special events and benefits at their festivals, a magazine subscription, a T-shirt, and other goodies. You also get a passport that you can take to participating breweries and collect stamps to win other prizes.

Make sure to check out their website at washingtonbeer.com to stay up-to-date with upcoming beer events around the state.

WASHINGTON BREWERS FESTIVAL

King County's Marymoor Park, 6046 W. Lake Sammamish Pkwy. NE, Redmond, WA 98052; WashingtonBeer.com/WA-Brewers-Fest

Fans of Washington beer will be right at home at the Washington Brewers Festival, held at King County's Marymoor Park in Redmond. Over 60 Washington breweries show up at the 3-day event along with a few out-of-state friends bringing over 200 unique beers. Held each year in June, the Washington Brewers Festival is one of the best places in the state to try multiple local beers in one setting. On Friday it's open to those 21 and over before it opens up to all ages on Saturday and Sunday. Kids are encouraged to attend the last two days with multiple activities going on for them, such as a kids' playground and root beer garden featuring plenty of soda crafted by local breweries. Throughout the weekend local bands take the stage to bring entertainment to beer lovers; another event is the annual brewers' keg toss. With plenty of great food and even a selection of local cider and wine, there are plenty of options to choose from. You can find many options for tickets depending on when you buy them and how many days you want to attend. Those who are members of the Washington Beer Lovers Club put on by the Washington Beer Commission will get a special tasting glass and the ability to try a special beer brewed just for WABL members.

July

RAILS-TO-ALES BREWFEST

At the Train Depot in South Cle Elum, WA 98943; RailsToAlesBrewfest.com

Always held on the second Saturday of July at the Authentic Milwaukee Road Depot, this annual festival includes 20-plus brewers, some hard cider, and even a winery or two. There are also nonalcoholic choices for designated drivers, or those just not partaking. This one-day festival features multiple bands as well as food vendors and prizes. The festival does have a railroad theme and you are invited to "relive the history of railroad glory days and the Milwaukee Road through an easy short interpretive trail hike around the railyard and a visit to the depot's museum." Tickets are $20 in advance and $25 at the gate. Admission includes 7 starter beer tokens for 5-ounce tastings, a commemorative 5-ounce sampling glass with event logo, as well as admission to the rail museum. There is also plenty of free parking and free shuttle service to the event. The proceeds for this event go to the Cascade Rail Foundation, a Washington nonprofit corporation that hosts the event. The profits will assist in future restoration projects and maintenance of the Historic South Cle Elum Depot, railyard, and substation. This is a 21-and-older event, so be prepared to show valid ID at the gate.

SEATTLE INTERNATIONAL BEERFEST
Seattle Center Fisher Pavilion, 305 Thomas St., Seattle, WA 98109; SeattleBeerfest.com

Taking place in July, the Seattle International Beerfest is a high-end 3-day beer festival that specializes in rare, hard-to-find, and exotic beers from all over the world. Sixteen countries are represented in the over 200 beers on tap at this festival, including many that aren't typically available at summer festivals, such as barleywines, imperial stouts, double IPAs, barrel-aged strong ales, farmhouse saisons, and sour ales. With multiple bands on the event list, attendees are sure to find a sound they like while tasting all of the unique beers that will be showcased. Of course, plenty of food is available as well. Tickets are $30 at the gate and include admission, an official SIB glass, and 10 tasting tickets. Free re-entry is also permitted all weekend if you have your glass and wristband. They also offer $5 tickets for those who aren't drinking, so if you're a designated driver you can still enjoy the good food and atmosphere. This is a 21-and-over event, so leave the kids with a sitter and bring a valid ID.

August

VANCOUVER BREWFEST
Esther Short Park, 301 W. 8th St., Vancouver, WA 98660; VancouverBrewfest.com

A 2-day festival, Vancouver Brewfest takes place in the heart of downtown Vancouver at Esther Short Park, at West Columbia Street and 8th Street. 2012 marked the first Vancouver Brewfest and will hopefully continue to be an annual event. Playing host to over 26 breweries from around the area, this is a typical festival that includes all of the essentials: food, beer, and music. This is also a dog-friendly event, so get the leash out and bring man's second best friend with you (beer being the first). This event is also a benefit for local charities. The profits from this festival will be going to DAV: Disabled American Veterans, Fish First, Multiple Sclerosis Society of Portland, Oregon, as well as the Second Chance Companions charity. Tickets to this event cost $21 and include admission, a drinking cup, and 8 sample tickets. This festival is 21 and over, so be prepared to show valid ID.

September

FREMONT OKTOBERFEST
North 35th Street and Phinney Avenue North, Seattle, WA 98103; FremontOktoberfest.com

Labeled as "Seattle's Fall Tradition," this beer festival has been voted by *USA Today* and Orbitz.com as one of the top places to toast Oktoberfest. A traditional 3-day festival, the Fremont Oktoberfest includes a tasting garden, 2 stages for live music, the Oktoberfest Village with kids' area, and a 5k run. There is also a Sunday Dogtoberfest, which means only on that Sunday dogs will be allowed in the Tasting Garden. The Fremont Oktoberfest village is free and open to all ages, while the Tasting Garden is for 21 and over. Tickets for the Tasting Garden are $25–$30 and include a 5-ounce tasting mug and tasting tokens to sample over 80 microbrews and German beers. A nontasting admission can be purchased for $15 and does not include a mug or tokens. Fremont Oktoberfest benefits the Fremont Chamber of Commerce with a portion of the proceeds going toward funding local schools, art groups, and community events. With multiple bands on the lineup for entertainment, there is always plenty of music to listen to. And if music isn't your thing, there is always the Texas Chainsaw Pumpkin Carving Exhibition. Those with the fortitude to put away the brew will want to visit the Buxom Beer Garden, where they can enjoy a 16-ounce, a ½ liter, or even a liter of beer.

SPOKANE OKTOBERFEST
Riverfront Park, 507 N. Howard St., Spokane, WA 99201; WashingtonBeer.com/Oktoberfest

Hosted by the Washington Beer Commission, the Spokane Oktoberfest Craft Beer Festival was first held in 2010 and is the premier craft-beer tasting festival for the WBC on the east side of the state. This Oktoberfest plays host to 24 Washington craft breweries, each bringing at least two types of beer. With over 50 types of beer being poured, many will be seasonal and Oktoberfest beers. Taking place at Gondola Meadow of Riverfront Park in Spokane, this Oktoberfest celebration pairs locally produced Washington craft beers with a high-peaked tent for a tasting garden, picnic tables, food, as well as live music to complete the celebration. Admission to this Oktoberfest is $15 for advance tickets, $20 at the door, and includes a commemorative tasting cup as well as five 5-ounce sample tastes. The Washington Beer Commission encourages attendees to designate a driver, and admission is only $5 for the DD. You must be 21 or older to attend this celebration, so bring a valid ID.

TACOMA CRAFT BEER FESTIVAL

Petrich Marine Dock, 1118 E. D St. Tacoma, WA 98421; TacomaCraftBeerFest.com

Taking place along the Foss waterway in downtown Tacoma, the Tacoma Craft Beer Festival kicks off in September. Tacoma has a beer history dating back to 1888, and in 2009 the first Tacoma Craft Beer Festival launched a new tradition. Whatever types of beers are brought to this annual festival, they can be tasted for a $25 admittance fee. This price comes with a 5.5-ounce commemorative tasting glass as well as 10 tasting tokens. If you find yourself running out of your tokens early on, you can get additional pours for the low price of $1.50 each. With over 55 breweries in attendance and seemingly endless beers to try, you're bound to find a beer or two that are well worth the trip. With all the profits going toward the Tacoma Historical Society, this event plays a role in supporting and maintaining Tacoma's rich heritage. As with most festivals, food, games, and live entertainment will be on the docket for the attendees to enjoy. This event is billed as a 21-and-over function, so be sure to bring a valid ID. Also, a quick look into the Tacoma Craft Beer Festival will also bring up their "Big Beer Festival," which is in February. This festival is dedicated to those high-ABV brews known as "big beers"!

October

FRESH HOP ALE FESTIVAL

Millennium Arts Plaza—East Yakima Avenue and South 3rd Street, Yakima, WA 98901; FreshHopAleFestival.com

Starting in 2003, the Fresh Hop Ale Festival has occupied the Millennium Arts Plaza in Yakima every year on the first weekend of October. This beer festival was set up to celebrate the world's number-one hops producer, the Yakima Valley, which produces almost 77 percent of America's hops used for brewing. Although it obviously emphasizes fresh hop ales, this event provides attendees with so much more. Craft beers, wine and ciders, homebrew, food, music, and even cigars are all a part of this yearly gathering. Among all the beer tastings and frivolity, a demonstration tent is also set up so attendees can learn how hand-crafted ales are made. The $35 admission includes a commemorative beer glass as well as $7 in scrip, which is used instead of cash. The website specifies that ID is required for everyone from 21 to 91, so get a babysitter for the young ones if you plan to attend.

December

WINTER BEER FEST

Hale's Palladium, 4301 Leary Way NW, Seattle, WA 98107; WashingtonBeer.com/Winter-Fest

Another festival sponsored by the Washington Beer Commission, the Winter Beer Fest gathering is specifically meant to showcase winter seasonal beers. Coming from 32 Washington breweries, the beers that are featured are dark malty stouts, winter warmers, barrel-aged beers, and many other liquid treats to imbibe in. This event, although centered on winter seasonal beers, will also include chocolate tastings and food pairings, as well as a holiday gift shop. More than 70 different beers will be flowing from the taps to wet the attendees' whistles. At this event, members of Washington Beer Lovers (WABL) will get extra perks, such as extra tasting tokens and access to the exclusive WABL-only beer. Tickets for this event are $25 for advance purchase and $30 at the door. These prices include a complimentary tasting cup as well as six 5-ounce beer tastes. This is not so much a child-friendly event; you must be 21 or older to participate.

BYOB: Brew Your Own Beer

Homebrew Shops

No other hobby can give you as much satisfaction as homebrewing. What other pastime allows you to drink beer while creating more for future consumption? From the excitement of drinking your first extract brew, to creating and fine-tuning your own all-grain recipe, every new brew provides hours of fun.

Washington state has a rich beer culture, and homebrewing shops have sprung up all over. That means equipment and ingredients are readily available for the novice and seasoned homebrewer alike. Most of these shops go above and beyond just selling you the products by answering questions and offering suggestions throughout your brewing process. Sure, you might be able to save some money shopping online, but you'll find great customer service and encouragement at shops all across the state.

To find a shop near you, make sure to check out the Washington Homebrewer Association website at wahomebrewers.org. Below you'll find a handful of recommended shops in the state to help you get started.

BADER BREWING
711 Grand Blvd., Vancouver, WA 98661; (360) 750-1551; BaderBrewing.com

In southwest Washington, Bader Brewing is by far the best place to go if you're looking to buy equipment and ingredients to brew beer or make wine, spirits, and even cheese. On one side of the shop they offer all of their winemaking supplies, while on the other side they offer everything you need to brew your next batch of beer. Whether you're a first-timer or an advanced all-grain brewer, you'll easily find everything you need at Bader. They also host regular classes that will teach you everything from brewing your first extract brew to advanced brewing techniques and how to formulate your own all-grain recipes. While the shop itself might not be the fanciest place around, the amount of grains, hops, and equipment they have alongside their very knowledgeable staff makes it the go-to place in the area for your homebrewing needs.

HOMEBREW HEAVEN
9109 Evergreen Way, Everett, WA 98204; (425) 355-8865; HomebrewHeaven.com

If you happen to be located anywhere near Everett and are interested in home-brewing or looking for equipment or ingredients, Homebrew Heaven is the place to go. Since 1996 they have been providing quality products and brewing knowledge to help you get started. They carry everything for brewing as well as for winemaking, cheese-making, distilling, cider- and mead-making, and even making your own soda. You can also buy one of their ingredient kits if you haven't worked your way up to creating your own recipes. Each of these kits comes with all of the ingredients and specific instructions. The staff at Homebrew Heaven know what they're talking about, as they are all homebrewers with plenty of experience. For those nowhere near a homebrew shop, they also have a fantastic online store carrying pretty much everything they offer in store.

SOUND HOMEBREW SUPPLY
6505 5th Place S., Seattle, WA 98108; (206) 743-8074; SoundHomebrew.com

When Sound Homebrew Supply opened in Seattle's Georgetown neighborhood, it filled a void for homebrewers located in the area. It's one of the newest shops in town yet has quickly become one of the best. Fridges full of hops and yeast, bins filled with a multitude of grains, and just about every other kind of ingredient you need to brew beers await you in the shop. They offer plenty of equipment for both beginners and advanced brewers at very reasonable prices. Along with beer they offer wine, cider, cheese, honey, liquor, and soda-making equipment and ingredients. You can also find a wide range of bottles ranging from normal 12-ounce brown beer bottles to full-size growlers. Or if you're into saving time and kegging your own beer, they have you covered with everything you'll need.

Homebrew Recipes

AIRPORT WAY PALE ALE
(CLONE OF GEORGETOWN BREWING CO.'S MANNY'S PALE ALE)

Go to most restaurants around Seattle and there is a good chance they have Manny's Pale Ale on draft. Now you can have it on draft at home. This very Northwest-style pale ale uses plenty of Cascade hops to give it a nice floral aroma without being too bitter. Since Georgetown uses its own yeast in its version, this recipe lets you choose what works best for you.

EXTRACT RECIPE

OG: 1.053, FG: 1.012, ABV: ~5.4%, IBU: 38

6 pounds Light LME
1 pound Light DME
12 ounces Crystal 40°L
.25 ounce Summit, 60 minutes
1 ounce Cascade, 30 minutes
1 ounce Cascade, 15 minutes
1 ounce Cascade, 5 minutes
1 ounce Cascade, Dry hop
White Labs California Ale WLP001, Wyeast American Ale 1056,
    or Fermentis Safale US-05

ALL-GRAIN RECIPE

OG: 1.051, FG: 1.010, ABV: ~5.4%, IBU: 39.9

9 pounds 2 Row
12 ounces Crystal 40°L
.25 ounce Summit, 60 minutes
1 ounce Cascade, 30 minutes
1 ounce Cascade, 15 minutes
1 ounce Cascade, 5 minutes
1 ounce Cascade, Dry hop
White Labs California Ale WLP001, Wyeast American Ale 1056,
    or Fermentis Safale US-05

COURTESY OF SOUND HOMEBREW SUPPLY (P. 245)

DICK DANGER ALE CLONE

Dick's Brewing Company's flagship beer, Dick Danger Ale, is a staple in Washington. While it is a dark ale, it defies any specific style guidelines. A nice roasted flavor comes from the black patent malt while the Mt. Hood hops added toward the end of the boil give it a slight spicy aroma. At only 5.2% ABV, this is one clone recipe where the 5 gallons you create may disappear very quickly.

EXTRACT RECIPE

OG: 1.054, FG: 1.011, ABV: ~5.7%, IBU: 39.4

6 pounds Light DME
10 ounces Black Patent Malt
8 ounces Crystal 80°L
.5 ounce Magnum, 60 minutes
1 ounce Mt. Hood, 10 minutes
1 ounce Mt. Hood, 5 minutes
White Labs London Ale WLP013, Wyeast London Ale 1028 or Fermentis Safale S-04

ALL-GRAIN RECIPE

OG: 1.054, FG: 1.011, ABV: ~5.7%, IBU: 39.4

10 pounds 2 Row
10 ounces Black Patent Malt
8 ounces Crystal 80°L
.5 ounce Magnum, 60 minutes
1 ounce Mt. Hood, 10 minutes
1 ounce Mt. Hood, 5 minutes
White Labs London Ale WLP013, Wyeast London Ale 1028 or Fermentis Safale S-04

COURTESY OF SOUND HOMEBREW SUPPLY (P. 245)

ELYSIAN BREWING'S THE WISE ESB CLONE

As the first beer brewed by Elysian Brewing Company upon opening, The Wise ESB is still a favorite of many regulars. It's a well-balanced ESB with a very solid malt backbone that holds its own to the bold citrus and grassy hops.

ALL-GRAIN RECIPE

9 pounds pale malt (we use Great Western Premium 2-row)
1 pound Crisp 77° crystal malt
1 pound Weyermann Munich malt
4 ounces Weyermann Cara-Hell
2 ounces Special B
8.4 AAU Chinook @Boil
$1/_2$ ounce Cascade & $1/_2$ ounce Centennial at 2 minutes before end of boil
$1/_2$ ounce Cascade & $1/_2$ ounce Centennial at whirlpool/end of boil

Mash at 154 degrees for 60 minutes; run off for 90 minutes; boil 90 minutes; pitch attenuative American ale yeast such as Wyeast 1056—they use Siebel BR96, a relative.

COURTESY OF ELYSIAN BREWING COMPANY (P. 4)

In the Kitchen

Pairing food with beer is always a good time, and cooking with beer in your recipes can make your dishes even more delicious. In this chapter you'll find recipes from a handful of the best brewpubs in Washington that use beer as an ingredient in their recipes. Below is selection of appetizers, entrees, and desserts you can create on your own using each brewpub's beers.

Food Recipes

BÊTE GALETTE

Elysian Brewing's Bête Blanche is an incredibly drinkable Tripel that is released each year in the spring both on draft and in 12- and 22-ounce bottles. Aside from being a perfect beer to pair with an array of dishes, it also makes just the right ingredient to add to their Bête Galette, a savory, buckwheat Bête Blanche crepe served with ham, gruyère cheese, and sautéed mushrooms, all topped with a pan-fried egg.

Serves 4

For Crepes
> *1 cup buckwheat flour*
> *¹/₂ cup all-purpose flour*
> *1 egg*
> *1 cup water*
> *12 ounces Bête Blanche (The Wise, Loser, Bi-Frost, and Men's Room work great too)*
> *3 tablespoons melted butter*
> *Salt and pepper*

Toppings
> *Sliced cremini (baby bella) mushrooms*
> *Sliced ham (rosemary ham works very well)*
> *Grated gruyère cheese*
> *1 egg per serving*

Sift buckwheat flour into a large bowl with all-purpose flour. Whisk egg and water together in a smaller bowl. Slowly whisk wet ingredients into dry ingredients to obtain a smooth batter. Add Elysian's Bête Blanche Tripel and mix until smooth. Let batter rest for 30 minutes.

Add melted butter and mix well. Batter should be the consistency of heavy cream or lighter. If needed, thin batter with water.

Lightly butter hot crepe pan (medium-high) and pour small amount of batter in (if you do not have a crepe pan, any 12-inch nonstick or cast-iron pan will suffice). Swirl to coat pan, cook, and flip. Voila! Make as many crepes as you can with the batter. Either begin to assemble the galettes or refrigerate (best within a couple of days).

Assembling the galettes: After making all the crepes, sauté the sliced cremini mushrooms until firm but not mushy. Turn off the heat and add salt. Have a small sauté pan (with lid) ready to fry an individual egg. In your crepe pan (medium-low heat), place one crepe. At the same time, pan-fry one egg per crepe. Top each crepe with ham, gruyère, and sautéed mushrooms. After the gruyère melts a bit, fold the galette and plate. Top with the fried egg; salt and lightly pepper. Serve with a side salad. Enjoy with an Elysian brew.

COURTESY OF ELYSIAN BREWING COMPANY (P. 4)

POTATO SAUSAGE CHEDDAR AND BEER SOUP

Beer and soup go hand in hand. Since beer is such a delicious addition to soups, it's no surprise that Snoqualmie Brewery created this mouthwatering recipe that utilizes its clean and hoppy Copperhead Pale Ale. Available year-round, this beer-and-soup combo can be enjoyed during any season.

Makes about 4 quarts

8–10 red potatoes, peeled
¼ cup butter, melted
1 large yellow onion, diced
2 tablespoons garlic, minced
4 cooked bratwursts, sliced (cook according to directions)
½ cup fresh parsley, chopped
Salt and pepper to taste
1 pint half and half
1 pint Copperhead Ale or pale ale
½ cube chicken bouillon
1 cup cheddar, grated, divided
1 bunch green onion, minced
4 tablespoons sour cream

Boil red potatoes till tender, drain, mash, and set aside. Sauté in butter yellow onion, garlic, bratwursts, parsley, and salt and pepper. Slowly add mashed potatoes, half and half, and ale, bringing to a very low simmer. Add bouillon. Stir in half of the cheddar and green onions, stirring often. Bring to desired temperature. Garnish with remaining green onion and cheddar, and sour cream.

COURTESY OF SNOQUALMIE BREWERY & TAPROOM (P. 68)

SILENT TREATMENT PALE ALE CITRUS VINAIGRETTE

Start your meals off right with a nice salad. Or just make the salad your meal. Choose your lettuce, add some fruit and nuts, and pour on this vinaigrette from No-Li Brewhouse. It uses 6 ounces of their Silent Treatment Pale Ale, which is also a nice lighter beer to start off your meal.

6 ounces Pale Ale
4 ounces orange juice
1 ounce white wine vinegar
14 ounces salad oil
1 teaspoon salt
$^1/_2$ teaspoon black pepper
1 teaspoon parsley
3–4 tablespoons sugar (to taste)

Whisk all ingredients together and serve on a salad with fresh fruit and nuts.

COURTESY OF CHEF LANE TRUESDELL OF NO-LI BREWHOUSE (P. 220)

CRYSTAL BITTER AIOLI

At No-Li's pub in Spokane, they serve fish and chips with this aioli made with their Crystal Bitter beer. Once you try this sauce on any of your seafood, you'll probably never switch back to boring old tartar sauce. It's easy to make and takes just a few minutes to put everything together.

1 cup mayonnaise
½ inch grated fresh ginger
1 cup Crystal Bitter Ale
¼ cup brown sugar
2 teaspoons lemon juice
1–2 cloves fresh minced garlic
1 teaspoon granulated garlic

Combine everything in a bowl and serve with seafood.

COURTESY OF CHEF LANE TRUESDELL OF NO-LI BREWHOUSE (P. 220)

FISH TACOS

No-Li's fish tacos are so good that there's even a chance that those who don't like sea-food will love them. They use cod, but you can substitute a similar style of fish and serve with a salsa you like. The recipe calls for only 4 ounces of their Silent Treatment Pale Ale, so just buy a 22-ounce bottle and you'll have a perfect beer to pair with your tacos.

6 ounces cod
½ tablespoon Cajun seasoning
4 ounces Silent Treatment Pale Ale
Cheddar-jack cheese, shredded
2 (6-inch) flour tortillas
Cabbage, shredded
Salsa

Sear cod in oil (any salad oil will do). Season with your favorite Cajun seasoning (No-Li uses ½ tablespoon of their house spice, sold at the brewery if you want to buy it). Deglaze pan with Silent Treatment Pale Ale and poach fish till fully cooked.

Melt a thin layer of shredded cheddar-jack cheese onto each tortilla. Add cooked cod to tortilla with a layer of shredded cabbage and your favorite salsa (No-Li uses a mango-peach salsa).

COURTESY OF CHEF LANE TRUESDELL OF NO-LI BREWHOUSE (P. 220)

CHUCKANUT ALE SAUCE

Sometimes having a flavorful and versatile sauce for a number of meats is just what you're looking for. Chuckanut Brewery and Kitchen uses this ale sauce on a few of their dishes. It's simple to make and tastes delicious. Add it to poultry, lamb, or game meats for a flavorful dinner.

1¹/₂ cups fresh cranberries
1¹/₂ cups Chuckanut Strong Ale or Alt
1 orange (juice and zest)
1 tablespoon honey
1 tablespoon white sugar
1 tablespoon brown sugar

Simmer the fresh cranberries in ale, all 3 sweeteners, and juice of 1 orange until tender and reduced to a good sauce consistency. Strain sauce to remove seeds and skin. Add zest of 1 orange. Spoon over meat and serve.

COURTESY OF CHUCKANUT BREWERY & KITCHEN (P. 86)

CHUCKANUT SHELLFISH BOWL

Calling all seafood lovers: Bellingham is located right on the bay and there is always an abundance of seafood. This recipe is a specialty at Chuckanut, but they give you the option to make it your own. Use clams, mussels, or pretty much any shellfish in this recipe that should impress your friends and family. Make sure to head to the brewery and get a growler of their Kölsch or a similar substitute.

Serves 4

> 1 stalk celery, chopped fine
> 1 onion, chopped fine
> 1 tomato, chopped small
> 2 cloves garlic
> ¼ teaspoon fennel seed
> ¼ teaspoon Herbes de Provence
> ¼ cup Chuckanut Kölsch
> ¼ teaspoon red chile flakes
> 3 tablespoons olive oil
> 4 cups cleaned shellfish, such as clams, mussels, or combination

In a heavy saucepan sauté celery, onion, tomato, garlic, fennel, and herbs on medium to low heat with olive oil. Cook until soft and bring to a simmer.

When bubbling, add Kölsch, chile flakes, and shellfish. Cover and simmer just until shells open.

Discard any unopened shellfish. Divide into 4 bowls and serve with toast or french bread.

COURTESY OF CHUCKANUT BREWERY & KITCHEN (P. 86)

DICK'S CREAM STOUT CHOCOLATE CAKE

If you enjoy a thick cream stout as well as a sweet chocolate layer cake, pick up two 12-ounce bottles of Dick's Cream Stout from Dick's Brewing Company along with the following ingredients to make a sweet treat perfect for special occasions. Make this once and you'll be sure to have people asking you for the recipe.

Cake Ingredients
  $1/2$ pound butter
  24 ounces Dick's Cream Stout
  $1^1/2$ cups cocoa powder
  4 cups sugar
  4 cups flour
  2 teaspoons baking soda
  $1/4$ teaspoon salt
  2 tablespoons vanilla
  $1^1/2$ cups sour cream
  6 eggs

Frosting and Filling Ingredients
  2 cups cream cheese
  1 $1/2$ cups heavy cream
  9 cups powdered sugar, divided
  2 teaspoons chocolate syrup

For the cake: Preheat oven to 375°F. Heat butter and Dick's Cream Stout in saucepan over low heat until butter is melted. Set aside to cool.

Line the bottoms of 2 9x13 baking pans with parchment paper.

Combine cocoa, sugar, flour, baking soda, and salt in a large mixing bowl.

Add vanilla to cooled stout mixture, then add sour cream. Add eggs one at a time to stout mixture.

Add stout mixture to dry ingredients and mix until smooth. Pour batter evenly into 2 prepared pans and bake for 40–45 minutes.

Allow cakes to cool completely before removing from pans and frosting.

For the frosting: Beat cream cheese and heavy cream in a stand mixer on high speed for about 3 minutes. Add 4 cups powdered sugar and beat until smooth. Add another 4 cups powdered sugar and beat until smooth. Transfer 1 quart of frosting to a container and set aside. This will be your outer frosting.

For the Filling: Add remaining 1 cup powdered sugar to leftover frosting in the bowl and beat until smooth. Beat in 2 teaspoons chocolate syrup.

COURTESY OF JULIE YOUNG OF DICK'S BREWING COMPANY (P. 162)

DICK'S ROOT BEER FLOAT CAKE

Although there is no alcohol in this recipe, it is a delicious layer cake that uses Dick's homemade root beer, brewed at Dick's Brewing in Centralia, in the cake, filling, and frosting. You can stop by and get a growlerful of it at their own Northwest Sausage & Deli to help make this one-of-a-kind root beer float cake.

Cake Ingredients

10 cups yellow cake mix

15 ounces Dick's Root Beer

1³⁄₄ cups prepared vanilla pudding

5 eggs

1¹⁄₄ teaspoon root beer extract

Buttercream Frosting Ingredients

¹⁄₂ pound butter

4 cups powdered sugar

1 tablespoon vanilla extract

¹⁄₄ cup heavy cream

2¹⁄₂ tablespoons Dick's Root Beer

¹⁄₂ teaspoon root beer extract

Filling Ingredients

³⁄₄ cup Dick's Root Beer

¹⁄₂ cup vanilla prepared pudding

6 ounces whipped topping

For the cake: Preheat oven to 375°F. Line the bottoms of 2 9x13 baking pans with parchment paper. Combine cake mix, root beer, pudding, eggs, and extract in a large mixing bowl. Stir until smooth. Pour batter evenly into 2 prepared pans and bake for 40–45 minutes. Allow cakes to cool completely before removing from pans and frosting.

For the frosting: Beat butter in stand mixer until smooth. Add powdered sugar 2 cups at a time and beat until smooth. Add vanilla and heavy cream and beat until incorporated. Add root beer by the tablespoon to reach desired consistency. Add root beer extract to taste.

For the filling: In a medium-size bowl, whisk together root beer and pudding. Mix in whipped topping until smooth.

COURTESY OF JULIE YOUNG OF DICK'S BREWING COMPANY (P. 162)

Pub Crawls

With so many breweries and bars that specialize in craft beer throughout Washington, you could easily come up with a long list of pub crawls around multiple cities. Being able to walk from one place to the next allows you to sample all kinds of beers in a fun and safe way, without having to worry about getting behind the wheel. Plus, walking is a great way to get a better feel for the neighborhood, especially for those of you just popping in for a visit.

Below you'll find six itineraries of pub crawls you can try in various cities. The key to a good pub crawl is just to have fun and don't worry about hitting every spot. If you find yourself at a bar or brewery you're really enjoying, stay awhile. But make sure to plan a safe way to get home since you'll be drinking a whole lot of beer.

Seattle: Ballard

There's no denying that Ballard is a neighborhood that loves its beer and local breweries. In just a few square miles you can visit all kinds of breweries, bars, or restaurants, all on foot. With so many places for beer lovers to enjoy, you could easily create multiple pub crawls through this neighborhood. Here's one that mixes the old with the new to give you a well-rounded taste of different beers. Keep in mind that Hilliard's and Northwest Peaks aren't open every day of the week, so you can either visit on a Thursday–Saturday or replace them if they happen to be closed. Don't forget to check their websites or give them a call before venturing out.

Jolly Roger Taproom, 1111 NW Ballard Way, Seattle, WA 98107; (206) 782-6181; maritimebrewery.com. Start your pub crawl right at the Maritime Pacific Brewing Company's Jolly Roger Taproom, named after their famous Jolly Roger holiday brew. If you're crawling during the holidays, you'll especially want to hit this spot. Since the next two stops won't have food, order an appetizer, such as their Lil' Sliders. Jolly Roger was serving sliders before they were cool. Have a pint or two of beer from the cask before heading out.

Head west on Northwest Ballard Way and turn right onto 14th Avenue. Walk a block and turn left onto Northwest Leary Way. Then walk a few blocks and turn right onto 15th Avenue Northwest (make sure to walk under the overpass first). Then turn left onto Northwest 49th Street and you'll see Hilliard's to the right.

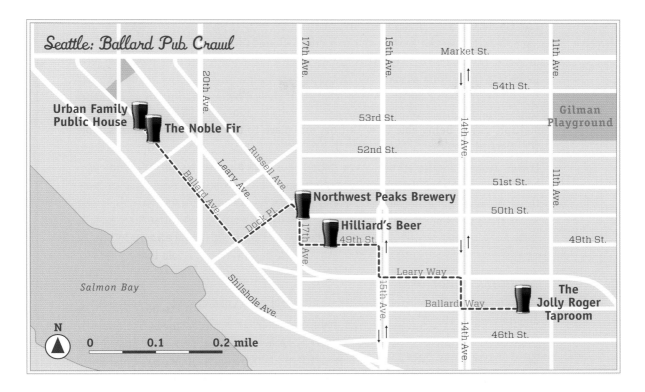

Hilliard's Beer, 1550 NW 49th St., Seattle, WA 98107; (206) 915-3303; hilliardsbeer
.com. Most of the time you'll be able to find Hilliard's beer only in cans, so now's
your chance to try it on draft. This is strictly a taproom, so sample what they have,
but don't linger too long. You have places to go.

*Head west on Northwest 49th Street and turn right onto 17th Avenue Northwest.
Northwest Peaks is in a small building right around the corner.*

Northwest Peaks Brewery, 4912 17th Ave. NW, Seattle, WA 98107; (206) 853-0525;
nwpeaksbrewery.com. Every time you visit Northwest Peaks Brewery, they will have
a different tap list. They do things a little differently than other breweries in that
they don't offer any beers year-round. Walking in the door is like rolling the dice.
But however the dice land, you know you'll be drinking delicious beer. They close at
8 p.m., so make sure to plan your pub crawl accordingly.

*Head north on 17th Avenue Northwest and take the first slight left onto Russell Avenue
Northwest. Take an immediate left onto Northwest Dock. Walk for 2 blocks and turn
right onto Ballard Avenue Northwest. After a short walk The Noble Fir will be on your
right.*

The Noble Fir, 5316 Ballard Ave. NW, Seattle, WA 98107; (206) 420-7425; thenoblefir .com. Now comes the part in the pub crawl where it's okay to drink beer from out of state. The Noble Fir's tap list is usually pretty loaded with options including local picks and those from abroad. All 16 taps rotate frequently and offer many rare and special beers. Grab a small plate of meats and cheese before heading to go get more substantial food just across the street.

Just walk across the street and look to the right.

Urban Family Public House, 5329 Ballard Ave. NW, Seattle, WA 98107; (206) 861-6769; urbanfamilypublichouse.com. If by chance you are still thirsty, have no fear. Urban Family Public House has a blend of both house-brewed and guest taps that spans the spectrum of styles. They have a small but tasty selection of food such as their Bacon & Blue burger or The Veg, a delicious black bean and quinoa based burger.

Seattle: Capitol Hill

If you're looking for a little nightlife, Capitol Hill offers plenty of it. Throughout the diverse neighborhood, you'll find all kinds of bars and restaurants. The following pub crawl runs the gamut of craft beer–loving establishments that welcome nightlife. Since they all stay open late, you can order up this crawl any way you prefer since you're not racing against the clock.

Stumbling Monk, 1635 E. Olive Way, Seattle, WA 98122; (206) 860-0916. The first stop is the infamous Stumbling Monk. Inside you'll realize it's not much to look at and they don't offer food. Forget about it! The selection of predominantly Belgian-style beers and laid-back atmosphere make it worth the stop. Keep in mind they don't open until 6 p.m., so come back later if you want a daytime crawl.

Head southwest on East Olive Way and turn left onto Melrose Avenue and you'll run into The Pine Box on your left.

The Pine Box, 1600 Melrose Ave., Seattle, WA 98122; (206) 588-0375; pineboxbar .com. Enter the chapel of beer. With 33 beers on draft, a built-in Randall that allows them to infuse beers with some delicious and crazy stuff, as well as over 40 whiskeys on draft, you could hunker down here for the night. They have a few food options here as well, and it may be wise to put something in your stomach such as a gourmet pizza or baked wings with hefeweizen mustard as you sample all this goodness.

Head south on Melrose Avenue. Right when you get to East Pike Street you'll see Six Arms on your left.

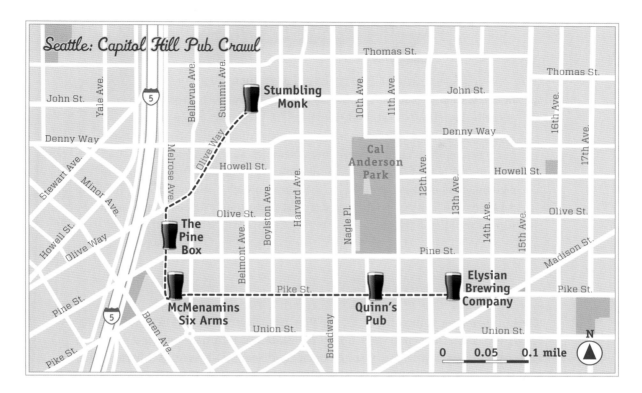

McMenamins Six Arms, 300 E. Pike St., Seattle, WA 98122; (206) 223-1698; mcmenamins.com. Now is your chance to get some really good grub and gulp down some McMenamins brews. The small brewery on site doesn't brew a lot, but there are always plenty of seasonals to try amid the standard McMenamins mainstays. Give the Rubinator a shot. While not on the menu, it's half of their Terminator Stout mixed with their Ruby ale brewed with raspberries.

Head east on East Pike Street for about 0.4 miles. Quinn's Pub will be on your right.

Quinn's Pub, 1001 E. Pike St., Seattle, WA 98122; (206) 325-7711; quinnspubseattle .com. After that nice walk you'll probably be thirsty. Luckily for you, Quinn's beer menu is a thing of beauty. Between 14 taps and a beer geek–approved bottle menu with a heavy focus on Trappist ale, you'll be drinking like royalty. If you skipped eating at the last few places, this is where you'll want to eat if you're looking for something a little more upscale. You can fill up on unique dishes such as wild boar sloppy joes, braised oxtail and potato gnocchi, or grilled giant pacific octopus.

Head east on East Pike Street for about 3 blocks and you'll see Elysian on your right.

Great Pumpkin Beer Festival

Held annually in October, Elysian Brewing's Great Pumpkin Beer Festival is a pumpkin beer lover's dream. Elysian tends to take their pumpkin beers very seriously and show their creativeness during the three-day festival. The event features around 60 pumpkin beers from breweries all over, although about 15 of them are brewed by Elysian and a handful are in collaboration with other breweries. You need to buy tickets to the event early, as it sells out quickly. They always have pumpkin carving, plenty of food, and a Great Pumpkin tapped each session with a new Elysian brew.

Elysian Brewing Company, 1221 E. Pike St., Seattle, WA 98122; (206) 860-1920; elysianbrewing.com. Well done. You've reached Elysian's original location. Congratulate yourself with a few rounds of their seasonal beers. By this time they probably aren't brewing, but you can still peek in through the glass and gaze at their beer kettles. Stay as late as you want—well, until 2 a.m., anyway.

Bellingham

Lace up your walking shoes and put on your raincoat. This Bellingham pub crawl involves quite a bit of walking. Have no fear; the biggest section is after your first destination, so just think of it as a little workout that allows you to drink more beer. While Bellingham is very much a college town, don't let that fool you into thinking the beer quality and selection will resemble a frat party. This is a fun and enjoyable crawl for anyone who appreciates good beer (in a glass, not a tube and funnel). To get things started right, begin at the award-winning Chuckanut Brewery.

Chuckanut Brewery & Kitchen, 601 W. Holly St., Bellingham, WA 98225; (360) 752-3377; chuckanutbreweryandkitchen.com. It's going to be hard not to fill up here because their food is so darn good. Maybe you'd like to start your pub crawl early and order lunch here. Either way, they brew up some killer lagers that won't wreck your palate early. They offer 6 rotating taps, so get a sampler tray if it's your first time. You pretty much can't go wrong with whatever beers you get. And though the

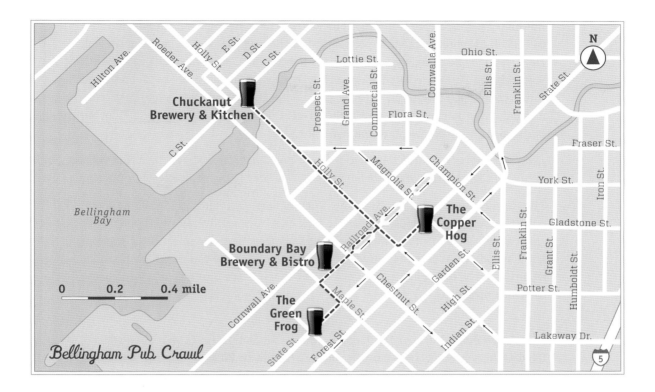

Bellingham Pub Crawl

food is good, resist the urge to eat yourself into a food coma. You have a 0.6-mile walk ahead of you.

Head southeast on West Holly Street toward the bridge. Turn left onto North State Street. Toward the end of the block The Copper Hog will be on your left.

The Copper Hog, 1327 N. State St., Bellingham, WA 98225; (360) 927-7888; thecopperhog.com. One thing Bellingham has going for it is that there is so much good food almost everywhere you go. The Copper Hog is no exception. Upon entering, either turn right and head into the dining room, or go straight into the spacious bar and rest your gut while you just have drinks. With 18 beers on draft, their selection is pretty respectable. Plus, they often have beers you can't find anywhere else in town. Pace yourself, though. The night is just beginning.

Head southwest on North State Street and turn right onto East Holly Street. Then turn left onto Railroad Avenue and walk about 1¹/₂ blocks. Boundary Bay will be on your right.

Boundary Bay Brewery & Bistro, 1107 Railroad Ave., Bellingham, WA 98225; (360) 647-5593; bbaybrewery.com. If you're not from Bellingham, by this point in the pub crawl you may be seriously contemplating moving here. Just wait until you quench your thirst at Boundary Bay. Try out any of their seasonal and small-batch brews and finish your time off with an oatmeal stout float. It's so good you might just order another. They do close at 11 p.m., but our next destination will have you enjoying our favorite beverage late into the night.

Head southwest on Railroad Avenue. Turn left onto East Maple Street. Then turn right onto North State Street and walk half a block. The Green Frog will be on your right.

The Green Frog, 1015 N. State St., Bellingham, WA 98225; (360) 961-1438; acoustictavern.com. Now is the time to kick back to some live music. If you're still thirsty, they offer plenty of Washington-brewed beers or a nice selection of whiskey if you're looking at stepping things up a notch. By this time you may have had a lot to drink and be hungry again. Try one of The Green Frog's interesting grilled cheese sandwich options.

Vancouver

Good thing you're not making this pub crawl back in 2010; otherwise you might be standing on the corner wondering why everything is closed at 6:30 on a Friday night. Slowly but surely the nightlife in what used to be a pretty boring downtown is improving and a new beer culture is popping up in the city. Keep in mind that this crawl is meant to be walked, or you'll be driving the wrong way on one-way streets and will certainly be pulled over. Also note that this crawl will only work Thursday through Saturday, as the first two stops are closed other days of the week.

Loowit Brewing Company, 507 Columbia St., Vancouver, WA 98660; (360) 566-2323; loowitbrewing.com. Start the evening out right at one of downtown's newest breweries, open at 4 p.m. Make sure to eat a little something before you start, as they don't offer food. Their tap list changes frequently so just order what sounds good, because it probably is. If you haven't tried the Shadow Ninja IPA, now is your chance. You won't be disappointed. While there make sure to play a game of *Street Fighter II* before you take off to your next destination.

Head north on Columbia Street and turn right onto West 9th Street. Walk a block and you'll see Mt. Tabor immediately on your right after you cross the intersection.

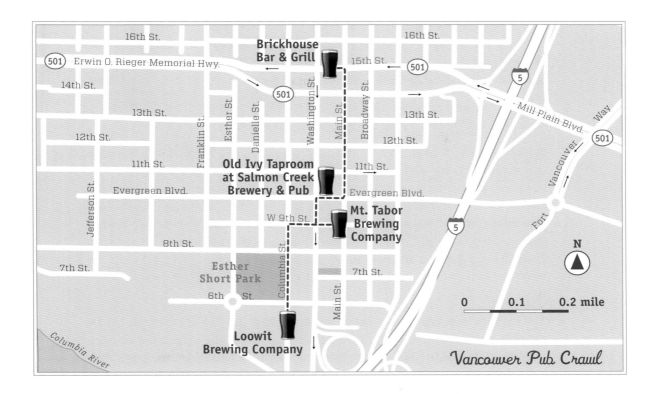

Mt. Tabor Brewing Company, 113 W. 9th St., Vancouver, WA 98660; (360) 696-5521; mttaborbrewing.com. Inside you'll notice that this is a tasting room pretty much literally inside the brewery. All of their kettles are right there, so you can see where your beer was brewed. There isn't any seating, but feel free to dance if there happens to be live music or a DJ. Sample their beers or just get a pint or two. Make sure to try the Hudson Bay CDA, but don't linger too long; you're probably getting hungry by now.

Head west on West 9th Street and turn right onto Washington Street. You'll see The Old Ivy Taproom once you cross Evergreen Boulevard. The signs still might say Salmon Creek Brewpub.

The Old Ivy Taproom at Salmon Creek Brewery, 108 W. Evergreen Blvd., Vancouver, WA 98660; (360) 993-1827. Depending on how hungry you are, you can either just get an appetizer or order a full-on meal; it's up to you. If you're not starving, just get an appetizer such as the jalepeño & cheddar stuffed tots served with chipotle aioli sauce. The hardest decision you'll make here is what to drink. With 24 taps to choose from, it's a daunting task. They usually have 4 or 5 of their own beers, but with the lineup of guest taps available, you probably won't be ordering the house-brewed beers. You could stay and end the night here, or if you're feeling adventurous, head to the Brickhouse for a good time.

Head east on West Evergreen Boulevard and turn left onto Main Street. You'll see the Brickhouse Bar & Grill on your left after about 4¹/₂ blocks.

Brickhouse Bar & Grill, 109 W. 15th St., Vancouver, WA 98660; (360) 695-3686; vancouverbrickhouse.com. You've finally made it to the end . . . or is it the beginning? Don't worry—Brickhouse stays open until 2 a.m. With plenty of quality beers on draft, 2 bars, a pool table, a stage for live music, and some killer food, you could be here awhile. Wings with a multitude of sauces, burgers, sandwiches and all kinds of other goodies await you. Head to the back lounge or stay up front. If it happens to be summer, grab a beer and head to the outdoor patio.

Olympia

Washington's state capital may not be home to a huge amount of breweries, but the city isn't lacking options for craft-beer drinkers. Scattered throughout the city, beer lovers can find a wide range of craft brews pouring at various locations. Here's a pub crawl that will take you to a handful of places around downtown. Just like other pub crawls, this is based on the idea that you're walking; you'll be driving into oncoming traffic down one-way streets if you follow these directions in a car.

Fish Tale Brewpub, 515 Jefferson St. SE, Olympia, WA 98501; (360) 943-3650; fishbrewing.com. Right across the street from Fish Brewing Company's production facility is Olympia's oldest brewpub. Start off with a sampler or two of their many beers. You can't try them all with just one sampler. If you're drinking any of their German-style Leavenworth Biers, pair them with an appetizer called the Fish Tale Sausage Sampler. Don't miss out on any of the Reel Ales series of seasonal beers if any are available.

Head north on Jefferson Street Southeast and turn left onto 4th Avenue East. You'll see the Eastside Club Tavern on your right.

Eastside Club Tavern, 410 4th Ave. E., Olympia, WA 98501; (360) 357-9985; theeastsideclub.com. Just remember you came to the Eastside Club Tavern for the beer. They don't carry their own food, but who cares—their beer menu will get you full. With 42 quality beers on draft, pool tables, table tennis, foosball, air

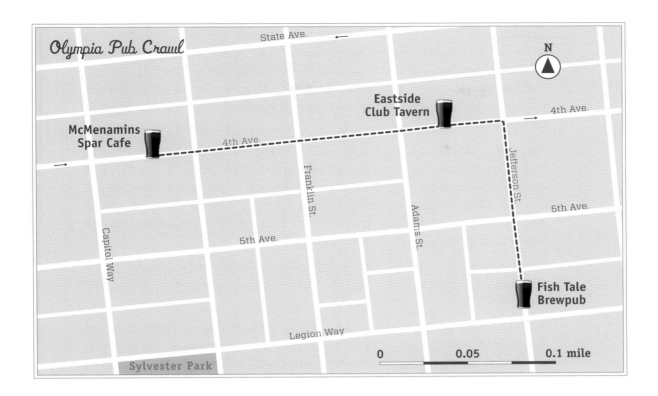

hockey, video games, pinball, and a jukebox playing good music, you'll most likely be hanging out here for a long time. Sure, you could spend the evening here, but you still have one more spot to hit before you call it a night.

Head west on 4th Avenue East and walk a little more than 2 blocks. McMenamins Spar Cafe will be on the right.

McMenamins Spar Cafe, 114 4th Ave. E, Olympia, WA 98501; (360) 357-6444; mcmenamins.com. Although the brewery in the Spar Cafe might be the smallest of the McMenamins breweries, you can be assured that they have plenty of fine beers including the regulars, such as Ruby and Terminator Stout, as well as a handful of seasonally brewed options. Chow down on their traditional pub fare or order any of their pizzas. If it's after 10 p.m. it's happy hour and you'll get both food and drinks discounted.

Spokane

While parts of Spokane are a wasteland for beer lovers, filled with bars and restaurants pouring a boring selection of brews, downtown has plenty of options if you're looking for unique craft beers. This pub crawl takes you to a few spots worth checking out—just make sure you wear comfortable shoes, as there is a bit of a walk toward the end.

Steam Plant Grill, 159 S. Lincoln St., Spokane, WA 99201; (509) 777-3900; steamplantspokane.com. Start your pub crawl at one of the well-known landmarks in the city. What once provided steam heat and electrical power to downtown Spokane is now a full restaurant and brewery. Share the taster tray filled with 11 of their beers poured in 5-ounce glasses. You can eat a nice steak or seafood meal or just nibble on some starters before heading out.

Head north on South Lincoln Street and turn right onto West Sprague Avenue. Walk a block and you'll see the entrance for the Post Street Ale House on the corner of Post Street.

Post Street Ale House, 1 N. Post St., Spokane, WA 99201; (509) 789-6900. If you didn't eat at Steam Plant, then Post Street Ale House is the place to get your grub on. Most entrees are under $10, so it's a little easier on your wallet. While not a huge menu, you can try dishes such as their Guinness braised short ribs, fish tacos, or blackened chicken fettuccini. They offer 26 rotating beers on tap, although a handful are typical macros. However, they do have a nice selection of seasonal and rare beers with some pretty fun events.

Continue heading east on West Sprague Avenue and turn right onto South Howard Street. The Blue Spark will be on your left as you near 1st Avenue.

The Blue Spark, 15 S. Howard St., Spokane, WA 99201; (509) 838-5787; bluesparkspokane.com. This is where the fun happens. With 26 beers on tap you'll find something good to sip on while listening to live music, playing pub trivia, or jumping up on stage during open-mic night. With some of the best deals in the area for beer, it can get packed, but don't sweat it; you're there to have fun.

Head north on South Howard Street and turn right onto West Sprague Avenue. You'll walk about 7 blocks to reach Jones Radiator.

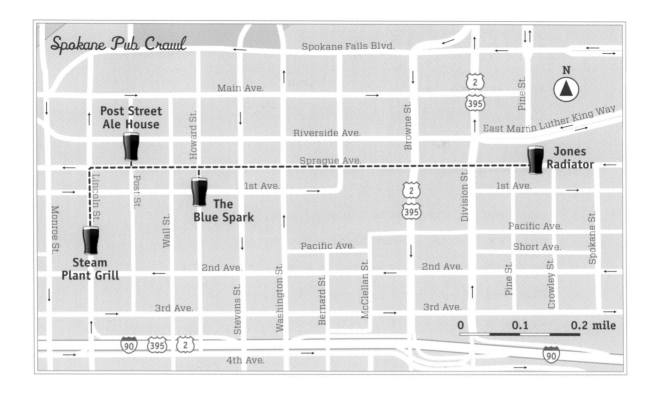

Jones Radiator, 120 E. Sprague Ave., Spokane, WA 99202; (509) 747-6005; jonesradiator.com. Before you head out to Jones Radiator, make sure you understand it's a little bit of a walk, but very much worth it. They offer 16 beers on draft, all artfully selected from all over the Northwest and beyond. Although it's small, you're bound to have a good time. If you time it right, there could be live music or trivia.

Appendix

Beer Lover's Pick List

Dark Cherry Stout, Horse Heaven Hills Brewery, Stout, 194

Dark Marc, M.T. Head Brewing Company, Cascadian Dark Ale, 143

Don't Fret Porter, Twelve String Brewing Company, Porter, 231

Dottie Seattle Lager, Emerald City Beer Company, Amber Session Ale, 7

Double Black Stout, Redhook Ale Brewery, Stout, 68

Double Diamond Winter Ale, Dick's Brewing Company, Winter Warmer, 163

Dragonstooth Stout, Elysian Brewing Company, Oatmeal Stout, 5

Fat Scotch Ale, Silver City Brewery, Scotch Ale, 123

Field 41 Pale Ale, Bale Breaker Brewing Company, Pale Ale, 191

Filthy Hoppin' IPA, Dirty Bucket Brewing Co., India Pale Ale, 58

Fireweed Honey Blonde, Rocky Coulee Brewing Company, Blonde Ale, 229

Folkvang Irish Red, Triplehorn Brewing Company, Irish Red Ale, 72

Heart of Darkness CDA, Two Beers Brewing Company, Black IPA, 33

Hellacious Repeats Double IPA, Ghost Runners Brewery, Double IPA, 165

Hilliard's Saison, Hilliard's Beer, Saison, 16

Honey Basil Ale, Northern Ales, Herbed/Spiced Beer, 223

Hoppy Redhead, Big E Ales, Extra Special Bitter, 83

Hoptopia, Scuttlebutt Brewing Company, Imperial IPA, 98

Hudson's Bay CDA, Mt. Tabor Brewing Company, Cascadian Dark Ale, 171

The Impaler, Iron Goat Brewing, Double IPA, 217

Imperial IPA, Boundary Bay Brewery, Double IPA, 85

Imperial Stout, Old Schoolhouse Brewery, Imperial Stout, 199

Industrial IPA, Diamond Knot Brewing Company, IPA, 88

Islander Pale Ale, Maritime Pacific Brewing Company, Pale Ale, 21

Jaywalker, Walking Man Brewing, Russian Imperial Stout, 173

Judge Porter, Barhop Brewing, Porter, 112

The Kentucky Dude, Naked City Brewery & Taphouse, Imperial Stout, 22

Lazy Boy IPA, Lazy Boy Brewing, IPA, 94

Lizzy's Lager, Orlison's Brewing Co., Lager, 224

London Calling Brown Ale, St. Brigid's Brewery, English Brown Ale, 203

Lucille IPA, Georgetown Brewing Company, IPA, 13

Make It So, Herbert B. Friendly Brewing, English Ale, 61

Mango Ale, West Highland Brewing, Pale Ale, 175

Mango Weizen, Northwest Brewing Company, Fruit Beer/Pale Wheat Ale, 145

Märzen, Alpine's Märzen, Marzen, 189

Masonry Oatmeal Stout, Brickyard Brewing, Oatmeal Stout, 56

Mild, Machine House Brewery, English Mild Ale, 19

The Monk, Gallaghers' Where-U-Brew, Tripel, 89

Monk's Indiscretion, Sound Brewery, Belgian Strong Ale, 126

Oatmeal Stout, Bellevue Brewing Company, Oatmeal Stout, 52

Odin's Gift, Odin Brewing Company, Amber Ale, 25

Old Madrona, Island Hoppin' Brewery, Imperial Red, 119

Old Man River Oatmeal Stout, Riverport Brewing, Oatmeal Stout, 228

Old Sebastes Barleywine, Anacortes Brewery, Barleywine, 82

Orangutan Pale Ale, Budge Brothers Brewery, Pale Ale, 215

Outburst Imperial IPA, Pyramid Brewery, IPA, 29

Pacemaker Porter, Flyers Restaurant and Brewery, Porter, 115

Pavlik's Pilsner, Soos Creek Brewing Company, Bohemian Pilsner, 149

Peach Hefeweizen, Laht Neppur Brewing Co., Hefeweizen, 218

Peeping Peater Scotch Ale, Port Townsend Brewing Company, Scotch Ale, 120

Pilsner, Chuckanut Brewery & Kitchen, Pilsner, 86

Point Defiance IPA, Harmon Brewing Co., IPA, 142

Poles Apart Milk Stout, Duo Brewing, Milk Stout, 137

Pomegranate Porter, Tacoma Brewing Company, Porter, 151

Porter, Lost Falls Brewery, Porter, 219

Postal Porter, Paradise Creek Brewery, Porter, 226

Quilter's Irish Death, Iron Horse Brewery, Unclassified, 198

Redoubt Red, Northwest Peaks Brewery, Red Ale, 23

Republic Pale, Republic Brewing Company, Pale Ale, 227

Rhubarb IPA, Slippery Pig Brewery, IPA, 125

Roggenbier, Reuben's Brews, Roggenbier, 30

Roslyn Dark Lager, Roslyn Brewing Company, Dark Lager, 201

Royal Tenenbaum Christmas Ale, Kulshan Brewing Company, Herbed/Spiced Beer, 93

Sacred Hop, Der Blokken Brewery, Double IPA, 113

Shadow Ninja IPA, Loowit Brewing Company, IPA, 169

Shticky Blonde Ale, 192 Brewing Company, Blonde Ale, 65

Sky Hag IPA, Airways Brewing Company, Imperial IPA, 136

Small Town Brown, Ancient Lakes Brewing Company, American Brown Ale, 190

Smoked Porter, Big Al Brewing, Porter, 3

Solar Trans Amplifier, Epic Ales, Witbier, 9

Spruce Tip, Twin Peaks Brewing and Malting Co., Imperial IPA, 127

Stash Box Pale Ale, Rainy Daze Brewing Company, Pale Ale, 121

Sternwheeler Stout, Ice Harbor Brewing Company, Stout, 195

Stouty Stouterson, Valhöll Brewing Company, Imperial Oatmeal Stout, 129

Index